REDLINING CULTURE

REDLINING
CULTURE

A DATA HISTORY
OF RACIAL INEQUALITY
AND POSTWAR FICTION

RICHARD JEAN SO

Columbia University Press
New York

Columbia University Press
Publishers Since 1893
New York   Chichester, West Sussex
cup.columbia.edu
Copyright © 2021 Columbia University Press
All rights reserved

Library of Congress Cataloging-in-Publication Data
Names: So, Richard Jean, author.
Title: Redlining culture : a data history of racial inequality and postwar fiction / Richard Jean So.
Description: New York : Columbia University Press, 2020. | Includes bibliographical references and index.
Identifiers: LCCN 2020022408 (print) | LCCN 2020022409 (ebook) | ISBN 9780231197724 (hardcover) | ISBN 9780231197731 (trade paperback) | ISBN 9780231552318 (ebook)
Subjects: LCSH: American fiction—African American authors—History and critcism. | American fiction—20th century—History and criticism. | Literature publishing—Political aspects—United States—History—20th century. | Authors and publishers—United States—History—20th century. | Literature—Data processing. | Race discrimination—United States—History—20th century. | Discrimination in employment—United States | Literature and society—United States—History—20th century.
Classification: LCC PS153.N5 S63 2020 (print) | LCC PS153.N5 (ebook) | 813/.609896073—dc23
LC record available at https://lccn.loc.gov/2020022408
LC ebook record available at https://lccn.loc.gov/2020022409

Columbia University Press books are printed on permanent and durable acid-free paper.

Printed in the United States of America

Cover design: Lisa Hamm

CONTENTS

Acknowledgments vii

INTRODUCTION   1

1. PRODUCTION: ON WHITE PUBLISHING   27

2. RECEPTION: MULTICULTURALISM OF THE 1 PERCENT   67

3. RECOGNITION: LITERARY DISTINCTION AND BLACKNESS   105

4. CONSECRATION: THE CANON AND RACIAL INEQUALITY   143

CONCLUSION   181

Notes   187

Index   215

ACKNOWLEDGMENTS

Every book is hard to write, but this one felt especially so. I began writing it during a time of intense hardship in my professional life, when I was out of a job and wasn't sure I would get to keep doing the work that I love doing. Doubt was constant. The nature of the work—a computational approach to the study of race and literature—provoked strong resistance. I struggled a lot—against the discipline, against colleagues, and, ultimately, against myself. Slowly, the nature of the work changed. It became more social. I met a group of like-minded scholars who were excited and deeply passionate about this kind of scholarship. We talked; we shared materials, ideas and projects; we collaborated. This community, more than anything, gave life to this book. Joy and pleasure in writing and research, something I had lost, came back to me. In the end, the ideas in this book alone were not enough to make me write it. The feeling that I was a part of something bigger, however—a new field of knowledge—was what kept me going.

I started doing this kind of work a decade ago with Hoyt Long, when we taught ourselves about computers and statistics and wrote a string of strange and experimental essays, which I now look back on with great fondness. I wouldn't be doing this work if it weren't for him. But more than that, I value his friendship and loyalty, which proved humanizing during a bad time. I've been talking about these ideas with Andrew Piper for a very long time. Those conversations have shaped my thinking in profound ways. They've no doubt made my work better and sharper, but even more importantly, they've helped me see how this work contributes to the formation of a broader intellectual movement, the thing that we care about most. Dan Sinykin and I have been on a long intellectual journey together for many years. We had no idea where it would take us or of what kinds of people and scholars we would eventually become. But I know today that I'm a happier and stronger person because we shared that path and helped each other.

Ted Underwood, Jo Guldi, Matt Wilkens, David Bamman, and Lauren Klein deserve mention for providing specific moments of motivation or guidance with this book and, more generally, playing such an important role in creating the field of cultural analytics and computational humanities. They've inspired me. Amy Hungerford and Jonathan Arac exhibited astonishing kindness and encouragement during a difficult and transitional moment in my career. Colleagues in the Department of English at McGill welcomed me with great warmth and support, for which I am grateful; in particular, I want to thank Trevor Ponech, Katie Zien, Allan Hepburn, Derek Nystrom, Fiona Ritchie, Michael Nicholson, Xander Manshel, Alanna Thain, Erin Hurley, and Michael Van Dussen. Finally, I want to recognize a cohort of younger scholars in this field who are doing important research and represent, I believe, the discipline's future: Melanie Walsh, Tess McNulty, Edwin Roland, Laura McGrath, Ryan Heuser, and Kent Chang.

Philip Leventhal at Columbia University Press saw promise in this book at a very early stage and continued to believe in it as it came to completion. At a late stage, revising this book with his help—page by page, and often sentence by sentence—not only made it immeasurably better but, intellectually, has been a highlight of my career. Funding for this book's research came from the following sources, which I gratefully acknowledge here: the Textual Optics Lab, directed by Robert Morrissey and Hoyt Long under the aegis of the University of Chicago's Neubauer Collegium; the University of Chicago Knowledge Lab, directed by James Evans under the aegis of the Templeton Foundation; the Textual Geographies Project, directed by Matt Wilkens under the aegis of the University of Notre Dame; the University of Pittsburgh Humanities Center; and the Hathitrust Research Center's Advanced Collaborative Support Grant. Data or access to data was provided by the Hathitrust Digital Library; the University of Chicago Textual Optics Lab; the McGill University Text Lab, directed by Andrew Piper; and the University of Kansas's Project on the History of Black Writing (HBW), directed by Maryemma Graham.

I've been talking about ideas with Hua Hsu for more than a decade now. Every day I look forward to our little chats. They are funny, weird, energizing, playful, and human, but most of all, they produce a vision of the world that I like, a world in which ideas matter and have a useful place, a world that I want to live in and write for. All of those chats amount to something bigger, and they saturate this book, more than he probably knows. They are its oxygen.

One's largest intellectual and personal debts are the hardest to articulate because they get so deep in you, they become a part of you. Xinyu Dong made this book better by constantly giving me an image of what scholarship should be through her feedback and the example of her own work: its rigor, its relentless and uncompromising desire to understand. Each morning, I got to work with the thought that I could do better. But it didn't stop there. Each afternoon, when the work was done for the day, she also gave me an image of what a good and full life should be: a life of attention, an aesthetic life, a life of care for the people and things that surround us. Each day she made me feel that I could be better and live better. An interesting life of the mind isn't worth much without an actually meaningful life. I have both because of her.

REDLINING CULTURE

INTRODUCTION

Sometime in the early 1980s, Toni Morrison had an important realization. Her writing career was going well. She had published three critically acclaimed novels—*The Bluest Eye*, *Sula*, and *Song of Solomon*—in the 1970s, each selling better than the last. But her own success had not meant a broader and penetrating success for other black novelists. As an editor for one of the largest and most powerful publishing houses in America, Random House, Morrison had seen this effect up close. The problem was that (in her words) "the market can only receive one or two Black women writers. Dealing with five Toni Morrisons would be problematic." Thus, by the early 1980s, Morrison the author likely had few regrets about her writing career. But Morrison the editor had one serious regret: She had failed to start her own book line, and she doubted she would have the opportunity to do so in the future. This would be the only way to break the racial logic of the literary market. "I feel no success as an editor," she said.[1]

Morrison's regret is surprising. As an editor, she published a number of successful novels by Toni Cade Bambara and Gayl Jones and discovered new literary talents, such as Henry Dumas. Today critics and scholars celebrate her for this work. Yet Morrison likely could not shake the feeling that all of these individual achievements were still not enough to offset a larger structural problem. That structure was the real problem, and she felt it all around her. But it was hard to see: it was no single publisher, editor, marketer, reviewer, prize committee, or reader. It was a pattern, a thick line that walled off nonwhite writers from the coveted resources of not only lucrative book contracts but also book reviews, literary awards, and bestsellerdom.

Living in New York City, Morrison had likely heard the term "redlining" at some point in the 1970s. Redlining describes the practice of arbitrarily refusing or limiting financial services (like bank loans) to specific neighborhoods (like Harlem) because its residents are poor or people of color. The practice started in the 1930s, when the Federal Housing Administration was created to insure mortgages. The agency identified financially "risky" areas and produced maps drawn by the Home Owners' Loan Corporation (HOLC) to mark those areas in bright red, so banks knew which neighborhoods to avoid. A *red line* separated the acceptable from the nonacceptable parts of the city, and the nonacceptable parts were typically populated by black people and immigrants. A HOLC map of New York in the 1950s has Harlem drenched in red. Redlining eviscerated the economic development of black neighborhoods, and while the practice officially ceased by the late 1960s, its aftereffects could still be felt well into the 1980s.[2]

What one hears in Morrison's frustration is the recognition of a similar kind of symbolic map, one focused on what we might call *cultural redlining*. It's widely recognized that large and mainstream book publishers like Random House can only publish so many black or Asian writers. Likewise, book reviewers at elite magazines like the *New Yorker* prefer to talk about white male authors like John Updike and rarely review minority authors. Book prizes might recognize a breakout star like Toni Morrison but almost no one else. And so on. We know all that as a kind of *talk*, as a series of historical anecdotes or stories. But what does all of that look like as a type of empirical structure or map? If we could draw the American literary field like a midcentury HOLC map, what red lines would we see? What patterns of enclosure, domination, and isolation would we find? For Morrison, the fact that book publishers could "handle" only one Toni Morrison was merely symptomatic of a greater cultural redlining in postwar American literature. She couldn't see this effect as a map on a piece of paper, but she knew it was real.

If we look at the publishing data, what we see is represented in figure 0.1. If we focus on the postwar period (a period I define, for this book, as the years between 1950 and 2000) and look at U.S. fiction and race, white authors represent 97 percent of the authors published at Random House. The data confirms what Morrison had intuited: an overwhelming whiteness and a scarcity of minority writers. Morrison, at last, would see the literary marketplace as a map of inequality. If publishers couldn't handle "five Toni Morrisons," this is what it looks like as a pattern.

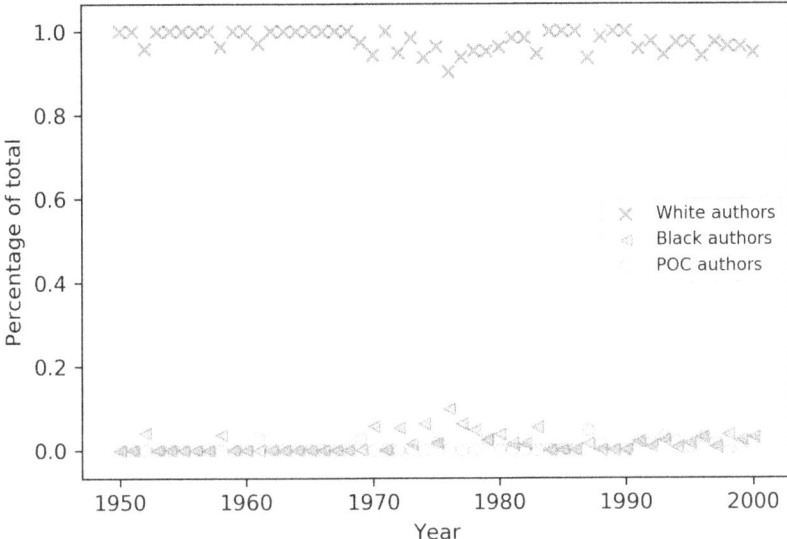

FIGURE 0.1 Percentage of novelists by racial identity (white, black and POC—Asian American, Latinx, and Native American) published at Random House by year between 1950 and 2000.

But the pattern doesn't end there. For instance, when we include information regarding American book reviews, book sales, and book awards—in order to understand the life of a book after it gets published and enters the wider literary marketplace, what she would see is represented in table 0.1. White authors also represent 90 percent of the most reviewed novelists in magazines and periodicals, such as the *New Yorker*. And when it comes to book prizes, white authors comprise 91 percent of novelists who win major awards, such as the Pulitzer. Even more starkly, racial inequality in the U.S. literary field is most pronounced in terms of sales: a staggering 98 percent of novelists who appear on bestseller lists are white.[3] This is all despite the fact that white people represent just 75.1 percent of the overall U.S. population in 2000.[4] A simple process of collecting some data and computing some basic statistics tells a clear story: through every phase of the literary field, from production (publishing) to reception (book reviews) to distinction (book sales and prizes), white authors exercise a distinct racial command over minority authors, particularly black novelists. And perhaps most surprisingly, these numbers do not change over time. Racial inequality, as a main feature of postwar literary production and

4 INTRODUCTION

TABLE 0.1 U.S. NOVELISTS, 1950–2000

RACE OF AUTHOR	PUBLISHING (%)	BOOK REVIEWS (%)	BEST-SELLERS (%)	BOOK PRIZES (%)
White	97	90	98	91
Black	2	6	0.5	5
POC	1	4	1.3	4

Percentage of novelists by racial identity (white, black, and POC—Asian American, Latinx, and Native American) in four contexts: mainstream publishing as represented by Random House, U.S. book reviews, U.S bestsellers, and U.S. prizewinners between 1950 and 2000.

reception, is resilient. Despite efforts by minority authors and activists to diversify and transform the American literary field—for example, the Black Arts Movement in the 1960s, the Combined Asian American Resources Project in the 1970s, and the ostensible "rise" of U.S. multiculturalism in the 1980s—none was strong enough to permanently undo the hegemony of white authorship in the field at scale.

This is not the usual story that scholars tell about postwar American literature. That story is typically far more celebratory. Scholars often say that American literature became less white and more racially diverse. They say that multiculturalism triumphed in this period. Darryl Dickson-Carr, in his introduction to *The Columbia Guide to Contemporary African American Fiction*, writes:

> The three decades between 1970 and 2000 constituted the most productive and successful period in African American literary history. Hundreds of African American authors . . . began or continued illustrious writing and publishing careers. . . . Prior to 1970, very few African American authors could hope to sell more than a few thousand copies of their books. By the mid-1990s, sales in the hundreds or thousands for individual works . . . were commonplace for several dozen writers. . . . The rewards have not been merely financial: African American authors also began winning some of the top literary book prizes. . . . Publishing houses that once dismissed manuscripts by and about African Americans out of a widespread belief that blacks do not read books have been proven wrong time and again. The doors of mainstream publication and distribution may remain open indefinitely to black authors.[5]

In his overview of postwar U.S. publishing, Michael Schudson declares:

> Multiculturalism by the 1970s was not just an academic anthem but a social fact. With changes in immigration patterns after 1965 immigration reform, Latin American and Asian immigrants altered the face of America. In publishing, Jewish American fiction, African American fiction, and Asian American fiction came to all but define the world of serious literature; a novelist like John Updike, late in his career, was seen to be an observer of northeastern white Anglo-Saxon Protestant nature rather than of generically "American" characters.[6]

However, I argue that scholars of U.S. literature have partly misread its postwar history by failing to recognize one of its signal features: unchanging racial inequality. I argue that the scholarly narrative of the rise of multiculturalism—a story that first took hold in the scholarship and then diffused broadly to the public—has in part obscured a more fundamental story. That story is about the economics of American literature—production, reception, and recognition—and how those economics have and continue to punish and exclude minority authors. Each chapter of this book explores a specific phase of the lifecycle of a novel—from publishing to reviews to sales to prizes—to uncover how racial exclusion enacts a core feature of each phase.

This exclusion, at the same time, has had a profound effect on the form and content of the postwar American novel. Cultural redlining is not just a demographic phenomenon; it also exists at the level of the text, the page, the paragraph, and word. Taking as its starting point the numbers asserted at the start of this introduction—97 percent, 90 percent, 98 percent, and 91 percent—I show that the history of postwar American literature and racial inequality are inseparable and that this inequality also directly shaped the development of the language, form, and narrative of postwar American fiction, both at the scale of thousands of texts and in terms of the individual works that scholars have identified as important, such as Toni Morrison's *Song of Solomon*. In particular, I argue that this inequality took the form of a vast literary whiteness that is felt across a wide range of fiction, prompting examples of both authorial acquiescence and subversion.

This book does not deny the validity and importance of our first scholarly narrative—the story of American literary multiculturalism—told by generations of historians and critics. This is valuable work: histories of the formation of cultural movements like the Black Arts Movement; readings of outstanding individual novelists, like James Baldwin and Flannery O'Connor, that illuminate the creativity and innovation of "American literature" on the page; readings of neglected minority racial authors, such as John Okada, that recover a marginalized literary tradition—interpretations of texts that precisely resist, rather than affirm, the intuited presence of some stultifying racial order from above. This has been the general approach to the writing of contemporary American literary history and race, and, again, I don't dispute its achievements.

My concern is that the first story has eclipsed our second story—the story of racial inequality and postwar American literature—or at least rendered it hard to see. I suggest that both stories can be true at the same time; one need not cancel out the other. But I also suggest that we know far less about the second story and that a greater awareness of it can lead to a powerful reorientation of our first scholarly narrative. In the pages to come, I attempt to realign these stories: the way that American fiction happens both at the scale of a single text or author and the scale of an entire publishing house and millions of book reviews. In my final chapter, I also try to parse how these stories became so misaligned in the first place. What is at stake is more than just the specific history of the postwar American novel. At stake is how we think about the relationship between data and cultural history and the relationship between numbers and reading.

Indeed, what largely animates this book's overall thesis is a methodological claim: literary scholars have missed the story of cultural redlining because our available methods, such as close reading and historicism, are not well equipped to discern such patterns. Cultural redlining, much like economic redlining, does not happen at the level of the individual writer, page, or text. It happens at a cognitive scale well beyond what a single person can observe or read. It happens in the tens of thousands of novels published by Random House, the hundreds of book prizes awarded by prize committees, and the thousands of book reviews printed each year. This book leverages the affordances of natural language processing and text mining to identify and analyze otherwise unseen patterns of language, form, and narrative. It does so to *foreground* what traditionally has been viewed as the mere *background* of literary history.[7] Inverting our usual orientation, I hope to show, not only gives us a new vision of American literary history writ large but also new and surprising readings of individual works of literature.

There will be costs. Quantification always means losing something; thinking about race with numbers risks reduction and reification. For example, one might argue that a white sociologist who lives in suburban Long Island, going door to door with a survey asking Harlem residents if they are "white" or "black," is incredibly naïve and reduces the complexity of racial experience to a crude binary. What about the differences between African Americans and recent immigrants from Nigeria? Doesn't this research risk pathologizing blackness as forever trapped in a state of poverty? Similarly, one might ask about the current project: what about the nonmainstream literary marketplace—black publishers like Broadside Press or minority-focused literary awards such as Premio Quinto Sol?[8] Didn't they do something to weaken the forms of racial inequality we see in the mainstream? Doesn't a literary history that only focuses on mainstream examples of racial inequality and thus neglects marginal, nonwhite forms of literary production and reception potentially just reinscribe all of those cultural redlines?

This book offers a modest first pass at a large problem—racial inequality and literary whiteness—that in 2020 continues to afflict American culture. It does not deny the inevitable limits of only focusing on mainstream versions of the literary marketplace. Yet I argue that reconstructing the most obvious and dominant forms of racial inequality in postwar U.S. fiction signals a useful, if not necessary, first step toward producing a more wide-angle vision of American writing and race, one I hope scholars with a greater knowledge of African American book history, Latinx cultural institutions, and so forth can build on. For example, despite all of its obvious problems, few would doubt that sociological redlining research, however reductive or naïve, was useful insofar as it helped to render vivid and concrete dynamics of power and racial exclusion. And this research enabled a series of more sophisticated follow-up studies, which, over time, helped effect real-world change in the present. This book has a similar aspiration. Cultural redlining in the postwar period invented a model that made possible and has helped sustain racial inequality in the arts and literature today. To defeat it, we need to know its history.

CONGLOMERATION, ENGINE OF RACIAL INEQUALITY

Over the past twenty years, scholars have identified multiculturalism as a signal, defining feature of postwar American literary history. A second defining feature that has more recently come to view is conglomeration.[9] The book business changed after the war. Facing twin pressures of a rapidly growing American population and rising literacy rates as a result of more people going to college, American publishers such as Random House started to expand and publish more books. Before the war, book publishing was run more like, as Jason Epstein describes, a "cottage industry": small and personal, with book deals secured on the basis of a handshake, and so forth. After the war, publishers moved toward a more "consumer-oriented" model that resembled a conventional business.[10] As a part of this transition, book publishers increasingly were acquired by larger media conglomerates, which were better equipped to meet the challenges of scale now facing book publishers. Random House offers a prime example. Random House was founded in 1927 by Bennett Cerf and Donald Klopfer, mainly to republish literary classics like *Great Expectations*. By the late 1950s, it had grown into a large and successful company, publishing major authors such as James Joyce and William Faulkner. By the 1960s, the publisher had attracted the attention of large corporations, and in 1965, it was sold to RCA for 38 million dollars, a media conglomerate principally known for interests in radio and television. More consolidations and mergers would soon follow. One historian estimates that by 1990, 60–80 percent of the total American and European book market was controlled by no more than five to ten individual publishing firms.[11]

Writers, critics, and scholars were predictably outraged by this turn of events and fiercely protested the commodification of literature. Specifically, they lamented the fact that books were now judged by their profitability, their status as commercial products, rather than, as it once was, as social goods that bore a responsibility to enlighten the public.[12] Editors were now under severe pressure to acquire and promote bestsellers, books with the potential for film adaptation in particular. Children's literature and genre fiction thrived; literary fiction suffered. Writers of the old regime worried that this new trend inhibited the spread and debate of serious ideas vital for a robust public sphere—democracy itself was threatened. In 1990, when Random House hired Alberto Vitale to ensure that every title at their Pantheon Books imprint be profitable, Kurt Vonnegut, Studs Terkel, and hundreds of other writers protested outside their offices.[13]

Multiculturalism and conglomeration thus appear to be two main drivers of postwar American literary history. But what is their relationship? Michael Schudson suggests a positive dynamic. He concedes that while the intense postwar corporatization of the book trade brokered the rise of a specific type of book, namely, the "bestseller," it also forced publishers to diversify their lists in order to reach new and broader reader constituencies. Moreover, the overall expansion of the book trade created opportunities for smaller presses to claim various niche markets, thus leading to a growing diversity of books published each year in general. This balancing market effect of diversification, Schudson implies, in part facilitated the emergence of black and ethnic literatures in the 1970s and 1980s. And we have evidence of this effect. Take Random House. In 1968, they hired their first black acquisitions editor, Toni Morrison, precisely to tap into a growing African American readership demographic. Morrison acquired and published books by Toni Cade Bambara, Gayl Jones, and many other black writers. When we look at figure 0.1, we indeed notice a spike in the number of black authors published at Random House. During a moment of peak conglomeration (the early 1970s), a publisher well known for embracing conglomeration hired a black editor in order to racially diversify and expand its fiction list.

But take another look at figure 0.1. What stands out is not so much the intensity of that spike but its ephemerality—its near-instant regression to the mean. And this trend line maps neatly onto Morrison's time at Random House: 1967 to 1983. As soon as Morrison leaves, the data suggests, the publisher returns to its pre-Morrison levels of black exclusion. Increasing authorial diversity at Random House, as a parallel or related effect of conglomeration in the 1970s on, is not a total illusion. But at best, at least based on the data, it is a passing trend.

Ultimately, conglomeration—or, more broadly, postwar industrial print culture—serves in part as an engine of racial inequality, one discernable in terms of both author demographics and the literature itself. I will argue that racial inequality is a specific feature of postwar print culture, an indissociable constant, even as this industry experiences perpetual and profound changes in its constitution. For example, in chapter 1, I show that conglomeration did in fact directly impact Random House—namely, an increase in its number of female novelists and young-adult novels. However, I also show that against this backdrop of conglomeration-induced change, the racial representation of authors, as well as how race gets represented in the novels themselves, remains unchanged or continues to benefit the racial status quo—whiteness.

At the same time, I track the extended effects of postwar print culture beyond just book publishing. Conglomeration, consolidation, and corporatization not only forced large American book publishers to change; it also had a reverberating effect within the broader book marketplace, from reception to distinction. Book reviews changed; bestseller lists changed; book awards changed. In chapters 2 and 3, I explore this afterlife to argue that despite all of these changes, the effects of racial inequality we see in publishing remain stable within each of these next phases. Racial inequality persists as a key feature in how these subindustries function. Yet I also show that inequality gets modified and nuanced, often in surprising ways, and takes on increasingly subtle demographic and textual shapes as we move deeper into the cycle.

What caused this inertia of whiteness in postwar print culture? One possible explanation, developed in greater detail in the next chapters, concerns one of conglomeration's most potent effects: rationalization, or, simply, the promotion of only a few books that the publisher thinks will be a bestseller or prizewinner, at the expense of promoting its entire list. In the postwar period, publishers discovered that it was more profitable and efficient to focus on just a handful of titles each season and push them very hard through marketing, in the hopes that one or two would become breakout hits, whether as bestsellers or film crossovers. This inevitably promoted a "star" system that necessarily drew resources away from a publisher's so-called midlist—authors who sell between ten thousand and one hundred thousand copies per book.[14] In short: big Manhattan book publishers publish hundreds of authors each year, but in their eyes, only a very few really matter.

Rationalization helps explain the main strangeness of figure 0.1: the fact that as soon as Morrison retires as an editor at Random House, the press reverts to its pre-Morrison levels of black authorship, about one black novelist per year. As I describe in chapter 1, Random House did not publish many black or other nonwhite authors, but those that it did, particularly during Morrison's time as editor and after, they put a good deal of effort into supporting. Writers like Toni Cade Bambara and Gayl Jones did not write bestsellers, but they got reviewed widely and sometimes won awards. They lent a certain critical prestige to the publisher. The problem, of course, is that supporting one or two prominent black authors ("known quantities") came to stand in for supporting a much larger and diverse group of black writers. It meant that writers like Bambara and Jones and others became synecdoches for the entire contemporary black literary field. The postwar evisceration of the midlist inadvertently meant the evisceration of a broad and inclusive field of black authors at large American publishing houses. Editors at Random House were unlikely untroubled by its immediate and severe "regression to the mean" for black authors after Morrison's departure simply because they didn't know it was happening.

Indeed, one thing I have learned about large book publishers over the course of my research is that publishers often do not have a good understanding in terms of how they operate at scale. I was unable to secure a reliable and complete list of novels and authors published at Random House between 1950 and 2000 directly from the press, and no such resource exists in the public domain.[15] It seems possible that, at least during this period, large American book publishers like Random House and others had a good grasp of how things were working at the day-to-day, interpersonal editorial level but a relatively weak understanding of how things were working at scale, such as what kinds of authors they were publishing or what kinds of stories and cultural representations they were producing. Reading through their editorial archive held at Columbia University, I found no attempts at quantitative self-analysis of what they were doing.[16]

The problem with this blindness is that it sustains the inertia of whiteness in print culture because no one is able to see its broad contours. It also has a reverberating effect within the larger pipeline of the book market. For example, in chapter 2, I show how Random House's valorization of a handful of black authors at the expense of acquiring books from many different black authors gets reproduced, if not amplified, in the world of book reviews, where an even smaller number of nonwhite authors grabs an outsized proportion of attention. And in chapter 3, I show how this pattern continues in the world of book prizes. Like their counterparts in publishing, book reviewers and prize committees have a good understanding of what they are doing at the local decision-making level, but they don't necessarily have a very strong grasp of what they are doing at scale—how those decisions accumulate over decades to constitute patterns regarding what types of authors get included and what kinds of stories get told.

Literary scholars have also been unwittingly complicit in this illusion. In 1992, about ten years after the numbers of black authors at Random House start to dip to their pre-Morrison levels, Henry Louis Gates Jr. identified a "proliferation of titles" being written by black authors and "high sales figures" for those books, guided by an overall upward trend in black authorship. He mentions "Toni Morrison" and "Toni Cade Bambara" as evidence.[17] Gates is not wrong that *certain* black authors are publishing more books and getting read, but he mistakes the success of a few individual authors for a transformation in the larger field. The larger field, from mainstream book publishing to book reviews to book sales to book awards, saw no enduring transformation. The trouble is that scholars like Gates, who serve as influential public proxies for the academy, have provided a false and potentially dangerous alibi to the literary world. They've helped promote the illusion that whiteness is attenuating in American fiction. Editors at Random House, book critics at the *New York Times*, and prize juries are more than happy to accept this university-sanctioned version of recent literary history. No one is to blame for a problem that doesn't exist.

"INEQUALITY" AS KEYWORD

How did literary scholars largely miss or get wrong this history? In chapter 4, I argue that a set of methodological commitments, close reading in particular, engendered a set of analytical blind spots for the discipline that prevented literary scholars, particularly Americanist scholars, from fully discerning an intense and unchanging racial inequality in the production, reception, and distinction of postwar American fiction, at the demographic as well as textual level. I also argue that the relative avoidance of an otherwise ubiquitous scholarly keyword—*inequality*—is both symptomatic and in part contributes to this interpretative blindness.

The simplest way to describe the American literary field's "red lines" is to call it an "inequality." For example, 97 percent is a value much greater than 3 percent; the number of white novelists published at Random House is massively larger than the number of minority authors it publishes. Literary scholars will likely concede that such numbers are useful in some way—as "facts" regarding the demographics of the publishing industry. But for the most part, many believe that such numbers flatten the dynamism and complexity of literature.[18] Literary critics and historians read literature precisely to understand why some are especially interesting or complex, and, thus, they avoid lumping them into large, anonymous piles and comparing those piles. For the most part, scholars of literature have eschewed the simple observation that *X is greater than Y* because it conceals more than it reveals in terms of the artifacts that we read and care about.

Indeed, "inequality" is rarely used by literary scholars. For example, if we look at a large collection of literary studies essays published in literary studies journals (ranging from *PMLA* to *Critical Inquiry* to *African American Review*) between 1950 and 2010 (a total of 63,397 articles), only 4.2 percent of articles use the term "inequality."[19] And despite the force of recent social events, such as Occupy Wall Street and #blacklivesmatter, which have installed "inequality" as a major keyword, literary scholars are only negligibly using this term more than they did in 1950.[20] The rate of increase is imperceptible—nearly indistinguishable from zero.[21] Another way to think about this is through comparison. Compared to their colleagues in the social sciences (such as economics or sociology), scholars in literary studies use it far less frequently. If we also look at a broad collection of academic articles indexed by the Web of Science database, which includes 198 peer-review journals, we find that the topic of "inequality" is over ten times more prevalent in the social sciences than in the humanities today. And the diachronic story is the same: since 1995, humanists, literary and cultural scholars in particular, have taken at best a marginal interest in the keyword "inequality," and that interest has not grown over time.[22]

It would be absurd to claim that such results indicate that literary scholars do not write or care about inequality or racial inequality. American literature is often centrally concerned with the problem of social inequality, and scholarship obviously registers this concern. The absence of a keyword like "inequality" does not necessarily equal a conceptual elision. Literary scholars, particularly scholars of modern American literature, care very much about inequalities of all sorts. They have simply found an alternative and, in their view, more generative and productive language to study social inequality as it manifests in creative works of writing.

However, I will make the case that the keyword "inequality," especially in the context of studying race and literature, has a particular affordance. But first, I want to revisit the obvious historical affordances of the keyword "power" for this context of study. The work of Michel Foucault and his critique of "power" have been intensely important for a range of scholars interested in race and racial difference, from Gayatri Spivak to Stuart Hall.[23] Hall, in *Representation*, his foundational introduction to the analysis of cultural representation, makes clear the value of Foucault's concept of power and the subject. He took interest in Foucault's notion of "discourse" as a "system of representations," or a way of talking about a topic or object. What is most important is that such a "discourse" governs—both makes possible and polices—the "rules" by which such an object can be discussed, and, thus, it makes knowledge about that thing.[24]

For Hall, Foucault's ideas offered a useful paradigm to study blackness and the historical constitution of the black subject. Discourse, as Foucault reminds us, is never just one statement or text; discourse only becomes meaningful as an aggregate of events spread out across a range of contexts and institutions, and only when aligned and coinciding does it produce a "discursive formation" relevant for the production of an object of knowledge, such as "blackness." Over time, such a formation then sustains a larger "regime of truth."[25] The critique of power and the subject especially appealed to Hall because it linked his interest in semiotics to the study of institutions, connecting the structural analysis of language to its impact on locations such as the state. By the mid- to late 1990s, Hall demonstrated a strong frustration with more social scientific renderings of the subject, which largely relied on fixed and historically insensitive empirical data.[26] Foucault provided a completely different conception of the black subject that deconstructed the very idea of that subject as ontologically stable or naturally out there. Hall instead wanted to trace the various discourses that historically have made available the idea of the black subject, discourses often tied to broader Eurocentric theories of "civilization" and "humanity."[27]

At a more immediate level, Hall was likely skeptical of various statistics regarding black poverty rates or correlations between race and crime because such empirical "facts" produce a conception of the black person as "bound to poverty" or a "criminal" rather than tell us something useful about how that subject became constituted through such tropes in the first place.[28] More generally, Hall also was dubious of the broader discourse of "inequality" as it existed in the 1970s and 1980s, particularly within the social sciences, such as economics. One not uncommon view held by many social scientists, starting in the 1950s and well into the 1970s, was that while economic and other forms of "inequality" exist in society, they represent merely an unfortunate side effect of capitalism, and as industrial societies naturally develop and become more affluent (as the United States did in the postwar period), such negative effects attenuate. And from this assumption there arises the belief that once issues of class injustice get worked out, other dimensions of social life, such as racial inequalities, get resolved as economic opportunities "naturally" get better distributed. David Grusky refers to this as the "benign narrative" of inequality in the social sciences.[29] He traces its origins (anticipating Thomas Piketty's major finding in *Capitalism in the Twenty-First Century*) to the postwar era of affluence and economic growth. For decades this benign narrative dominated social scientific understandings of "inequality," and only through the efforts of more recent scholars has it been critiqued and displaced.[30]

One way to summarize Hall's position is that "inequality"—whether in its *X is greater than Y* formulation or simply the keyword itself—is a mere *symptom* of power. When we look at the discursive constitution of categories rather than just what the categories indicate, we get closer to unmasking the forces of "power" that induce "inequality" as a social effect.

However, the data so far suggests some basic affordances to thinking about U.S. literary history and race through the optics of "inequality." Most simply, it allows us to understand literary whiteness not only as a kind of discursive regime with various instantiated norms and rules but also as a pattern with concrete ebbs and flows. For example, few historians and critics, least of all Eric Lott or Toni Morrison,[31] would doubt that whiteness constitutes a driving force in the articulation of canonical American fiction before and after the war, but few knew, for instance, that the pattern has proven so "sticky" and "unchanging" and that a rupture seen in U.S. publishing in the 1980s was merely passing and ephemeral. Moreover, there exists a value to quantifying the force of that whiteness. While there is obvious value in understanding whiteness as a permeating social consensus, as something that cannot be confined to a specific location or quality, there is also value in observing degrees of intensity, the distinction between domination and absolute and total domination. It is the distinction between 97 percent and, say, 75 percent (or whatever value we determine to signify racial oppression). Such a distinction cannot tell the entire story of literary whiteness. But marking that distinction is important for discerning the precise contours of that force and how it evolves through time. The simple observation that 97 percent is much, much greater than 75 percent has utility in framing "power" as a matter of measurable degrees and strength.

Broadly, I argue that we can think of "power" and "inequality" dialectically. Inequality might register as just a symptom of power, but it is a very useful symptom for diagnostic purposes, and symptoms (as we all know) often can take on a debilitating force of their own. I demonstrate how an awareness of quantitative patterns of racial inequality—what I have called "red lines"—in terms of both demographic authorial representation and literary representation—can be useful to the work of the critique of power and the subject, the unraveling and interruption of the discourses that make certain forms of racial subjectivity available and normalized. One might think of such red lines as the necessary staging ground for such discursive regimes. For example, in my chapter on Random House, I show how its 97 percent authorial whiteness engenders specific textual forms of racial representation, particularly regarding white characters, that circumscribe the terms by which white as well as black characters can be known and thus rendered.

A greater rhetorical and methodological attention to "inequality" helps correct, I argue, an implicit, regular, and problematic assumption in American literary history. Literary scholars tend to believe that postwar U.S. fiction largely emerges through a formal model of cultural democracy. For example, Mark McGurl, in *The Program Era*, argues that the institutions of American literary fiction of the Cold War period, particularly the modern university, represented a kind of laboratory of democracy in which talented individuals from underprivileged backgrounds were identified, trained, invested with cultural capital, and thus afforded social mobility.[32] In general, this is how literary elites at the university, as well as at publishing houses, magazines, and prize committees, thought of their work: as the instantiation and maintenance of a diverse and inclusive chorus of excellent voices. The problem, as Walter Benn Michaels and Kenneth Warren have argued, is that this model of cultural democracy, with its marked emphasis on individual creative genius, has all too easily coexisted with class and social inequality.[33] Postwar American literary culture, both its fiction and criticism, has generally favored a conception of formal democracy in which gross social inequality has not been viewed as a burden.[34]

We see this effect in a range of recent and not-so-recent studies of American literature. Whenever one writes a book on postwar American literary history and some topic, such as "postmodern belief" or "the end of man,"[35] one implicitly produces a quantitative racial representation of authorship in its selection of case studies. One usually has three or four chapters on white authors, such as Thomas Pynchon or Flannery O'Connor, and one or two chapters on a minority author, such as Ralph Ellison or Toni Morrison. One does this, of course, to produce a more inclusive vision of "U.S. fiction." But this otherwise salutary democratizing move has had the unintended consequence of actually *overrepresenting* nonwhite racial authorship in the postwar American literary field as it existed on the ground. Admittedly, literary critics do not claim to reflect some kind of authorial demographic reality when they make such choices. But these choices can be misleading. They can make the racial inequality of the field vanish. They can confuse a scholarly vision of U.S. literature for a vision of the field that is not real.

FUGITIVE SCIENCE, 2020

The idea of using quantification to assist in the project of racial critique upends our usual notions of the relationship between science and race. Historically, we understand empirical methods as typically creating racial stratifications and hierarchies, often supporting white-supremacist ideologies and denigrating nonwhite subjects as inferior. For example, in the late nineteenth century, a number of statistical methods, like regression, now foundational for the discipline, were in part invented to bolster eugenics.[36] Their legacy is inscribed in a longer history of using statistical measurement to create racial categories that have identified white people as genetically or mentally superior to nonwhite people, especially blacks.[37] It is also inscribed in the statistical tools and methods that continue to be used as the theoretical basis for today's ever more sophisticated forms of machine learning, like principal component analysis.[38] Scientific inquiry is driven partly by a desire to build better quantitative methods to measure differences between things. In the context of measuring differences between people, however, such methods all too often have been mobilized to support or intensify prevailing racial ideologies.

In recent years, skepticism toward science and technology and its ability to represent or articulate race has only intensified. For example, Cathy O'Neil and Safiya Umoja Noble have documented how computational algorithms used by banks and online search engines intensify racial stratification and oppression by articulating racial minorities as fixed, quantified types that reinforce existing patterns of inequality. O'Neil refers to such technologies as "weapons of math destruction."[39] Noble calls them "algorithms of oppression," which enable a form of "technological redlining."[40] The innate tendency for statistical methods to reproduce racial ideologies have only become strengthened, not resolved, by the invention of more sophisticated computer-based tools rooted in those now canonical statistical methods, such as linear regression and statistical inference. In "Why Are the Digital Humanities So White," Tara McPherson connects the historical dots. She shows that the history of present-day computation and computers is deeply intertwined with the history of racial formation in the United States since the 1960s.

Yet critical suspicion can also lead to critical adaptation. The association of quantitative methods with structures of racial oppression can be—*must be*—interrogated from the inside.[41] This book attempts to bridge the gap between "cultural analytics" and the critical analysis of race (or "critical race studies"). It does so by discovering generative points of contact between two methods typically viewed as antithetical: data science and racial critique. Cultural analytics is an emerging field where humanist scholars leverage the increasing availability of large digital corpora and the affordances of new computational tools. This allows them to study, for example, semantic patterns in the English-language novel at the scale of centuries and across tens of thousands of texts. While scholars in cultural analytics are taking on a variety of topics, race remains relatively understudied. The reasons for this elision are not hard to grasp. As my brief history makes plain, traditional statistical methods have often historically meant the quantification of one's objects of study and the reification of race. Such labeling works against the aims of critical race studies, which takes as its very mission the deconstruction of racial categories.

Indeed, as Stuart Hall has reminded us, the problem is with racial categories—the way that they contain and reduce individuals to discrete, measurable features. The task for cultural and literary studies, as Hazel Carby has argued, is to discern how "difference exists in the creative articulation of the racialization of a subject and to tease out the political implications of the type of narrative subject being invented."[42] Rather than reify categories of "white" or "black," scholars should expose how such categories are innately unstable and incoherent.

For the most part, this has been the approach of Americanist literary scholars who write on race. Yet there has also emerged a robust and alternative approach in the quantitative social sciences that embraces the insights of Hall, Carby, and critical race studies in general while still mobilizing a quantitative apparatus. The challenge of the *category* remains central. Social scientists like Tukufu Zuberi and Angela James argue that using "race" as a categorical variable (such as labeling a subject in an experiment as "white" or "black") can be useful in determining the relationship between race as a social marker and whatever phenomena one is studying, such as diabetes. One can effectively track the *association* of racial identity and other effects, such as a disease. For example, African Americans are far more likely to have diabetes than white people. The danger is in treating "race as an unalterable characteristic" and imputing causes to its posited presence or absence.[43] Being black does not *cause* one to get diabetes. The more effective way of including racial categories in one's study is to understand race as a *proxy* for a host of other potential economic, social, and cultural factors, such as income rates, education, etc. One needs to "contextualize" racial identity. But again, as Zuberi and James stress, the problem is not with using statistics based on categories of racial identity. It is how we use them.[44]

Most literary scholars, I think, would accept this as a valid view, but scholars who work on literature still have not had much use for even this relatively more enlightened approach to quantitative methods. That is, we study texts as well as authors, and texts represent infinitely complex and multifaceted objects: one can think of every word as a "variable," and in addition to every word, every effect produced by such words, such as "affect," or by the accumulation of words that constitute a broader narrative effect also can represent "variables." Social statistics might be able to decompose the figure of "the black person" into an array of social elements, such as income, gender, and education, to predict voter behavior. But historically, there has not existed a robust-enough quantitative method to decompose a work of literature into a meaningful body of aspects that can capture the complexity of racialized authorship. For example, it would be absurd to define "Asian American literature" as the odds of using a specific word or set of words, such as "woman" or "South Korea," or a literary style, such as stream of consciousness.

Yet recent advances in statistical and computational methods have generated a rich set of affordances for textual analysis that brings quantitative methods into useful orbit with literary and cultural studies. New methods like natural language processing (NLP) can observe and assimilate millions of observations and variables; for example, every word in every novel in a corpus of thousands of texts. But this is a lot of information—usually, far too much to identify coherent patterns. A lot of noise. But the innovation of NLP (and other data science methods, like social network analysis) is that they can turn fuzzy or rough patterns into hard, meaningful signals. Much like a human, the more information it sees, the better it gets at figuring out what's real in the data and what's noise, and it learns to generalize about that data. In the past, literary scholars have tended to avoid quantitative methods in literary studies because it meant turning the endless complexity of the written page of novels into crude measurements, like the number of times the word "manners" appears in novels by Jane Austen versus Charles Dickens. By contrast, an NLP-inspired version of quantitative criticism creates "models" of literary texts. Rather than produce simple measurements of textual behavior, it *models* texts as complex systems of a near-endless array of interacting features, interactions that then produce new features. Like a human, it sees all the words in a text as that text unfolds, and as it sees more of the text, it updates its understanding of what that text is, learning to generalize better the more it discerns. And it can do this at the scale of thousands of texts, not just a handful, with both consistency and rigor.

This approach to analysis—what scholars call "literary modeling"—has produced an energized version of quantitative criticism.[45] Part of this is driven by the capacity of computational analysis to produce complex representations of texts and authors, representations that change as it "learns." Moreover, this method allows opportunities for new readings. The machine never learns on its own. We collaborate with the machine through a recursive process of feedback—as it sees things, we see things that prompt new readings of texts, and these new readings compel it to learn new things and see more. Literary modeling is the dialogue between human and machine, close and distant reading. Recently, Ted Underwood, Andrew Piper, and Katherine Bode have used this approach to track patterns of language and discourse in large corpora of literary works and use them to build new theories of genre and form as well as new readings of individual texts.[46]

However, this book will argue that a modeling approach to literature brings a specific affordance to the study of literature and race. A simple measurement approach confirms the worry held by Hall that quantification puts individuals into artificial boxes of "white" or "black." Yet a modeling approach does the opposite. When we build a literary model to study some distinction or effect in a large corpus of texts—say, realist versus modernist novels—we must start with these categories to set into motion our experiment, but we understand that these categories are not fixed or definitive but instead constructed and contingent. So, when the model returns a set of results (say, realist novels tend to have a greater rate of dialogue than modernist texts), the results are meaningful insofar as they tell us something about the social constructedness of the categories we started with, that is, "realist versus modernist novels." But we could do something further with the model. We can *decompose* it—break it down from the inside—to explore and indeed "deconstruct" the categories we started with, testing their a priori cogency. Additional analysis might tell us, for instance, that the distinction between literary realism and modernism attenuates over time or that in fact it was never particularly stable or coherent. It might tell us that the distinction is highly vulnerable or precarious, reliant on authorial gender or a set of specific words. Ultimately, a model reveals insights not only about the effects of one's categories but also about the constructedness of the categories themselves. In this way, the machine is not an ontological thinker. It is a relational thinker. It helps you understand how different things relate to one another.

This approach, I argue, can align with the goals of critical race studies. Stuart Hall calls for a version of cultural critique that deconstructs those categories to show the diversity of human experience that inheres within them.[47] More recently, Alexander Weheliye contends that race, racial relations, and racialization represent a set of practices that exclude nonwhite subjects from the universally posited status of "the human"; he similarly argues for a black studies that "advocates the radical reconstruction and decolonization of what it means to be human."[48] A critical version of data science can enhance this project. For example, in chapter 3, I use a literary model to demonstrate the inherent instability of racial categories of "white" and "black" within fiction, deconstructing their putative difference, while in chapter 1, I develop a model to identify and track the historical invention and transformation of literary whiteness over time. In its most ambitious form, this book attempts to practice what Britt Rusert has called a "fugitive science" (and what Jessica Marie Johnson has similarly referred to as "black digital practice")—the use of "the rich imaginative landscape of science to meditate on slavery and freedom, as well as the contingencies of black subjectivity"—for our contemporary technological moment.[49]

GETTING LEVERAGE

So far, I've mainly been talking about "red lines." I've argued that what most defines the postwar U.S. literary field is a *red line* that separates white and nonwhite authors, depriving the latter of the resources and opportunities of publishing, reception, and recognition. And I've argued that a machine can help us understand that line, how that line reveals the strength of race as a social construction, and how its expression mutates and evolves over time. But here I will argue that a study of cultural red lines must also be a history of racial recovery. That seeing red lines should also mean seeing the things that stand outside or beyond that red line. That those things are just as important as the red line itself. That to only gaze upon that red line to the exclusion of the things it aims to erase is to unwittingly participate in that process of erasure.

Much of the current enthusiasm of computational criticism centers on "scale." This enthusiasm, however, seems deaf to the present interests of scholars in minority race studies. Many literary and cultural scholars in African American and ethnic studies often want to move in the other direction. Rather than get bigger and wider, they want to see what technology and capitalism precisely erases when society attempts to get bigger and wider with its new methods of surveillance. They want to recover how racial minority subjects get excluded from normative accounts of "what matters," accounts increasingly impacted by technology. Christina Sharpe, quoting Saidiya Hartman, writes: "We must become undisciplined. The work we do requires new modes and methods of research and teaching . . . of undoing the 'racial calculus and political arithmetic that were entrenched centuries ago' and that live into the present."[50]

In the context of the digital humanities, Kim Gallon adds to this list of exclusions *technological belonging* and makes the case for a black digital humanities invested in tracking "how computational processes might reinforce the notion of a humanity developed out of racializing systems." Here, Gallon articulates a conceptual motivation for the work of Noble and O'Neil. But Gallon makes a second, perhaps even more valuable argument. Her polemic is not a totalizing riposte against the use of technology and numbers in humanistic research. She can imagine a version of computational criticism and cultural analytics in which "studying and thinking about the category of blackness may come to bear on and transform the digital processes and tools used to study humanity." But there is a caveat. Such a version of a cultural analytics invested in the study of race must take as its basis what she calls a "technology of recovery, characterized by efforts to bring forth the full humanity of marginalized peoples through the use of digital platforms and tools."[51] Pattern recognition isn't enough. Scale isn't enough. Cultural analytics scholars need to work at both ends. We need to see the lines and shapes that cut through our vast troves of data, discovering pattern and signal, but we also need to see the single texts or authors that break from those patterns, the individual objects that refuse to be assimilated. In other words, we need to find the noise in our data, the things that precisely confound our models. These things are important because they typically recover examples of minority cultural expression that deform and subvert the very patterns that attempt to define, contain, and control them.

Social scientists and scientists construct statistical models to identify patterns in large datasets. And they have methods to determine which specific individual observations do not fit those patterns or trends. We call them "outliers" and often cast such observations as deviations or problems in the data, simply removing them. Such individual items can, in the eyes of researchers, distort or obscure the "true" underlying pattern within the data. Literary and cultural scholars will naturally flinch at this language. All too often, such outliers in literary and cultural history are women or racial minority authors or texts. More typically, our historical gaze drifts precisely to outliers rather than to the authors and texts that stand at the very center of literary history's dominant trends. It is those outliers, we feel, that meaningfully defy such patterns and, therefore, over time may reconstitute them in interesting ways. It is in this sense that literary history potentially works in the opposite direction as statistics. Scientists usually want to discern the lines that best fit their data. Literary scholars typically want to see what does not fit.

But there is a concept that bridges the gap. What makes our "outlier" observation so interesting is that it has (what statisticians call) "leverage." That is, if that observation didn't exist, our patterns would look very different. They would have a different shape. That one point, despite being just one single observation in a large dataset of many observations, has *leverage*. It has more influence than all of the other single observations. In this book, I present *leverage* as a concept that splits the difference between the statistical search for large-scale, encompassing patterns, a search that attempts to tame the very incoherence and heterogeneity of one's data, and the literary historical search for individual texts and authors that defy such patterns and trends, the unique and exemplary works of literature that refuse to be assimilated. Such an approach does not erase such "outliers" to make the red line of American literary history look neater. It uses the affordances of statistical methodology (paired with close reading) to understand precisely the very force and impact that a single author or text can have upon an entire literary field.

We can start reimagining American literary history as a history of leverage. For example, a red line runs through postwar U.S. book publishing. That red line represents the 97 percent of white authors that get published at mainstream presses like Random House. That red line is the voice of literary whiteness: the language, forms, and concepts that enact racial inequality as a literary practice. But there is a novel that does not fit that line. As I describe in chapter 1, that novel is Henry Dumas's *Jonoah and the Green Stone*. That specific novel breaks our pattern. It bears a set of forms and ideas that meaningfully deviate from that red line's norms. But even more so than just deviating from set patterns, it defies them in purposeful ways, gesturing toward the emergence of new patterns that over time further deform what has preceded it. Dumas's novel has, in other words, *leverage* over the field. It is distinct, and we know this, not least of all, because it is one of the few novels by a nonwhite person published by Random House between 1950 and 2000. But it is distinct in an interesting and significant way. It is distinct because it acts upon the field of publishing in a way that very few, if any, other novels of that time can. And what that text does is meaningfully alter or subvert the broader pattern that aims to contain it.

U.S. minority literary history has always been, in a sense, a history of the outlier. Literary historians recover works of literature, like John Okada's *No-No Boy*, that break through the literary field, interrupting the status quo and enabling new forms of expression. But what a human reader discerns as distinctive and thus special is different from what a machine will discern through the lens of data: the literary field as a set of systematic patterns. There exist two forms of cognition—human and machinic. The first we know a great deal about, and that mode has done a great deal to recover a cohort of important minority authors and texts. The second we know very little about, assuming it has little to teach us about literary history. But that mode itself can bear a form of leverage. In rising above the entire literary field and seeing it at once at scale, it can see micropatterns of authorial relation and language that reveal other outliers.

This book argues that a literary history of red lines must also be a history of leverage. The technology that makes it possible to write a history of racial inequality and literature also makes possible a history of recovery. One cannot exist without the other; whenever there is a line on a graph, there must also be points that resist that line, that lie somewhere far from it. In terms of a literary history written through the lens of data, the lesson of technology is that no red line ever remains coherent or stable. The technology and data point us both to the contingencies and ruptures that ultimately define that line and to the defiant outliers that cry out for recovery. And what we find within such moments of contingency and rupture are *racial minority authors meaningfully subverting and transforming the systems of power that seek to contain them*. Again, such cultural red lines are never totalizing. Contained within them are sites of their own undoing. Here, more than anywhere else in this study, the value of close reading becomes apparent. Distant reading gives you the pattern and signal. But close reading helps you understand the outliers and noise—the spaces of exclusion—that in part constitute the shape of the pattern itself.

CHAPTER SUMMARIES AND WHY I WROTE THIS BOOK

This book consists of four chapters. Each chapter focuses on a major phase of the American literary field: production (publishing), reception (book reviews), distinction (prizewinners and bestsellers), and finally, consecration (scholarship). Each chapter combines traditional literary studies methods, such as close reading and historical research, with data analysis. As for the latter, each chapter introduces and emphasizes one computational method. Part of this book's aspiration is pedagogical, to make clear the affordances of data science for literary history. As such, the introduction of each computational method is done in lay terms; technically minded readers can consult a series of footnotes for more elaborate details and explanations.

A word about periodization: earlier I describe the historical scope of this project as the "U.S. postwar period," which I defined as 1950 to 2000. While somewhat arbitrary, I have selected this period as representative because this book is focused on American print culture, particularly its relation to race, and, following U.S. book historians and scholars, this block of time represents a coherent period for this interest.[52] For example, 1950 marks the rise of print culture's conglomerate era, in which book publishers assumed their modern form, while 2000 marks its contemporary digital transformation, in which new online platforms and web services, such as AO3 and Amazon, have dramatically altered the way that books get written, read, and sold.[53] Similarly, it is during this time that racial identity rapidly grew to become a central concern of American culture, fiction in particular.[54] Again, I dispute the extent to which "multiculturalism" actually affected the overall literary marketplace in this period, but I agree that "race" became a major flash point of public debate and interest for writers and readers, especially by the late 1990s.

Chapter 1, "On White Publishing," studies the racial inequality of American book publishing, focusing on Random House as a case study. The question I aim to answer is: does the dominance of white authors at Random House between 1950 and 2000 (97 percent white) produce a distinctly "white" aesthetic—a white style, form, and content? And if it does, what does that aesthetic look like? Answering this question is important in understanding how structural racial inequality at the level of literary production affects the content and form of novels. I approach this question from three different perspectives: (1) I study the archive of Toni Morrison, who was an editor at Random House between 1967 and 1983, to understand how racial inequality appeared "on the ground" at the level of daily decision making and interactions. (2) I use the quantitative method known as "word embeddings" to study Random House fiction at scale. I collected a digital corpus of approximately 1,400 Random House novels—representing about 33 percent of all U.S. novels published at the press during this period. I then use this method to track patterns of discourse in this corpus. In particular, I am interested in how writers in this corpus represent racialized characters, that is, characters marked as "white" or "black." And finally, (3) I combine this pattern-recognition analysis with close readings of individual novels—for example, Henry Dumas's *Jonoah and the Green Stone*—to parse how such patterns materialize at the level of the text. I am especially interested in how specific texts, like Dumas's novel, enact and/or subvert such patterns.

Chapter 2, "Multiculturalism of the 1 Percent," studies the next phase of the literary field—reception—through the lens of book reviews. How does the system of reviews, which decides which books are worth reading and which are not, extend the racial inequality we see at the level of publishing? To answer this question, I collected "metadata" for the top 1 percent most-reviewed American novels between 1965 and 2000 (approximately one thousand novels). Metadata describes which novels were reviewed when and where. I find that racial inequality persists in the literary field, albeit in a more attenuated way: 90 percent of the most-reviewed novels in this dataset are written by white authors; less than 10 percent are written by nonwhite writers. However, I wanted to understand this data more rigorously in terms of whether the most *influential authors*—that is, the authors reviewed in the most prestigious magazines—are white versus nonwhite. Here, the method known as network analysis allows us to study book reviews as a system of influence. It thus allows us to detect which authors are deemed most worthy of attention by book reviewers—which authors are granted the most influence. I introduce and use this method to track how such patterns of attention often correlate to racial identity. How does the literary elite—the gatekeepers of the world of letters—think about race and literary excellence? And when they do admit a nonwhite author into this literary pantheon, what are the rules of inclusion?

Chapter 3, "Literary Distinction and Blackness," continues our study of the postwar American literary field and race by looking at literary distinction: bestsellers and prizewinners, respectively marking how some novels become popular and/or prestigious. As novels enter this next phase of the literary cycle, does racial inequality still persist? I find that it does. I created a corpus of 224 bestselling American novels and 225 prizewinning American novels from this period. A staggering 98 percent of bestsellers and 91 percent of prizewinners (a figure that surprisingly does not change even into the 1990s) are written by white authors. But I wanted to know more about the specific content of these novels to ask: do postwar U.S. bestsellers and prizewinners have a distinct "white style?" And thus, is the postwar field of literary distinction marked by an exclusion of nonwhiteness or blackness? I created a third corpus—229 novels written by black authors identified by the History of Black Writing Project at the University of Kansas. I introduce and implement the method known as textual classification to understand how these three corpora are similar or different in terms of content, style, and form. This is an important question to answer because a strong assumption of postwar American literary scholarship is that a defining aspect of this period is the distinction between "high" and "low" culture, that is, between bestsellers and prizewinners. In this chapter, I show that what also distinguishes the field is a simultaneous aversion of both high and low to literary blackness. I combine this quantitative analysis with close readings to understand how individual texts potentially can also subvert these distinctions.

And chapter 4, "The Canon and Racial Inequality," looks at how scholars have talked about American literature. The major question I aim to answer is: how did literary scholars ignore or miss this story of redlining? There is a dissonance between how scholars increasingly focused on U.S. multiculturalism in the 1980s and 1990s—reconstructing the canon—and what was happening "on the ground" in the U.S. literary field. I am interested in tracking how the discipline honed in on a set of keywords such as "hegemony" and "power" to the exclusion of other terms such as "inequality." And I track how this tendency had a profound effect on how literary scholars understood the U.S. literary field at a time when it sought to transform the canon. Here, I use the method known as "topic modeling" to reconstruct the evolution of how scholars talk about "race" in American literature. With the help of JSTOR scholar services, I created a corpus of 63,397 academic articles published in literary studies journals from 1950 to 2010. Topic modeling allows me to track "race" as a theme in academic discourse and parse how its keywords get articulated and transformed over the second half of the century. This approach helps answer the question of why "racial inequality" never became an explicit keyword of this discourse and, thus, of the scholarship itself. Finally, I perform a close reading of Toni Morrison's *Beloved*—one of the most discussed novels by Americanist literary scholars between 1950 and 2010[55]—to see if and how this novel can begin to teach us how to read for "inequality." How can we start to model a form of literary criticism that attends both to the qualitative and quantitative aspects of racial oppression?

Indeed, as I started researching this book six years ago, I was struck that it was usually writers and activists, and not literary scholars, who were most aware of the forms of inequality determining their professional world. Here I am thinking of a slew of recent pieces in magazines decrying, for example, the whiteness of book publishing and of literary organizations, such as VIDA: Women in Literary Arts, which have collected troves of data regarding gender inequality and book reviews.[56] It became clear that academics and scholars were lagging behind writers and activists in understanding what was actually going on and were producing a largely inaccurate picture of how multiculturalism unfolded (or failed to unfold) during a pivotal moment in American literary culture. This error not only hurts scholarship but also impedes activist efforts to build a more equitable literary culture. If there has been a critical blindness, the real blind spot has been our incapacity to see what we can't see. To truly fight this problem of racial inequality in culture today, we need a clearer picture of the past. That's why I wrote this book.

1

PRODUCTION

On White Publishing

GREAT CHANGE AND NO CHANGE

The story of American book publishing after the Second World War is typically told as one of change and loss. Before the war, the industry experienced what Jason Epstein has called a "Golden Age" of book publishing, albeit short lived: "a cottage industry, decentralized, improvisational, personal."[1] Contracts were secured on the basis of handshakes; novelists like John O'Hara lounged in the offices of Random House; editors like Maxwell Perkins were close friends with their authors. After the war, the publishing field experienced a profound rupture, what many have dubbed the "Great Change."[2] Large, multinational corporations began to take an interest in publishers. As book historians have documented, "over the course of the 1960s and 1970s, most of the major [New York City] Midtown publishing houses were bought by large publicly owned corporations that both capitalized and rationalized an industry that had remained a genteel backwater during the first half of the twentieth century."[3] This began an era of conglomeration and corporatization. If in the previous era book publishers were generally committed to aesthetic evaluation without strong regard for the bottom line and saw their "mission" as elevating the intellectual standards of American society, the new era's watchword was "the bestseller."[4]

The history of Random House, perhaps more than any other American publishing firm, encapsulates this great transformation. Random House was founded in 1925 by Bennett Cerf and Donald Klopfer. The two began with the modest goal of reprinting literary classics, such as *Great Expectations*, while occasionally "publish[ing] a few books on the side at random."[5] By 1950, they had published major authors such as James Joyce, Sinclair Lewis, and Robert Graves and had come to represent U.S. literary publishing at its most prestigious and influential. Then came the buyouts and mergers. In 1959, Random House sold 30 percent of its stock to the public, allowing it to then buy Knopf in 1960 and Pantheon in 1961. This move signaled a massive change in Random House's disposition. Cerf decided that it was time to run Random House like a modern corporation. Mergers between large publishing houses would allow their owners to expand and diversify. This attracted the attention of larger corporations, such as RCA, which bought Random House in 1965 (later selling it in 1980 to Advance Publications once they found that book publishing would not bring as much profit as initially anticipated and hoped for). In 1998, the German multinational corporation Bertelsmann AG purchased Random House. By the 1990s, book publishing had turned international, and Bertelsmann believed that the American company could become more profitable if it shifted its orientation to a global marketplace.[6]

If the reality of postwar American book publishing has largely been defined by endless conglomeration and corporatization, the discourse around that reality has chiefly focused on intellectual outrage, critique, and protest. As early as 1946, James T. Farrell anticipated the major contours of this discourse. In his essay "The Fate of Writing in America," he writes: "the tendency toward combinations and concentration in the book industry will increase the difficulties of operation for small and independent publishers."[7] He continues: "the scale of publishing will be enlarged and money will talk more than ever. . . . Now more than ever, publishers will be forced to be receptive to bestseller books." In 1980, Thomas Whiteside published a series of well-received essays in the *New Yorker* that critiqued the publishing world's "Blockbuster Complex": the increasing imperative to publish novels that sell in order to attract the attention of Hollywood at the expense of literary quality and social value.[8] And in 1990, after the notorious "yacht-lover" Alberto Vitale was hired to head Random House, the entire editorial staff of the esteemed in-house imprint Pantheon resigned, while several hundred people, including Kurt Vonnegut and other writers and editors, demonstrated in front of the Random House building.[9] Again, a story of change and loss. Book publishers have lost their society-elevating mission. Novelists no longer write thoughtful or complex books. Readers have lost a golden age of good writing.

Again and again, whether in the scholarship or the biographies of publishers and famous novelists, we encounter this narrative. Granted, a handful of sociologists, such as Lewis Coser, have usefully nuanced this story to argue that because of publishing's low financial barriers to entry (compared to, say, making a movie) the field is also highly "decentralized," with literally thousands of small book publishers hovering at the edges of large publishers such as Random House or Doubleday. The "great change" has been partly tempered by decentralization. By way of explanation, Coser drolly adds: "for every publisher who has sold out to a conglomerate, there is an editor who has set himself up as a publisher."[10] Yet still, the perception and general reality of mainstream American book publishing is that of relentless conglomeration and a consequent devaluing of "literary quality." After all, even if there are hundreds of small presses springing up each year, studies have shown that 60–80 percent of the American book market by the late 1990s was controlled by just five book publishers, of which Random House is one.[11]

Scholars and writers tend to assert a narrative of change and loss when describing the postwar field of American book publishing. But there is a simultaneous yet suppressed narrative of profound *nonchange* that underlies the more apparent story. In my introduction, I produced a graph that documents the percentage of white versus nonwhite novelists (black and nonblack persons of color) published at Random House between 1950 and 2000.

The graph shows that between 1950 and 2000, 97 percent of novels published by Random House were written by authors who are white.[12] Black novelists constitute a mere 2 percent of that total.[13] What is even more striking is the stability of that statistic, year after year. Excluding two small blips in the 1950s and then a slight period of increased activity for black authors in the 1970s and early 1980s, Random House does not publish novels by black writers. This might come as a surprise; American literary historians tend to think of Random House as particularly progressive in terms of racial representation. What about Ralph Ellison's *Invisible Man*? What about Toni Morrison, the editor? Looking back at our graph, one of those pre-1980 blips in the 1950s represents *Invisible Man* (1952); the rise in activity we see in the 1970s corresponds almost perfectly to Morrison's tenure at Random House (1968 to 1983). Even if Random House at specific moments was pushed to publish or highlight works of African American literature, such moments were consistently short lived. After Ellison and after Morrison, the publisher quickly regresses to the mean: less than 5 percent novels per year by black writers. After 1983, we're back to a nearly flat line. As for other minority writers, they are even more marginalized than black authors.

I've focused on Random House precisely because we'd anticipate Random House, of the various large publishers in the postwar period, to present the least amount of racial inequality between white and black authors. This, at least, is the perception: this is the house that published Ellison, Stokely Carmichael, and Toni Cade Bambara; brought out *The Black Book*; and hired the industry's most prominent black editor, Morrison. But the raw statistics tell a different story. 97 percent is a staggering figure. The story here is clear. Despite the popular and scholarly perception that major U.S. publishing houses like Random House took an interest in civil rights in the 1970s and had begun to embrace "multiculturalism" by the 1980s,[14] the reality is that mainstream publishing stayed averse to printing novels by black people throughout this entire period. I don't have data on other publishers, for example, Penguin, but it's unlikely that their numbers significantly differ. Random House made it publicly known their commitment to black literature.[15]

This chapter takes as its starting point the following conundrum: postwar American book publishing is defined simultaneously by a profound change in its basic structure and means of operation and a profound lack of change in its racial representation of authors. Change and the lack of change stand side by side. Pairing our statistical analysis of race with the scholarship, we see that as one (the publishing industry) endlessly mutates, the other remains unaltered. In this chapter, I focus on the latter to argue that our elision or ignorance of this pattern has caused scholars to overlook a persistent and dominant whiteness not only at the level of what types of authors get published at major publishing firms but also the types of stories that get published in the American literary field at large. Methodologically, I draw from historical and sociological research to parse why this is likely the case and what this looked like at the ground level of editorial decisions and authorial careers. However, I also employ computational, text-mining methods—word embeddings in particular—to study the impact of this racial inequality on literary narrative and language, at the scale of thousands of novels. I conclude with a close reading of a single novel—Henry Dumas's *Jonoah and the Green Stone*—in order to understand how this inequality manifests at the level of the page and how an individual text can subvert its pattern.

WHITE PUBLISHERS

The concept of "white publishers" and its critique is an old one. As early as 1926, W. E. B. Du Bois attacked mainstream American publishers for producing stereotypical representations of black people: "Can publishers be criticized for refusing to handle novels that portray Negroes of education and accomplishment on the ground that these characters are no different from white folk and therefore not interesting?" Later scholars, such as Barbara Christian, would invoke this article as a seminal version of the African Americanist critique of racial bias in U.S. publishing.[16] But perhaps the most eviscerating critique was written by Zora Neale Hurston in 1950—ironically, at the dawn of the publishing world's *great change*. In an essay titled "What White Publishers Won't Print," Hurston argues that the typical white person cannot conceive of black people outside of racial stereotypes, and because book publishers are in business to make money, they will produce stories that conform to such stereotypes, rather than challenge them. She does not entirely fault publishers for doing so. But she contends that literature ought to "mirror" social reality, and publishers, as the "accredited representatives of the American people," have a valuable role in propagating more accurate visions of social reality.[17] But most literary institutions are failing at this, and those that fail fall into the category of "white publishers."

Beginning in the 1970s, studies of the book industry by sociologists and literary historians and autobiographical accounts by publishers such as Jason Epstein are noticeably mute or quiet on the question of race.[18] For example, John Thompson's landmark book on the publishing industry makes no reference to race as a major factor in the postwar transformation of the field, whether as the identity of publishing staff, editors, marketers, or the authors they publish.[19] "On-the-ground" sociological studies from the late 1970s by Coser, Walter Powell, and others are more attuned to race, but they usually mention it as an incident in the data-collecting process (as when they note that they encountered only one black editor during their many interviews with editors at the major presses).[20] And the rash of publisher memoirs that arose in the 1980s, which largely double as self-hagiographies, avoid sticky questions of race and inequality in narrating the rise of their respective publishing empires. The history of postwar book publishing, again, is a story of change and loss. Race—even its mere mention—is very hard to locate.

Thus it is also difficult to give a substantial account of the state of race and racial inequality in book publishing between 1950 and 2000. However, while what we might call "mainstream" scholarship on U.S. publishers has generally seen race as a side effect or afterthought to larger processes overtaking the field, African Americanist critics and historians, following the insights of Du Bois and Hurston, have taken a long-standing interest in this question. There has yet to appear a definitive account of racial inequality in postwar publishing, but we can glean useful pieces of evidence from work by earlier sociologists and book historians.

First, the personnel of major publishing houses during this period, particularly the position of editor, were overwhelmingly white. In their exhaustive sociological study of major book publishers in the late 1970s, Kadushin, Coser, and Powell encountered only one black editor.[21] In a later study, researchers found that Toni Morrison had been the first black person promoted to a senior editorial position at a major publishing company and that after her retirement in 1983 blacks would remain just 1 percent of the staff at large publishing houses into the 1990s.[22] Finally, in another study from this period, interviews with minority staff reveal a largely "homogenous, unidimensional staff" among editors. Racial minorities are typically only hired as token gestures, and "young up and coming" colleagues are always "young, white males from the East or Midwest."[23] (Gender inequality and the intense maleness of publishing, of course, is also touched upon in these studies.) Given the lack of follow-up studies in the 1980s and 1990s, it is hard to infer if such dynamics have altered. But a slew of recent studies of the U.S. publishing industry suggests that not much has changed, and, thus, nothing likely changed in the 1990s. One study from 2016 reports that racial minorities account for just 2 percent of "publishing executives."[24] In sum, scholars, both then and now, tend to view the American publishing world as a "white male WASP province."[25] This is the great nonchange of the postwar era.

The lack of change stands in direct contrast to the profound change overtaking the American reading public in terms of racial demographics. As Donald Franklin Joyce has documented, "the era between 1960 and 1974 witnessed rapidly rising literacy rates and educational levels among African Americans, as well as increased government funding for public education and libraries in African American communities, expanding the economic viability and cultural autonomy of the black reading public."[26] He further argues that "among Blacks in the 1960s and 1970s there was a growing self-awareness of their present and past culture that resulted in an increased demand for books about Black history and culture." In response, "white book publishers" attempted to satisfy this heightened demand for books about black topics and people.

Indeed, by the late 1960s and for much of the 1970s, "Black [was] marketable," as a *New York Times* article declared and as book editors, such as Toni Morrison, would later recall.[27] But as our previous statistical analysis shows, even during the height of black marketability, publishers like Random House merely were now willing to publish a few books, rather than just one or zero books, by black authors. As Morrison recollects, it was impossible to publish more than two black authors per season—and two was an accomplishment.[28] The 1970s facilitated a greater interest in black authors and resulted in a handful of bestsellers, such as Alex Haley's *Roots*, but at scale, this was a mere blip in the overall publishing habits at major houses. And by the 1980s, they regress to where they were at in the 1960s. In his memoir, André Schiffrin—the former publisher of Pantheon—offers some insight as to why this was the case. Big publishers like Pantheon became interested in civil rights and wanted to publish books on this topic. He writes: "the growth of the civil rights movement helped create a massive audience for writing on racial issues."[29] But the problem was that "those who demonstrated at Selma, Alabama and elsewhere did not need our books to tell them what was wrong." Black readers weren't buying their books. White readers were interested, but that interest ebbed and flowed based on current events.

Here it is important to mention that the emergence of the black reading public brokered the rise of small black publishers in the 1960s. As Dudley Randall, the founder of Broadside Press, has argued, "Until the 1960s . . . black writers have had to address themselves to a largely white audience, through white magazines and white editors and publishers. If the white editors thought a book was too militant, or would not interest white readers, the author was told to tone down his message, or the book was rejected."[30] It is for this reason that in the 1960s many small black publishing firms began to appear. Randall continues: "They found a wide black audience, stimulated by the civil rights struggle intensified in the fifties." These presses included Jihad Productions (Newark), Broadside Press (Detroit), and Third World Press (Chicago). The years between 1960 and 1974 witnessed "the most rapid proliferation of new Black book publishers in the century."[31] While we lack hard empirical evidence, it seems that black publishers satisfied the needs of an expanding black reading public in a way that white publishers could not, but doing so lessened the commitment of mainstream publishers to invest further in black authors, continuing an already vicious cycle. In any case, despite the "hotness" of black issues in the 1970s, excluding a few exceptions, large publishing houses remained largely white in both demographics and content. They weren't really publishing more books of interest to black people and therefore weren't inspired to hire more black people as staff. Again, no real change.

Last, the persistence of white publishers raises one more question: does the state of racial inequality in large publishing houses like Random House produce racial inequality in terms of the kinds of stories they publish? Does white publishing lead to stories that privilege white characters? Can an all-white publishing industry produce racially progressive fiction, or is that fiction doomed to reproduce racial stereotypes? Given the difficulty of studying the content of texts at scale, this represents the most yawning gap in the current state of research. However, an empirical study carried out by Nancy Larrick in 1965 titled "The All-White World of Children's Publishing" produces some striking findings. Larrick finds that of the 5,206 children's trade books published in the late 1950s by major trade presses, only 349 included one or more Negro characters (less than 7 percent).[32] In terms of publishers, she finds that eight out of sixty-eight publishers surveyed featured all-white casts. And she finds that not much is changing. Surveying books that came out in 1965—the height of the civil rights movement—only 9 percent of children's books feature a single black person.[33] Result after result shows that major American book publishers, at least in terms of children's books, do not care about representing black people. Most damning, one editor interviewed states that "the effect on sales" of featuring black characters was "negative."[34] Larrick concludes with a call to action: "white supremacy in children's literature will be abolished when authors, editors, publishers, and booksellers decide that they do not need to submit to bigots."[35]

THE VIEW FROM THE ARCHIVE

Random House published a small cohort of black authors in the 1950s and 1960s. Most famously, they released Ralph Ellison's *Invisible Man* in 1952, but they also worked with writers such as Lucille Clifton in the late 1960s, publishing several of volumes of her poetry. Based on editorial correspondence held at the Random House archives, we find that editors such as Alice Mayhew (a white woman) were deeply committed to Clifton and held her work in high regard, even though it didn't sell many copies. For example, Mayhew, via Random House, sponsored Clifton for a prestigious Guggenheim fellowship. She begins her letter of reference by declaring: "Random House considers Lucille Clifton one of the most important poets it has published and a major discovery for the literary world."[36] The publisher had few black authors, but the small handful that they had they took rather seriously. Further, they appeared to know how to promote them and who their ideal audience was. In correspondence with the firm's marketing department, editors like Mayhew and Nan Talese shared lists of "black editors" at various "black journals" and magazines to which they planned to send copies of Clifton's work.[37] Random House was far from being a great promoter of black writing in the 1950s and 1960s, but they were not completely oblivious to the present state of African American fiction and poetry.

This nascent interest in black authors paved the way for Toni Morrison's arrival and rapid ascent at Random House in the late 1960s and through the 1970s. Morrison started her career at Random House in 1964 as a textbook editor based in Syracuse, New York. She was transferred to the firm's Manhattan offices in 1968, where she more properly began her work as an editor of fiction and trade literature, although she continued to edit textbooks into the 1970s. Within a few years, Bob Bernstein, the president of Random House, promoted Morrison to the position of trade editor—a position of significant authority at the press. She became the press's first black trade editor. As commentators have noted, the period's "political and academic tide was lifting Morrison's boat."[38] Morrison used her extensive literary and academic connections, spanning Harlem and Yale, to find talented new black writers, such as Gayl Jones, as well as promote them with the help of already established black authors. Each time one of her author's books was about to come out, Morrison solicited blurbs from distinguished writers, such as James Baldwin and Ishmael Reed, and when the book came out, she regularly hosted popular release parties uptown in Harlem. Morrison retired from Random House in 1983.

My earlier statistical analysis of novels by black authors published by Random House indicates that Morrison was given a certain amount of authority to acquire and publish books by black authors between 1968 and 1983. It's unlikely that she published *every* Random House book by a black writer in this period, but she served as the press's most visible point of entrance for aspiring black authors. As is now well known, Morrison acquired a run of novels by black female authors such as Toni Cade Bambara and Gayl Jones as well as nonfiction by authors such as Huey Newton. Unsolicited manuscripts and letters of inquiry sent to Morrison by the late 1970s show that Morrison had built a substantial reputation in the New York literary world as the field's premier and most influential black editor. The archive also shows that Morrison commanded the respect and attention of Jason Epstein, the press's editorial director, in identifying and promoting young black authors.[39] It appears that they only truly clashed once—regarding the commercial viability of Gayl Jones's *Palmares*, a novel that Epstein disliked and thought was unmarketable.[40] Overall, it seems that Morrison's general influence at the press was enough to cause a slight directional change in the number of books written by black people published at Random House. Again, the spike we see in our graph neatly aligns with her time at the press.

So far, I've described Random House as a "white publisher." I now closely study Morrison's archival papers from her time there to better understand what practices made the press "so white." My guiding assumption is that Morrison's time at Random House represented a pressure point in that process, and in studying her time there, we can gain insight into what particular decision-making and dispositional factors molded that alleged whiteness.

Reading Morrison's extensive collection of correspondence in the archives is, for the most part, a relatively mundane affair. But several things stand out. Morrison is a generous though exacting reader of manuscripts. Each day she read a half-dozen unsolicited manuscripts from aspiring writers: poetry, novels, and nonfiction. Almost all of it, of course, is rejected. But for nearly every submission, Morrison typically provides constructive feedback; rarely does she insult or dismiss. What most stand out are her preferences for writing. For fiction, she loathes the high modernist style, such as stream of consciousness. She doesn't have much of an ear for poetry and often encourages poets to submit their work to other presses even when she intuits that the work is good. For nonfiction, she dislikes academic jargon and rarely accepts manuscripts from professors. Overall, her two most common reasons for rejecting a submission are (1) the writing is poor and (2) the book's topic is too specialized or narrow, inappropriate for a trade press. In letter after letter, she replies to authors that his or her writing style requires more practice or work or that the topic is only appropriate for a purely academic or poetry-reading audience.

Race virtually never comes up as a factor in her selection process. Her main criteria for selection, again, are (1) is the book interesting and original? and (2) will the book have an audience and sell copies? Of course, what very well may make a book interesting to Morrison is precisely whether it deals with race or blackness. But she is clear—both in her correspondence to writers and in her post-factum documentation of the process to her superiors—that good writing will always trump a thematic interest in race or the fact that the author is black. Morrison has excellent aesthetic and literary judgment, was confident in that judgment, and was intent on conveying to her authors and colleagues that if she accepted work, it was not because the author was black or because the book was about black topics. It was because the work was excellent. For example, in a memo sent to other editors, Morrison rejects a manuscript by a distinguished black author called "The Black Critique" because "in trying to use his blackness as *the* important critical qualification, he underestimates or ignores the importance of artistic analysis."[41] Very likely, as Random House's first black editor, Morrison was initially subjected to various types of casual racism and assumptions about her ability to judge literature untouched by a presumed racial bias, and she was eager to demonstrate her aesthetic judgment to her white colleagues. In any case, by the mid-1970s, she had demonstrably proven herself to her superiors like Epstein.

The only time that an attention or awareness of race enters the process is usually at its back end: publicity and marketing. Morrison often took an assertive hand in helping to get the promotion right with the press. In a memorandum sent to the publicity department regarding the design of her author Toni Cade Bambara's soon-to-be-published novel *The Salt Eaters*, Morrison insists that the book's jacket have a "strong and colorful type with special care in the choosing of the type design" because the book's title refers "to a large group of Black people of many backgrounds and interests."[42] Overall, Random House had established mechanisms to promote relevant books to a largely black and/or Southern audience. They knew a "Black market" existed. Morrison knew how to leverage those mechanisms for her authors when the time was right.

Even in letters to close friends like Toni Cade Bambara, which assume a highly personal register, Morrison never mentions things like "whiteness" or "racial inequality" at the press. For the most part, the correspondence and relations between Morrison and her white colleagues are extremely collegial. Morrison identifies and promotes a handful of promising black writers; editors from Mayhew to Epstein acknowledge and respect Morrison's wishes and are eager to help publish these authors at the press, largely deferring to Morrison's evaluations. The books are published, Morrison is enthusiastic about the authors she has edited, and higher-level editors like Epstein are happy that the press is recognizing more black authors. The only time that she seems to betray any frustration or antagonism is during an interview carried out years after she had already retired from the press. She says: "the market can only receive one or two black women writers. Dealing with five Toni Morrisons would be problematic."[43] And even in this rhetoric, racial inequality is displaced onto the market, not Random House. There is nothing in the archive to suggest that Random House put restrictions on what Morrison could publish or what types of authors she could promote; if anything, Epstein sought to empower her to find more black authors.

The only time that the whiteness of Random House is named as an explicit problem by Morrison (based on her archival records) occurred following the posthumous publication of Henry Dumas's *Play Ebony, Play Ivory* in 1974. I describe Dumas's biography in greater detail in my next section, but Dumas was a young and black New York–based poet whom Morrison championed in the in the 1970s after his untimely and tragic death in 1968 (he was shot and killed by a New York City police officer after jumping a subway turnstile). She had discovered his work in the early 1970s through a family friend. *Play Ebony, Play Ivory* was one of several of Dumas's books that Morrison published at the press. She was proud of their publication.

The book did well, and Morrison was elated, but not everyone was happy. A scolding letter came from Hoyt Fuller, the executive editor at *Black World*, a Chicago-based literary magazine. Several of Dumas's poems that appeared in *Play Ebony, Play Ivory* had originally been published in *Black World*. But the Random House volume did not acknowledge this. Fuller writes, "we were more than a little offended." And he ends by noting that "only the paperback editions of Dumas' books were sent to *Black World* while hardcover editions were sent to the local white press," a not-so-subtle jab at Morrison's ostensible complicity with "white publishers."[44]

Morrison was irked by Fuller's letter but likely brushed it off—she didn't personally know Fuller, and dealing with jealous colleagues in the literary world in the wake of a successful book was not uncommon. But a week later came a letter from another colleague at *Black World*, Carole Parks, whom Morrison respected, liked, and considered to be a friend. Parks's letter is eviscerating. She echoes Fuller's general critique but adds a harsh, personalized twist:

> For you see, it's not just that you have given people absolutely no inkling that a *Black* publication gave Dumas his first national exposure. It's that you have at the same time added to the myth that Black genius would languish unappreciated were it not for some white liberal or far-sighted *individual* like yourself. Dumas *chose* to write for NEGRO DIGEST, to speak to a Black audience whenever he could. He was, in turn, honored and *nourished* by those people.[45]

Most damning, Parks concludes her letter with an attack on Morrison's entire project of publishing and promoting black writing at Random House: "I see a rather ugly pattern developing around your 'event' books. One could infer that you are not just interested in advancing your already prestigious career but in singlehandedly (perhaps even unconsciously) advancing your own version of 'Black history.'?"[46] Parks essentially attacks Morrison for using her position of power and influence at Random House to advance her own career and to curate a personal vision of black literature rather than helping to uplift the broader black cultural community and its many artists and writers. Not incidentally, a small university press with ties to the black Chicago literary world—Southern Illinois University Press—had also earlier in 1970 published a version of *Play Ebony, Play Ivory*, but under the more populist title of *Poetry for My People*.

Morrison's response is curious. It is difficult to read. In the thousands of letters of correspondence to writers and editors in the archive, Morrison is consistently confident and sure, rarely if ever betraying a sign of weakness or nonclarity. Here, she begins her letter by saying "Hoyt's letter bothered me.

Yours hurt me deeply." She continues by offering a defense of her own actions and that of Random House, but much of it sounds like disingenuous and special pleading ("I don't have a career, you know. I just work"). And she admits that "the omission of credit was *my* error." Much of the response is framed by rhetorical questions, a tactic she rarely uses. She writes: "I think publishing black books *is* an event. Perhaps they should be done quietly? Secretly? Perhaps I should leave white publishers to their own devices?" It is also the only time I have read Morrison use the expression "white publishers" in the archive. The letter ends rather abruptly and with a rare declaration of melancholy and vulnerability: "More than that, I will miss your friendship. I thought you knew me."[47] Given the substantive list of complaints forwarded by Parks and given the fact that, indeed, the omission was entirely Morrison's fault, this is an unsatisfying response from an editor and writer who typically gets the last word.

It would be a mistake to read too much into a single letter exchange in a career that spanned fifteen years and consisted of hundreds of other positive interactions with black literary magazines, including *Black World*, and black editors. Literary historians like Cheryl Wall frame Morrison's work at Random House as a great success ("As an editor, she helped to define two decades of African American literary history")[48] even if she sometimes encountered resistance. There is much to support this view. But Morrison made it a point to preserve this correspondence in her archives. It clearly troubled her. Parks's letter forces to visibility the racial inequality that underlies the work being done at Random House and other large Manhattan book publishers. It is ungenerous of Parks to accuse Morrison of trying to produce her own self-serving version of "Black history," but it usefully makes clear the larger mechanisms at Random House that pursue black literature for the tastes and preferences of white booksellers and readers. And thus, it cannot be said truly to benefit the black community. Importantly, Parks forces Morrison to refer to her own publisher as a "white publisher." What, essentially, is left unnamed in the daily grind of getting authors signed and books marketed and published and in a day-to-day system of interpersonal interaction that is largely collegial finally explodes to visibility. Let me stress that it would also be a mistake to dismiss Morrison's valuable editorial work as a kind of white complicity. Yet, Parks's letter reminds us that *outside* of Random House, there was a widely held perception that publishers like Random House promoted racial inequality even as they sometimes published high-profile works by black authors like Gayl Jones. It is clearly something that Morrison struggled with and could not fully reconcile, much less name. And this pained her: "I thought you knew me."[49]

RANDOM HOUSE BY THE NUMBERS

Morrison's troubled encounter with Parks reveals higher-order processes of racial inequality at Random House. It marks a limitation in what can be discerned through traditional methods of historical research or textual analysis ("close reading"); these are things that historical actors like Toni Morrison or Carole Parks could *feel* or infer from their day-to-day work lives but that remain operative at such a vast scale to otherwise evade human perception or attention. In the rest of this chapter, I pivot to quantitative methods to render such processes visible.

First, my data. This chapter takes Random House as its case study to study the postwar U.S. publishing scene. I chose Random House for two reasons. First, scholars tend to identify Random House as one of the three most important publishers in this period, and thus whatever trends we expect to see in "mainstream" book publishing at large will be generally captured by Random House.[50] Second, this chapter focuses on the question of race and racial inequality. Scholars have also identified Random House as keenly interested in black cultural topics and writers.[51] Dynamics at Random House should signal an upper threshold for racial tolerance and equality, and thus whatever negative effects we see should be worse or equal at other large presses. This study, of course, could have included not just one but several publishers. It could have included other large mainstream publishing houses, such as HarperCollins, or smaller presses, such as Grove. I have chosen to focus on a single, large U.S. publisher for two reasons. First, the decision to analyze just one large press allows me to develop an argument that can get at some of the granularity of processes at the press, such as specific interactions between editors and writers, as well as attain some mastery over its archive. This would have been simply impossible at the scale of three or four presses. Second, I have chosen to exclude smaller presses like Grove or Graywolf because I first wanted to understand how racial inequality happens in its most normative form: at perhaps the most prestigious and influential publishing house of the postwar era. No doubt we would see different patterns at publishers such as Graywolf. My hope is that in first understanding how racial power and inequality happens at "the top," as it were, we can then better understand how smaller presses have over time tested and perhaps altered that power.[52]

Earlier, I described some of the basic demographic aspects of this corpus. Here, I present a more comprehensive account. The corpus consists of 97 percent white authors, 2 percent black authors, and 1 percent nonblack, person of color authors. The corpus is 58.5 percent male and 41.5 percent female and 73.5 percent American and 26.5 percent non-American. A rigorous and careful process was used to identify the social identity of each author.[53] In terms of genre, we have the following breakdown: 30 percent literary fiction, 28.6 percent young adult fiction, 8.5 percent detective fiction, 8 percent romance fiction, and 2.7 percent historical fiction. (I have chosen to focus only on the five most popular genres in the corpus.)[54]

An observation about gender. The ratio of men to women authors is not as "bad" as the ratio for white to nonwhite authors, but it is still offensively unequal. One might argue that gender representation enacts a form of inequality as trenchant and durable as racial inequality. I have no doubt that sexism and gender discrimination were and continue to be potent at Random House, but in terms of "head count," women steadily gain traction as the decades wear on, and by 2000 have achieved essential numerical parity with male authors, at least in terms of representation (fig. 1.1).[55] And along similar lines, one might argue that the publisher's racial inequality is keenly inflected or determined by gender: what about a possible "white male effect?" The data counters this thesis. White male authors, following the broader gender trend, are notably declining in this period, while white female authors are on the rise.[56] The story here is that within the field of whiteness at Random House, there is a great deal of action. White women are trading places with white men. White men are on the outs. But the

FIGURE 1.1 Percentage of novels written by identified male versus female writers published by Random House, 1950 to 2000, as a function of all novels published in that period, by year.

broader racial dynamics of white and nonwhite remains unchanged. The decline of white men does not mean an increase of black novelists.

Last, to facilitate computational, text-mining analysis, I have assembled a corpus of 1,371 digital texts. This corpus was provided by the HathiTrust library and is commensurable with the full corpus in terms of its breakdown of gender, race, genre, and chronology.[57]

THE GEOMETRY OF WHITENESS

The question I want to explore is whether the vast racial inequality of white authors to black authors at Random House has affected the *content* of the literature it produces. Does this inequality at the demographic level translate into a form of discrimination at the level of narrative and language? Do white publishers like Random House create what we might call "white fiction?" And if so, what does "white fiction" look like at the level of form and content?

In the late 1980s and early 1990s, cultural theorists and historians such as Geoff Dyer, Ruth Frankenberg, and Eric Lott articulated a set of arguments that aim to explicate "whiteness" as a visible cultural identity. One major thesis is that whiteness names what Frankenberg calls a "standpoint."[58] By this, she means that the person who identifies or is identified as "white" sees his or her own racial identity as "unmarked" or standard. This naturalizes whiteness as the baseline upon which all other racial identities are measured, and from this naturalization there flows a cascade of social privileges. Whatever traits that are associated with white identity are viewed as natural or "normal"; those that are not are marked as deviant. A second thesis is that whiteness is defined as absence or noncontent. That is, whiteness is "empty" or merely relational to other racial forms of identity, particularly blackness. It has no autonomous qualities. It is simply reactive and responsive, filling itself with the qualities manifested by other races. This argument has become especially important for literary studies of whiteness. In her study of canonical U.S. fiction and race, Toni Morrison has argued: "Whiteness alone is mute meaningless, unfathomable, pointless, frozen, veiled, curtained, dreaded, senseless, implacable."[59]

Early work in this area named whiteness as a thing that is there but largely devoid of meaningful content. It's there but not there. This framework is useful, but as scholars like Sara Ahmed, Hamilton Carroll, and even Frankenberg herself have noted, it courts a peril in naming the effects of whiteness as somehow unreal. It elides the actual force of whiteness in the world. To meet this critique, Frankenberg identifies a cohort of "discursive repertoires," such as "racial incognizance" (refusing to acknowledge that race is a factor in social relations), that white subjects sometimes practice.[60] Ahmed describes whiteness as narcissistic; its "content" is to always see itself as the subject of discourse.[61] Much of this work is to understand whiteness as not just a standpoint but a series of specific, content-based practices with effects.

This work signals an improvement over more coarse attempts by U.S. historians of whiteness such as David Roediger, who have sought to locate whiteness through a "keyword" approach. For example, individuals who espouse a white identity and ideology are more likely to use racial slurs like "coon."[62] Whiteness thus is constituted by a vocabulary that consists of epithets and semantic stereotypes. The limit of this approach is that it assumes that the discursive expression of whiteness is explicit or self-aware. But this is not always true. Whiteness often expresses itself covertly. Frankenberg parses whiteness as a set of situational interactions in which whiteness grows manifest through a "repertoire" of recurring gestures. Often these gestures are miniature in nature. They are contingent and contextual. The power of this approach is that it exposes whiteness where it seeks to disguise itself in otherwise ordinary social interactions.

But Roediger's approach still has value when studying a large corpus of texts—say, a collection of U.S. Southern newspapers from the nineteenth century or, as in our case, 1,371 novels published by Random House between 1950 and 2000—in terms of tracking the semantic evolution of language associated with white identity. The challenge is pairing a method that works at scale and diachronically with one that retains the sophistication of Ahmed's or Frankenberg's, which are more attuned to the microdynamics of situational articulations of whiteness. In the rest of this section, I introduce a computational method that I believe splits the difference.

A keyword approach to race is guided by the intuition that as experts in history or culture, we generally already know what words tend to signify whiteness and how they do so, whether positively or pejoratively. Hence the keyword "coon." An intuitive move would be simply to count the number of times this word appears in a corpus and track that over time, perhaps also linking such counts to types of authors or periodicals. But here we limit our understanding of racial expression to a narrow notion of "choice." Yes, a particular author chooses to use the epithet "coon" when he or she writes a novel. But that author is making many more choices, perhaps unconsciously, when he or she does that. He or she, to start, is indirectly or directly choosing to use other words with that word—what we call a "collocation," or what one can think of as the words that appear near that word. When that author uses the word "coon," he or she might typically also use the word "stupid" or, more ambitiously, "job stealing" or "poverty" with it. Each use of a word thus encodes a greater action into the vast ocean of all possible words that is language. Getting a list of those words and relative frequencies would tell us something important about not only the appearance of "coon" in our textual corpus but also *how* it is used.

A collocations approach imagines language as a probabilistic distribution in which one is interested in the words that are most likely to appear next to that word. This is still a fairly coarse approach to studying language. But it signals a robust extension to the keyword approach. At scale, it can be revealing and powerful. In particular, when our keyword is not only a single word of interest like "coon" but something more like a figure such as *black or white characters in novels*, it can be especially telling. My corpus is novels and not newspapers, and so I will be tracing a content to whiteness not only at the purely semantic level but also at the representational one. I'll be looking for whiteness as both a semantic form and character type.

We can do even more with collocations. To start, take the approach I just described. Here we might observe that some words (like "dog") are more likely to appear near certain words (like "bone") than other words (like "neuron"). But if we only focus on those words, it doesn't tell us much about the word "dog," our original term. We can also look for words that bear a more conceptual relation to the word "dog." Under this rubric, we would find words like "cat," because "cat," unlike "bone," is more conceptually similar to "dog." These words provide a higher-order conception of the word "dog." The key is to find the words that tend to share the same co-occurring terms, not just the words that tend to appear next to each other in sentences or paragraphs. John Firth described this principle as "you shall know the meaning of a word by the company it keeps."[63] Over the past decade or so, this approach has become popular in computer science and computational linguistics as a language model: "word embeddings."

This approach is robust because it allows us to think of the relations between all of the words in our corpus as a sprawling *geometric space*. Suppose that our corpus has 2,000 words. We can think of all those words falling into a vast 2,000-by-2,000 geometrical space where each word is a point (a vector of quantitative values, technically) within that space. "Dog" and "cat" will appear close to each other based on Firth's principle, but they will also have quantitative proximity or distance to every other word in that corpus based on that same principle. When we compute the distance or semantic similarity between words, it is based on that *n*-dimensional space. Again, it constructs that geometric space in order to understand how all of the words relate to one another as it also computes the relation or similarity between two specific words. The key is to imagine the relationship between words in multidimensional, geometric terms.

A vector semantics approach to whiteness and texts allows us to split the difference between Frankenberg and Roediger. Counting the number of times a word like "coon" appears in a large corpus of texts has obvious value. But what Frankenberg and others have taught us is that whiteness is subtle and stealthy. It reveals itself more as an alignment of otherwise plain elements, an intensity that only emerges when certain things so subtly come together. It's never just a single word, and it is rarely an explicit declaration or claim. It is a disposition that is pieced together. The power of word embeddings is that it allows us to think about whiteness as arising from a vast environment of language, an incredibly complex, layered, and multidimensional landscape of words. The method allows us to peer deeply into that space and recover even the most subtle of its effects. It affords the power of precision and scale while allowing for the exposure of occluded lacunae and silences that also substantively form whiteness's expression.

PATTERNS OF LITERARY WHITENESS

Our question: does the demographic dominance of white authors at Random House between 1950 and 2000 translate into any discernable literary effects at the level of content and form? In this section, I'll implement the "word embeddings" approach to get at this question, but with one important twist. What defines a discourse of whiteness is less the use of specific words or phrases and more a broader orientation to how one thinks about racial identity. In the context of novels, a decent proxy for this orientation is characterization—the representation of persons as characters within the space of narrative. I am interested thus in how white writers represent characters marked as "white" versus "black." As I mentioned earlier, the figure of the character articulates a useful category to think about the intersection of discourse and narrative in our corpus: that is, analyzing character representation allows us both to account for a potential "white language" associated with novels by white authors and a "white storytelling"—that a certain form of represented world is particular to authors identified as white. Here, I implement a collocations approach to the question. What words most commonly occur with racialized characters? When a white or black character appears, what language is used to represent them?[64]

46 PRODUCTION

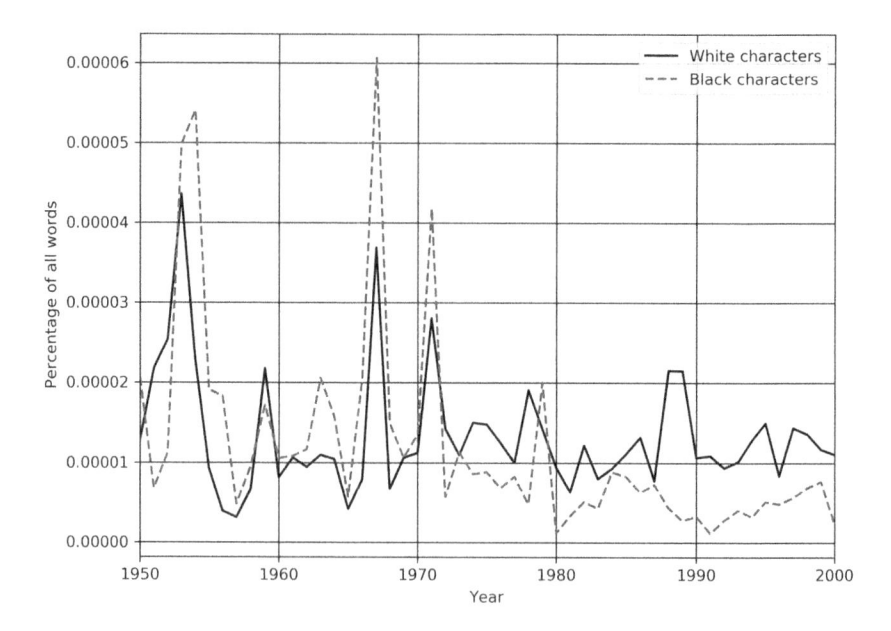

FIGURE 1.2 Percentage of references to identified "white" versus "black" characters in Random House novels, 1950 to 2000, as a function of all words, by year.

Before we start this analysis, just one more exercise will be useful. Are there any time-based trends to racial representation in our corpus? Are the number of white versus black characters increasing or decreasing in Random House fiction between 1950 and 2000? We can simply count the number of times white versus black characters appear in these texts and plot those counts by year (fig. 1.2).[65] The results are rather noisy. We see two spikes in the mid-1950s and late 1960s. But we find no obvious upward or downward trends. Perhaps most surprising, despite the sharp uptick of racial-minority authors published at Random House in the 1980s, we also find no proportional uptick or surge of racial representation in that decade.

These results puzzled me, so I dug a bit deeper into the results. We can break down our results by race (white writers versus black writers), identifying the rates at which they respectively produce representations of white and black characters, and compare them. Here is a graph that plots the number of times characters marked as "black" appear in novels by white versus black authors in this corpus (fig. 1.3).[66] What stands out is the relative amount of attention paid to black characters by black novelists compared to white authors from the mid-1970s to the mid-1980s; the first dwarfs the second. And this attention closely

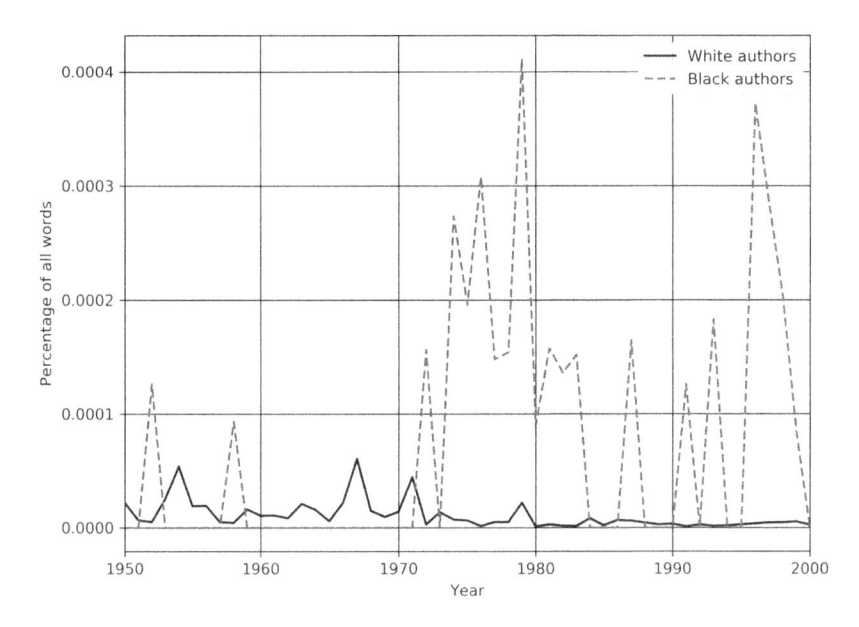

FIGURE 1.3 Percentage of references to identified "black" characters in Random House novels, 1950 to 2000, as a function of all words, by year, in novels by identified white versus black authors.

maps onto the statistical increase in the number of black novelists published at Random House—again, the mid-1970s to the mid-1980s, roughly the same period that Morrison serves as an editor. By contrast, white authors experience no discernable increase or decrease in its representation of racialized characters.

This analysis helps explain this puzzle: literary attention to white and black characters in Random House fiction is increasing in the 1970s and 1980s, a time of increasing nonwhite authorship at the press. But that signal, which is being generated by nonwhite authors, is drowned out when we look at the corpus as a whole. At Random House, the number of black novelists is tiny compared to the number of white novelists, and thus, whatever effect produced by the former is largely masked by the publisher's other 97 percent. This is an important point that I will return to later in this chapter. But for now, we can start our word embeddings analysis of the content of these racial representations. First, we transform the novels in our Random House corpus into a geometric space that reports the words most associated with the appearance of white and black characters and quantifies the relationship between these words as spatial distances.[67] We do this twice: one to describe the semantic geometry of "white characters" (fig. 1.4) and one to describe "black characters" (fig. 1.5).[68]

48 PRODUCTION

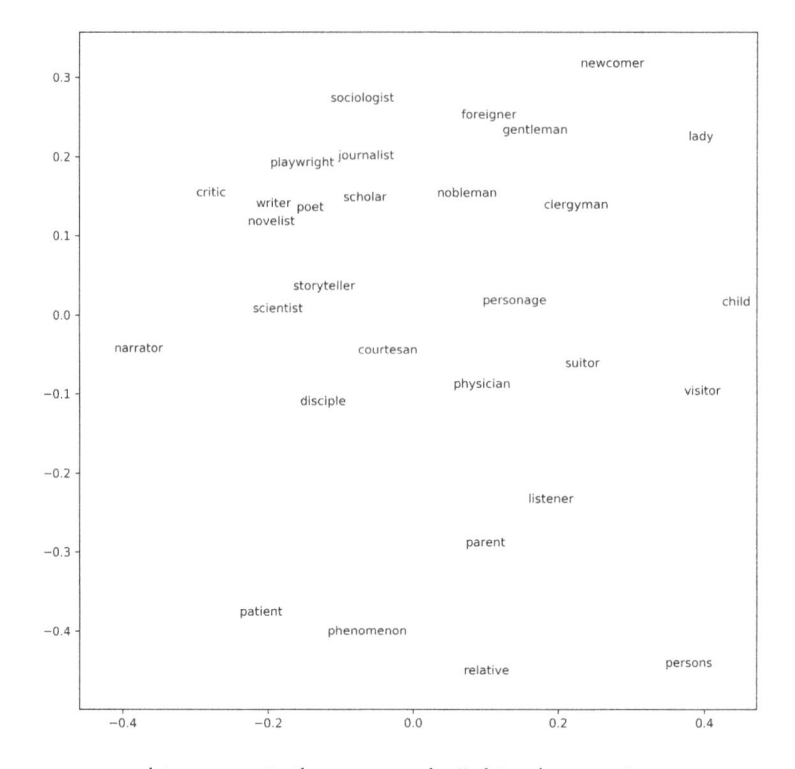

[scatter plot with terms: newcomer, sociologist, foreigner, gentleman, lady, playwright, journalist, critic, writer, poet, scholar, nobleman, clergyman, novelist, storyteller, personage, child, scientist, narrator, courtesan, suitor, physician, visitor, disciple, listener, parent, patient, phenomenon, relative, persons]

FIGURE 1.4 Top thirty most similar terms to the "white character" vector as computed by the Gensim word2vec embeddings model, rendered in two dimensions by a multidimensional scaling algorithm.

Here I need to anticipate a likely critique. In my first analysis, I identify "white" and "black" characters by using an algorithm to find every time a character is explicitly marked as white or black. The limitation with this approach, of course, is that white characters are typically not marked or described as "white." Word embeddings, however, offer a partial solution. It looks for words that tend to appear near explicit mentions of white characters, but it also looks for words that tend to resist association with black characters in order to locate whiteness as the thing that is not explicitly racialized.[69] Through our model, "white characters" thus emerge as a discourse that registers both explicit whiteness and the absence of racial distinction, which critical race studies scholars have described as itself marking a form of whiteness.[70]

A clear and simple story emerges from the data.[71] White characters in this corpus are portrayed largely in positive and flattering terms, while black characters tend to be rendered via negative stereotypes. (Granted, there is a small

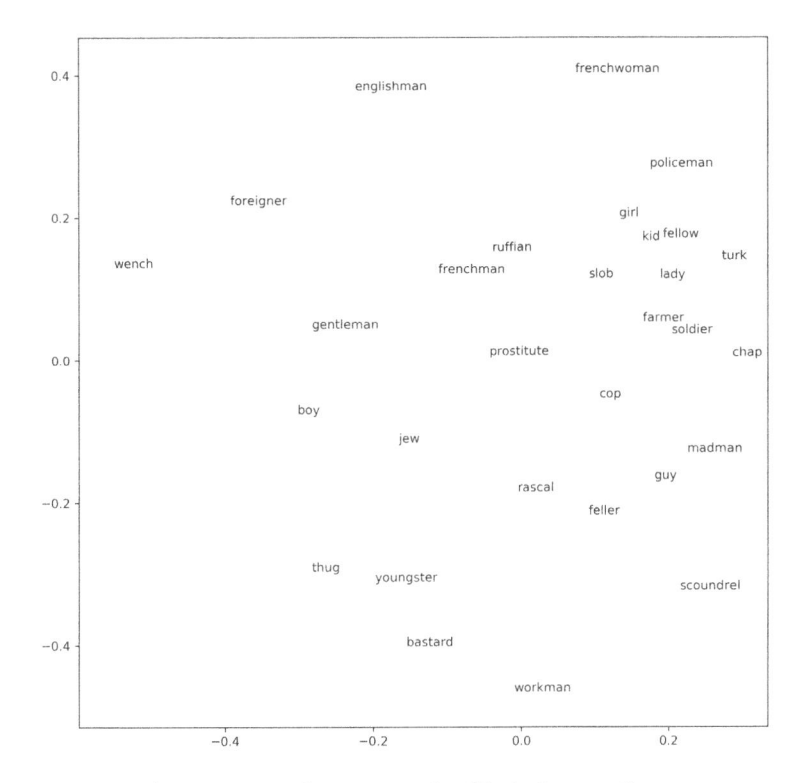

FIGURE 1.5 Top thirty most similar terms to the "black character" vector as computed by the Gensim word2vec embeddings model, rendered in two dimensions by a multidimensional scaling algorithm.

degree of overlap—"lady" appears on both graphs—but we can discern an overall pattern of distinction in which one has more pejorative terms than the other.) White people tend to be "persons" and "parents," whereas black people tend to be "rascals" and "thugs."[72] This is depressing if also predictable, to a degree. Yet what is revealing is the specificity of the types associated with white characters; we find a robust cluster of *literary* positions, such as "critic" and "sociologist," more associated with white characters. White people in these novels are *literary types*. They read books. They listen. They write. By contrast, black characters overall tend to be rooted in more familiar racial stereotypes: "thugs" and "bastards." However, the opposite of this formation is not merely being an imagined good "person." To be the opposite is to be literary or intellectual. The large mass of white authors at Random House in part write their own whiteness into the fabric of their stories by writing about their professional *habitus*. In Updike's *Rabbit Is Rich* (1981), Harry Angstrom's son, Nelson, tells him that the reason he's so tight with money is because "you got the habit of poverty when you were a child, in the Depression. You were traumatized." Nelson of course knows what he is talking about: "I took this course in sociology at Kent."[73]

A logical next step, echoing our earlier character-counting analysis, is to break down our corpus into white and black authors and compare how they represent racialized characters. The analysis we have just performed is for the entire corpus, which is more than 97 percent white. What about black authors? Here we arrive at a methodological limitation. We simply do not have enough texts by black authors (or in general, for the entire corpus) to perform a word embeddings analysis. Having fewer than one hundred texts of novel length will produce unreliable results. And in general, the massive imbalance between the number of novels by white authors and black authors would make any quantitative comparison (such as a most-distinctive-word test) rather dubious.

Instead, we'll focus on searching for patterns of literary representation at the scale of the corpus, and the scale of the corpus articulates race primarily as whiteness. This is not to say that our minuscule group of novels by black novelists *does not matter*. But it might be more effective to think about those novels as representing a space of exclusion. That is, we can reconstruct the forms of pressure that they put upon our more dominant space of "whiteness."

A simple test enables us to get traction on this question. The test works as such: I ran the word embeddings model on the full corpus, which includes white and black writers. Now, let's try a counterfactual. We run the model twice: once only with white authors and once with white and black authors. If black authors exert a statistical force on the model's geometry of racial representation, these two models should be different. If they don't, the models will be exactly the same. Those two geometries will be identical. I ran this test and came up with a negative result. This was a dispiriting result. It is difficult to accept, at least in statistical terms, that black writers do not exert a substantial-enough force in the quantified space of literary representation to change the overall dynamics of Random House fiction and how it depicts race. But it's not entirely surprising. White writers outnumber black writers by a factor of more than thirty.[74]

But clearly novels by black authors are doing *something*, even if such effects are not able to be registered in statistical terms of "significance." The key here, to borrow a conceptual approach from Morrison at the scale of the text, is to decipher the haunting presence of blackness within the archive of whiteness, how it places otherwise invisible pressure points in how that whiteness articulates itself. If thus far we have used various computational methods to track and parse a broader semantic and narratological pattern of whiteness, we now need more robust methods to decompose that pattern into finer parts. Doing so allows

TABLE 1.1 THE "WHITE CHARACTER" VECTOR BY DECADE

1950s	1960s	1970s	1980s	1990s
clergyman	situation	lady	creature	gentleman
decorum	reader	listener	child	suitor
humility	patient	gentleman	patient	creature
Christian	method	affection	certainty	parent
tact	physician	posture	situation	stranger
necessity	poet	frankness	physician	lady
relative	criticism	irony	possibility	child
piety	ritual	sentiment	lady	listener

Sample of the top eight out of fifty most similar terms to the "white character" vector by decade as computed by the Gensim word2vec embeddings model.

us to better trace the latent force of blackness as a force of exclusion, a constitutive outside—the thing that doesn't register as a pattern but is there, shaping the very thing that attempts to erase or obscure it.

The first decomposition I want to do is to break down our pattern of whiteness in Random House fiction by time; specifically, I want to track the "evolution" of whiteness by decade. I am interested in whether literary whiteness is stable through this period or if it changes. And if it changes, I am interested in how rapidly it changes and what precisely constitutes that transformation. Using an extension of the word embeddings language model, I can identify the terms most associated with white characters in this corpus by decade. In table 1.1, I report a sample of the eight terms most highly associated with white characters.[75]

Moving through the decades, the contours of a story about whiteness in this corpus starts to emerge. In the 1950s, the portrayal of white characters is most associated with religion: "clergyman" and "Christian."[76] One can make a few possible inferences. One is that this discourse reflects an early U.S. Cold War valorization of Christian and religious identity as a response to Soviet communism,[77] or it might signal a residual or lingering nineteenth-century association between whiteness and religious identity, the image of whiteness as innately holy.[78] But what stands out is that this discourse essentially vanishes by the 1960s. Here the image of the white person in fiction is expressed through the image of the person of letters. To be white is to be literary. This new trend likely reflects the ascent of "serious" literary fiction by white novelists—Jane Smiley, John Updike, and others. Whiteness sheds its more tamed and banal association with religion and links up with the literary. To be white is to be sophisticated, cosmopolitan, and well read. But in the end what stands out most about the period's overall trends is how this 1960s transformation morphs into a more general discourse of manner and refinement. By the 1970s and 1980s, to be a white person in a novel is to be a "lady" or "gentleman." It is to have "posture" and "affection." Here, we see the disposition of the man of letters combine with the disposition of the refined person. To be white is to have such manners but also and at the same time a cultivated sense of "irony." While there are obvious little nonalignments, for the most part we see a general trend, and that trend is a movement away from religion and toward literary sociability.

Let me pause to anticipate a possible critique: what about genre? A legitimate concern might be that the effects we see here are primarily linked to a specific genre. This would introduce what in statistics we call a "confounder" in our trends. After all, as I point out in my introduction, Random House and most other major publishers are publishing more genre fiction over time—genre is becoming more important. My question became: are the effects that we see specific to genre fiction or literary fiction only, or is it generalized across the entire corpus regardless of genre? To test this, I created a simple basis of comparison: literary fiction versus genre fiction, which includes detective, romance, and historical fiction, aggregated together as one category. I used the same extension of our word embeddings model, but I now compare genre against genre rather than decade against decade. Table 1.2 documents the results.

The results reveal both distinction and continuity. Literary fiction predictably links white characters to literary identity ("writer" and "novelist")—if anything, these results just underscore how self-fixated white writers at Random House are on their own racial identity as refracted through their work identity. If a white person shows up in their novel, he or she is likely to be some kind of novelist or literary person. And somewhat predictably, genre fiction tends to link white characters to genre roles, like "the lover." But what is also clear from the results is a sense of continuity. "Gentleman" appears on both lists, and the figure of the "poet" appears in genre fiction, while the figure of the "parent" (likely an effect of young-adult fiction) appears in literary fiction. The notion of the white person in Random House fiction as both literary and cultivated cuts

TABLE 1.2 THE "WHITE CHARACTER" VECTOR BY GENRE

LITERARY FICTION	GENRE FICTION
writer	child
listener	parent
parent	stranger
suitor	gentleman
physician	lady
disciple	listener
novelist	lover
gentleman	poet

Sample of the top eight out of fifty most similar terms to the "white character" vector as broken down by genre: literary fiction versus genre fiction.

across genre. One can spot a slight skew based on genre, but there is a consistency. In any case, this sense of continuity is strong enough to suggest that genre is not driving the effects of racial characterization that we see at the scale of the entire Random House corpus.

Next, I want to look at the representation of black characters. Using the same procedure, I decompose our account of black character representation (table 1.3). These results are somewhat curious. Two things stand out. First, the representation of black characters in our corpus is relatively stable compared to its representation of white characters. A core set of terms appear in nearly every decade: "boy," "gentleman," "fellow," and related terms. There is, in other words, not a great deal of semantic *variance* in portraying black characters. When a black person appears on the page, there is less discursive action around that character. In sum, the literary imagination of black characters is not particularly dynamic or changing. It is, for the most part, just one thing, and that thing does not discernibly evolve through the years. Second, that core discourse is generally benign. Terms like "fellow" are comparatively neutral, indicating no explicit positive or negative association. Black characters are *just there*. Granted, and as we saw in our earlier, overall word embeddings account, we find a number of

TABLE 1.3 THE "BLACK CHARACTER" VECTOR BY DECADE

1950s	1960s	1970s	1980s	1990s
Frenchman	Jew	gentleman	Jew	Jew
gentleman	fellow	Jew	fellow	guy
soldier	soldier	guy	soldier	foreigner
fellow	chap	chap	chap	fellow
boy	guy	fellow	farmer	kid
girl	boy	cop	boy	scoundrel
guy	farmer	thief	girl	whore
gambler	murderer	madman	gentleman	thug

Sample of the top eight out of fifty most similar terms to the "black character" vector by decade as computed by the Gensim word2vec embeddings model.

racial stereotypes and epithets, like "murderer" and "thug," picking at the edges of our lists. Such a discourse indeed exists and often arises to describe black people. But this discourse is less central to black character representation than its benign one. In Ann Beattie's *Another You* (1995)—a novel about an emotionally crippled university professor who fantasizes about having an extramarital affair—a "black man" appears at a key moment during a funeral, but merely as a stage prop, literally just to help one of the main characters get around: "Now, the black man held the handles of the wheelchair, his orange leather gloves enormously puffy, as if two small life rafts had inflated his hands."[79]

Finally, I performed our genre analysis, this time breaking the corpus into literary fiction versus genre fiction, and again found no meaningful distinctions. Black characters tend to be represented the same through this banal language regardless of genre.

The broader story that emerges from this computational analysis is that the history of Random House fiction between 1950 and 2000 is in part the story of white character evolution, from one type of person to another more specific type of person, against the backdrop of a largely unchanging, stable, and banal black representation. White people in this corpus keep *becoming something*, such as a writer or academic. By contrast, black characters stay the same—a generalized form of a person, with always the nagging threat of danger or debasement ("thug" or "madman"). We might infer that these two things rely upon each other. In figure 1.2, we recall that the rates at which white and black characters appear in our corpus over time are nearly the same (while, again, acknowledging the nontrivial caveat that my model only identifies marked examples of whiteness). White and black characters tend to appear with the same frequency in Random House fiction over time. But one has a semantic space far more varied and robust than the other. To move into a different register, one type of character is more "round," while the other is more "flat." And we might then speculate that the very "roundness" of white character representation partly depends upon the relative flatness or banal presence of "black guys and fellows." One final way to describe this distinction is to say that white characters are allowed to be more *human*. That is, if being human is imagined to consist of the capacity to inhabit and express a spectrum of subject positions, white characters are allowed to exist on a far broader and longer scale.

Our computational model gives us a way to visualize this pattern of change and nonchange in the corpus over time. For example, when we compare the representation of white or black characters in novels published in the 1950s versus the 1960s, and so on, we can quantify the amount of semantic change that has occurred between these two decades. We can then plot these values over time, and the results will tell us which specific decades presented the greatest amount of change for racial character representation (fig. 1.6).[80] So, for example, this chart shows that from the 1950s to the 1960s, white characters experience a semantic change of 0.153 (a score computed by our algorithm), while black characters experience a change of 0.024. The chart overall reveals a clear and consistent picture: through every decade change (1950s to 1960s, 1960s to 1970s, and so forth), white characters have a far greater amount of semantic variability compared to black characters, particularly from the 1970s to the 1980s (fourteen times greater!).

With this final result, we can begin to draw together the different parts of our computational analyses. First, Random House fiction is defined by a profound racial inequality at the authorial-demographic level. Ninety-seven percent white is an astonishing figure. The most apparent effect of this inequality on fictional content is the production of a set of racial representations rooted in what appear to be racial stereotypes. These representations substantively privilege white characters in consistently rendering them as cultivated, literary, and intellectual compared to black characters, who tend to be represented

56 PRODUCTION

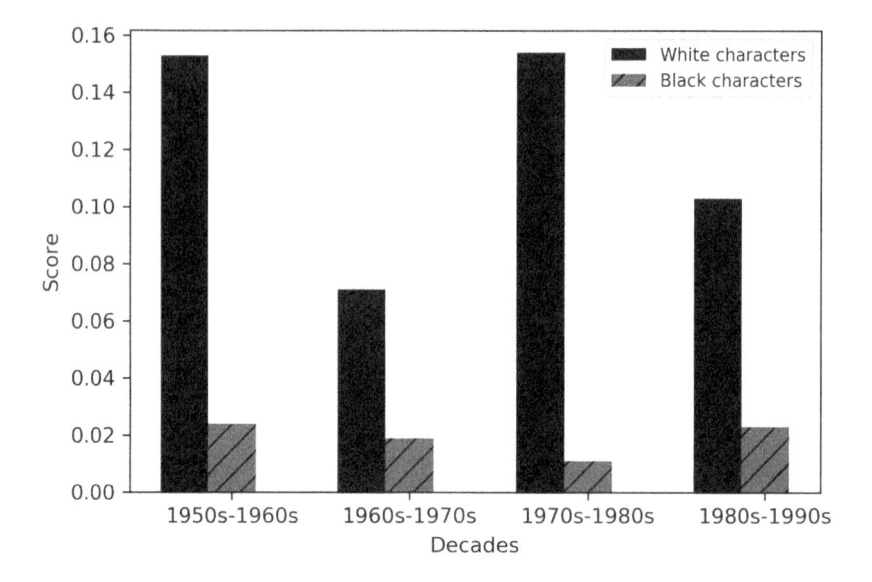

FIGURE 1.6 Amount of semantic variance associated with white versus black character vectors by decade. The score quantifies the degree to which the top twenty-five words most associated with white or black character vectors change between decades. An elevated score thus indicates a high degree of semantic change associated with white or black character vectors over time, e.g, from the 1950s to the 1960s, and so forth.

as relatively more banal or degraded. But beyond this substantive difference, we also find that white characters are just allowed to be more semantically variable, if not *more human*—white characters are perpetually evolving, decade by decade. By contrast, black characters are semantically stable and unchanging, despite discernable changes in U.S. race relations in this period, such as the emergence of the civil rights movement. In sum, this is how the demographic racial inequality of Random House gets translated into a kind of content, a "literary whiteness," at the scale of thousands of novels and on the page.

Yet, at the same time, we find little fractures in this story. Yes, in statistical terms, the handful of black novelists published at Random House, particularly in the 1980s, are not enough to change the overall direction in how Random House writers, in the aggregate, portray race. And yes, it is rather damning that our first graph shows that as soon as Toni Morrison leaves the press, Random House largely regresses to its pre-Morrison levels of black literary authorship. However, even as we have shown literary whiteness to be unusually durable and strong, it is not entirely monolithic and unchanging. Through a decomposition of our language model, we find that the way that white authors think about *white characters* changes over time, peaking between the 1970s and 1980s. Not incidentally, this is also the historical window in which black authors start getting published more at Random House and becoming increasingly visible at the press and in the public. The story of race at Random House is the story of how they briefly tried to introduce more black editors and writers in the late 1970s and 1980s and how white writers responded to this modest attempt at change (one, we know, that did not last or endure) by writing more about white people, constantly rethinking and reimagining the representation of people like themselves. Again, the data is limited such that we cannot directly "prove" the impact of one upon the other. But we can infer a ghostly or allusive impact of blackness upon this archive at scale.

This argument both confirms and extends existing historical and theoretical accounts of whiteness in postwar American culture. Our results echo the historical claim made by Nell Irvin Painter that the most recent articulation of whiteness in U.S. society centers on its emergence as a "visible norm" or as a marked identity.[81] Against the backdrop of black political mobilization in the 1960s and the growing visibility of "black" as a political identity, there developed a concurrent, responsive view of "whiteness" as an "ethnic" identity, (and in the eyes of white nationalists, an increasingly "minority" and besieged group, not unlike African Americans). We see this in force by the 1990s. This story gets refracted in the history of mainstream American fiction by white authors in two ways. First, we find that indeed white authors at least indirectly respond to the growing number of black authors in their midst by rethinking their representation of white characters, particularly the figure of the cultivated, literary person—a cipher for *themselves*. But at the same time, despite the occasional derogatory description of black people as "thugs," their energy is spent on rethinking white literary portrayal, not black representation. This resonates with Robyn Wiegman's thesis that whiteness is innately "narcissistic."[82] And it puts a fresh spin on Mark McGurl's argument about "autopoesis" and postwar U.S. literature in the age of the Master of Fine Arts (MFA) degree (the institutionalization of creative writing). McGurl finds that a defining feature of American fiction produced in the MFA environment is a self-reflexivity in which creative writers trained at MFA programs tend to write about being trained at MFA programs and the university in general.[83] Here, we see a racialized version of this effect. A core aspect of postwar U.S. fiction for authors identified as "white" is a reflexive or autopoetic narration of what it's like to be a white person writing novels in a time of growing racial diversity.

BREAK THE PATTERN: HENRY DUMAS

Our first decomposition of the language model provides some traction in understanding how novels by black authors latently impact the overall corpus's articulation of race, particularly in terms of character representation. But it still elides the force of individual novels. Thus far we've only studied this corpus as a whole. In this final section, I perform a more aggressive breakdown of the corpus. Rather than analyze by time, I analyze by text.

We've constructed two semantic fields, or "vectors," to represent in geometric or multidimensional terms "white characters" and "black characters." We have so far kept them separate in our analysis, but we can combine them into a single vector to represent a general "racial character representation" semantic field. In broad strokes, this semantic vector accounts for how the novelists at Random House between 1950 and 2000 think about race. As a next step, to decompose our corpus by text, we can measure each novel's semantic proximity to that vector. Much in the way that we can measure the distance between words and a "white character" vector within our geometric space, we can also imagine individual texts as collections of words, then treat each text as a point in that space and measure its closeness to that character vector.[84] This is a useful approach to get some more granularity with our analysis. We know what constitutes our "white character" and "black character" vectors at scale, how it internally works, and how it operates over time. As a next step, we can parse how that vector works in single texts.

I implemented this approach, assigning a "score" to each novel in our corpus in which the score indicates that text's semantic proximity to our overarching racialized character vector space. Again: closeness indicates that the text is highly engaged with this vector, while distance means that it is relatively disinterested in racial representation, as measured by the model. Here is a sample of the list, highlighting individual novels of interest (table 1.4). The very top of the list holds few surprises and confirms expectations. We have works of "literary fiction" (Faulkner's stories and Styron's *The Confessions of Nat Turner*) that deal explicitly with race, often producing problematic depictions of black characters. We recall the firestorm of controversy that Styron's novel provoked upon its publication. And we have instances of genre fiction (James Michener and Margaret Long, or adventure and romance) that reproduce stereotypes about white and black people as part of its more general narrative landscape of generic tropes. Michener: the *noble African* who helps our white female protagonist as she journeys to Mozambique. Or Long: the *beautiful and earnest white woman* who returns home to the South to find herself.

TABLE 1.4 SAMPLE OF EIGHT NOVELS

RANK	TITLE	AUTHOR	YEAR
1	*The Faulkner Reader*	William Faulkner	1954
3	*The Confessions of Nat Turner*	William Styron	1967
10	*Affair of the Heart*	Margaret Long	1953
13	*The Drifters*	James Michener	1971
19	*Band of Angels*	Robert Penn Warren	1955
21	*Invisible Man*	Ralph Ellison	1982 (reprint)
31	*Jonoah and the Green Stone*	Henry Dumas	1976
38	*Flags in the Dust*	William Faulkner	1973 (posthum. edition)

Sample of eight novels drawn from the top forty most semantically similar to our "race vector," which approximates the degree to which a novel expresses an interest in the textual representation of white and black characters.

This decomposition first allows us to understand more precisely what a discourse of whiteness looks like in this corpus at the level of the page (as well as its "narcissism" as represented through white characters). Take Michener's *The Drifters*, a novel released in 1971. The novel is a geopolitical romance that features a cast of six different characters from six different parts of the world, as they grapple with political, economic, and social changes. The story is anchored by George Fairbanks, an investment analyst for the fictional "World Mutual Bank" based in Switzerland. The events of the story are reported through his eyes, and his perspective is a not so thinly disguised Cold War U.S. ideology.

The novel is full of musings that ponder the future of society, in particular the crisis of race relations and postcolonialism. In one moment, a character worries:

Man's supreme problem today is finding a way by which he can live with technical advances. Really, if he doesn't, he's lost. And it is the white man who is grappling with this problem. I don't mean that it was white scientists and a white nation that put a man on the moon. I mean that it is the white man who is struggling with the matter of automation, of air pollution, of urban control, of whatever is significant in the world today.[85]

We likely could not find a better example of "white narcissism" in our corpus; this is nothing more than a special pleading for the white man's burden for the postwar age. But what stands out is how aggressively whiteness is figured as occupational station. It is the white man who is the scientist. It is the white man who is the thinker and intellectual, the person—the only person—who can think our way out of this current crisis. Michener reflexively writes his own status as a white thinker into the fabric of the story itself.

But this second analysis does something even more important. As we read through this list, we also note the strong presence of novels by black authors, such as Ralph Ellison, but also lesser-known authors like Henry Dumas. Dumas stands out in particular. If we look at the top forty novels on our list (or top 3 percent overall), only two authors have more than two novels on that list—Faulkner and Dumas, and only one of them is black, Henry Dumas. The active presence of African American novelists like Dumas gestures toward an impact of black writing in this corpus that cannot be registered by our previous statistical test, which was not fine-grained enough to detect individual signals. Despite the empirical evidence, elicited through statistical tests, that the thirty-eight novels by black authors in our corpus are not "enough" to alter the contours of racial discourse at Random House, single novels like *Jonoah and the Green Stone* are doing something. In our decomposition, this *something* registers as a single or handful of novels breaking the surface of our more systematic discourse of race and characterization. There is only one way to parse what this breaking of surface consists of, though—to close read the text. In this final section, I bring our story full circle by returning to Henry Dumas, focusing on his unfinished novel *Jonoah and the Green Stone*, his most substantial work of fiction, edited by Morrison.

Henry Dumas was a charismatic and ambitious writer. He worked hard to succeed but was thwarted for most of his life. Writing primarily in the 1960s, during the early years of the Black Arts Movement, he was largely ignored or refused by established black authors and mainstream book publishers. He had made contact with Ralph Ellison while studying at Rutgers University in New Jersey, but Ellison was repulsed by his writing and avoided him. Dumas sent his work to Viking Press—in a bid to become its "black writer" as it currently lacked one—but never heard back. He started a literary magazine that failed within two issues. Dumas died at age thirty-three. Ever restless, he labored to connect with other writers and produced at a feverish clip, yet publishers passed on his work. He left the world frustrated and denied.[86]

Dumas got his big break a few months after his death. In the late 1960s, Toni Morrison would ask her friend the poet Quincy Troupe to babysit her children. One day, as she went to pick up them up, she spotted a few editions of Dumas's poetry on Troupe's bookshelf. She picked up a copy and read several pages. She was impressed and asked to borrow more volumes. Over the next months, Morrison kept reading, and while she rarely fell in love with poetry, she grew captivated by Dumas's voice. Morrison took his work to her colleagues at Random House, championed it, and by the late 1970s, edited and published two poetry chapbooks and three volumes of fiction, including Dumas's unfinished novel, *Jonoah and the Green Stone*.

It's unsurprising Morrison would take such a strong interest in Dumas. His work, particularly his fiction, eschewed standard conventions of realism. Rather than articulate "blackness" as a sociological fact or direct lived experience, his writing typically mixes realism and fantasy/mythology, injecting into otherwise naturalistic stories of modern black life otherworldly scenes and persons that could not exist in this world. His prose is often quite strange, full of images and symbols culled from African American myth or folklore. Time is usually nonlinear; representation unstable; and point of view unreliable, told more often than not through the confused eyes of a child. Literary scholars in the 1970s and 1980s interpreted Dumas's work as an early or anticipatory version of "fabulist" fiction, labeling his interventions as a form of "surrealism."[87] More recently, scholars and historians have traced his affiliations with the Black Arts Movement (Sun Ra especially) and have identified his aesthetic as an incipient type of "Afro-Surreal Expressionism." Dumas's writing is, in the words of Amiri Baraka, "weird." It is estranged from reality and the language of reality. It bears an intense commitment to nonmimetic representation, "mysterious black symbol worlds of shimmering utterance," that takes as its purpose the revision of reality.[88] Here, Dumas's literature both supports and aligns with Toni Morrison's ambitions for her own novelistic writing as it would unfold over the next three decades.

Dumas stands out in black literary history as an outlier. While he presents a major departure from the immediate postwar black literary aesthetic (Ellison, Baldwin), he also has yet to be fully claimed by historians of the Black Arts Movement that would follow. He remains understudied and undercanonized.[89] Dumas also stands out as a kind of statistical outlier within our computational analysis. In terms of our notion of an imagined geometry of whiteness, Dumas's work is clearly doing something. Perhaps this is hardly surprising: Morrison deliberately brought Dumas into the Random House fold precisely *to do something*—namely, to disrupt the standard outflow of novels by white authors at the press and to challenge the prevailing orthodoxies of black fiction in the existing postwar moment. Looking back, we have ample historical evidence of that impact. And while the statistical results support that evidence, they also help us understand the why and how of that impact at the scale of the page. How does Dumas help interrupt Random House's pattern of whiteness or at least (to invoke a keyword from this book's introduction) exert a kind of "leverage" that allows us to look at that pattern in a new light?

In this section, I close read *Jonoah and the Green Stone*. The novel was written in the 1960s, although never finished. Dumas's executor, Eugene Redmond, had to piece together several drafts of chapters to mount the final version. However, the text was published by Random House in 1976 as a novel, and I read it as such. The novel's first part takes place in late 1937 in Mississippi during a great flood. The story's protagonist, Jonoah, a young black boy, is separated from his parents and rescued by a passing black family, who pull him to safety on a small raft. This section recalls in vivid and terrifying detail their encounters with a white man, Whitlock, whom they also have pulled onto their vessel. Whitlock, a racist working-class man, quickly turns on them. He becomes violent and threatens them until he is thrown from the boat. In the rest of the chapter, the story recalls the aftermath of the flood through the troubled eyes of Jonoah, who has become gravely sick. In the next section, the story jumps to the 1960s. Jonoah is now living in Connecticut and is active in the burgeoning civil rights movement. The section describes his return to the South and his run-ins with the racist police state. Throughout, both sections focus on Jonoah's effort to make sense of the deep hatred whites have for black people.

Our language model has been drawn to this novel because of the intensity by which it invokes racial language, particularly in how it describes characters in the novel through racialized tropes. And indeed, especially in the book's first section, there is a great deal of this type of language. When Whitlock boards the black family's vessel, the encounter is framed entirely in racial language. Whitlock is a white man. Jonoah and his new family—Papa Lem, Mamada, and Jubal—are black. In this encounter, the terms by which they can interact are determined by who they are as racial persons. "We were Black against white," Jonoah recalls.[90] And as the stress of the encounter builds, so does the strength of this racial binary. The terror that Whitlock brings to the ship is the terror of whiteness; what makes them vulnerable and hated is their blackness. "White man," "Black," and "nigger" pixelate the physical text, the image of a stark racial order becoming clearer as each of these words materialize. This is what the model notices.

But there is a surplus to this language that our model helps draw attention to yet cannot fully register. For example, when Whitlock first appears in the text, he appears as the image of a "white man" riding a "white horse": "the white man with the muddy white horse!"[91] Our algorithm will detect the figure of the "white man," but it will miss the "white horse." Yet this figuration is essential for Dumas.

Here his writing drifts into the mythological. The terror of whiteness—in the eyes of black people—extends beyond the mere presence of *characters*. It has become naturalized as a feature of the lived environment, assimilating both animals and the natural world. As the story progresses, the chain of "white" literary signification extends even further. There is not merely the white man with his white horse, humans and animals colluding to terrorize black men and women. As Jonoah discerns, the flood itself has become a terrible whiteness. It crushes down on him and his new family. And finally, the name "Whitlock" also bears symbolic signification. Again, while our algorithm will miss this, most readers will see the word "white" embedded in this name, as well as the word "lock." Whitlock brings whiteness as a form of enslavement, the veritable "lock" that will turn Papa Lem back into chattel. Here, the story's white character serves to enact a chain of white signification as well as to self-allegorize it.

Dumas writes this scene as a kind of high-stakes, terrifying game. Whitlock will smile and then threaten. Papa Lem will meet and parry the threat, then rebuke it with some action or word. Back and forth it goes. Jonoah: "I watched a strange and terrifying game of black and white."[92] What the algorithm has observed in particular is that the game achieves its intensity through the close proximity by which white and black coexist in the text as semantic entities. "White and Black." "White man, nigger." The terror of Whitlock and Papa Lem confronting each other in such close quarters—a small raft—is mirrored in the close quarters of the text. As the game unfolds in the diegetic space of the novel's story, there is a simultaneous game unfolding in the text's language. Dumas uses the words "Black" and "black" in the text, and this effect creates a deliberate ambiguity. For example, the game being played is between a "white man and Black man," but it is also one of "black and white." In other words, Dumas shifts between sociological and mythical modes. We see conflict between a white man and a black man and between good and evil. Our model will miss this effect (the text-parsing process is not case sensitive). However, again, we locate a linguistic excess to how the author invokes the language of race. His strategic creation of textual aporias facilitates the mutation of the real into the mythical.

Furthermore, the story's overall guiding metaphor—the river—encourages the reader to further explore this interplay of meaning and interpretative ambiguity. The figure of the river allows for the mutation of whiteness into the natural world and back: again, the river is a kind of horrifying whiteness. Jonoah thinks of the white man as the flood itself. But the river also comes to allegorize the experience of reading the text. The narrator states that the river has a "code,"[93] and his task, as the flood overtakes his world, is to decipher the meaning of that code—or perish. The reader continuously encounters the fading out of the real (the natural world) into proxies for the mythical (the terror of whiteness), back into the metaphorical or allegorical. Overall, racial signification is unstable. The text participates in what scholars have called "racial abstraction."[94] The river is an apt metaphor. Literally, it unmoors the reader from familiar landmarks of racial meaning. As the reader immerses herself in the steady rush or flow of the narrative's language, whatever piece of familiar land she might grasp at quickly disintegrates at the touch. The real becomes mythical becomes metatextual. In constantly seeing double and inevitably missing things, the reader encounters "race" as a fugitive substance, ephemeral yet inexorably present. This design is built into the diegetic space of the narrative. Jonoah passes through the world as the reader passes through the text, grasping for elusive signs of meaning.

This is the work that *Jonoah and the Green Stone* does as an outlier to the field of Random House fiction published from 1950 to 2000. The novel is striking in how it appears on our list, a black novel falling amid other more familiar touchstones of white literary canonicity, whether highbrow (Faulkner) or middlebrow (Michener). Its presence interrupts this otherwise coherent list of books. But again, Morrison brought Dumas into the Random House fold precisely to disrupt things, and it seems that Dumas himself had prepared for this encounter. He carefully studied the works of canonical white writers like Faulkner as a college student and in particular was drawn to Faulkner's short story "Dry September," which describes the murder of a black man, Willy Mayes, by a posse of Southern white men for allegedly raping a white woman. Even before he was published by Random House, Dumas imagined a literary conversation with Faulkner, a conversation that continues at a much larger and distant scale—the scale of literary pattern.

Faulkner's short story ends with a domestic scene in which one of the white men who killed Mayes, McLendon, now terrorizes his wife. The last line reads: "The dark world seemed to lie stricken beneath the cold moon and lidless stars."[95] This ending, with its drift toward a higher abstraction of white versus black, gestures faintly to the kind of mythological abstraction that so inspired Dumas. In Dumas's hands, however, the conflict between white and black is intensified tenfold: "They were the white trash, the nigger haters, and great white hunters hunting the great black buck."[96] Here, the conflict extends far beyond a final, quiet projection onto the universe; it is naturalized into the regular order of the world, humans hunting animals. White men and black men become white hunters and black bucks. The semantic mutation here is far more direct and visceral than Faulkner's more oblique and harmless "dark world." In Dumas's work, race is abstracted in order to make its horror and violence isomorphic with every aspect of the world, not just a semblance one might notice when one looks up at the sky.

Henry Dumas is an "outlier" in several senses. In terms of postwar American literary history, he does not quite fit in with either the 1950s–1960s postwar scene or the 1970s–1980s Black Arts scene, and he has yet to be fully recognized by contemporary black artists or scholars. He does not belong to the conventional black literary canon. At the same time, he has also come to attention as a statistical outlier. Based on my analysis of word vectors, he is the only black author to have three different texts in the top forty novels that engage most directly with Random House's language of race—a semantic space that frames race and racial identity in highly stereotypical terms. Dumas stands out, and I hope to have shown with my close reading why this is so. The value of a computational approach to literary history is that it reveals persistent patterns of language and form. But perhaps just as importantly, it draws our attention to the individual works and authors who interrupt the pattern. Close reading allows us to discover moments of curious and revealing noise amid all of the signal. Such noise enables us to understand how that pattern can and often is subverted. That it has vulnerabilities and is tenuous.

Jonoah and the Green Stone exerts what I have called *leverage*. By this I mean that Henry Dumas's novel shows how the overarching patterns of racial representation that otherwise define Random House fiction at scale—stereotypical discourses of "white poets" versus "black thugs"—can be meaningfully deformed and transformed. It reveals how the entire representational axis of "white" and "black" can be fundamentally shaken, rendering the semantic foundation of "race" suddenly strange and alien. Perhaps most importantly, his novel captures a dynamic and potentially explosive surplus of meaning that can inhere in otherwise ordinary racialized language, the use of "white" or "black" to describe a person. Again, from our current data alone, it is impossible to estimate the specific impact that Dumas's text had on other Random House novels. But it points to a break or rupture, as a way to escape from ossified patterns.

THE STILL UNTOLD STORY

Yet beyond Random House, how broadly was Henry Dumas's impact felt? Did it send shockwaves across the American publishing world, or was it confined to Random House, where, ultimately, its impact was largely contained? Perhaps the most disturbing bit of data I have shared in this chapter is the first one I refer to: the graph documenting the demographic racial inequality of Random House, likely the most influential and dominant publishing house in the United States in the second half of the century. Ninety-seven percent white. This graph is disturbing because whatever upward trend we see in racial authorial representation in the late 1970s is quickly reversed as soon as Morrison departs. The graph's charting of ephemerality, its tiny little peak of change, seems to mock the intuitions of black literary history—the notion that Morrison could affect enduring institutional change at Random House in terms of increasing its authorial racial diversity. And our content analysis only amplifies this story: with the exception of a few outliers like Henry Dumas, Random House fiction, at the scale of the entire press, largely produces racial stereotypes in which white people are represented as more intellectual and sociable and afforded a greater range of semantic representation, what it means to be human.

This is a troubling story, one defined largely by containment, and it is one in part supported by the data. But one immediately speculates upon other potential stories, stories in fact occluded or disguised by the data. What about racial representation at smaller book presses, like Grove or Graywolf? What about black publishers? Perhaps what we see as containment or failure at Random House in the early 1980s unfolded as expansion and success in literary domains outside of Random House. Perhaps the rupture we find with Dumas in the 1970s was the spark for greater change outside of the spaces that sought to control it. For example, we can think of the explosion of black publishers like Broadside Press in the 1960s–1970s; by the early 1980s, at least thirty-four black publishers were actively publishing books by, for, and about black people.[97]

The story of Random House's postwar racial inequality is an important story, one essential to understanding the wider contours of mainstream American fiction in this period. But I should stress that it does not stand as a synecdoche for the entire field; it is a part of that field, and it is a vital part, but it is not a part that is the whole. What has been most interesting about documenting Random House's history has been uncovering the dialectics of change that exist within its state of nonchanging, the little tremors and subversions. The important question to ask—what I hope will be the basis for future scholarship—is how such internal ruptures induce a broader dialectic at the scale of the entire literary field. Such stories are well beyond the scope of the data and analysis I present here, but we need all of them to understand the whole as a whole.

2

RECEPTION

Multiculturalism of the 1 Percent

RACE AND REVIEWS

Complaints about book reviews are nearly as old as book reviews themselves. Book reviewing, of course, has a long history in the English-language literary tradition. The profession emerged in the late eighteenth century and played an important role in the commodification of literature, particularly novels. Reviewers served a busy and literate (and increasingly expanding) modern audience interested in reading books for both pleasure-seeking and professional reasons. Readers were hungry to read new things but usually did not have the time to read entire novels. Reviewers did the time-saving work of filtering and gatekeeping. As Cheryl Wilson, Frank Donoghue, and Jon Klancher have argued, the book review represented an "important component" of the literary marketplace in the nineteenth century.[1] They also argue that it is during this time that writers learned to adjust their habits to meet the expectations of book reviewers, reviewers learned to anticipate the interests of readers and the marketplace, and readers learned to accept (or reject) the opinions and judgments of individuals paid to write about books.

It's also during this time that writers of all sorts learned to criticize and complain about book reviews. In 1890, Eliza Lynn Linton lamented how "the work of reviewing has fallen into comparatively few hands," the results of which could be "instant fame or obscurity for a new writer depending on his or her connections."[2] Complaints of this type would continue unabated into the twentieth century. However, by the postwar period, anger and resentment toward the profession of book reviewing took on a specific cast. In my previous chapter, I described the increasing corporatization of the book industry and the perceived negative effects of this process on literary quality. Publishers were focusing too much on the bottom line. Talented writers were getting ignored or being pushed out for not writing for a mass audience. By the late 1960s, a slew of prominent commentators had begun to notice the extended effects of cultural corporatization on the evaluation of literature. No fewer than three essays in major magazines decried the "decline" or "waning art" of book reviews. Robert Avrett wrote: "the reviewing of books, a highly respected segment of the literary scene, has fallen into a state of decadence."[3] In *Harper's Magazine*, Elizabeth Hardwick declared: "sweet, bland commendations fall everywhere upon the scene; a universal, if somewhat lobotomized, accommodation reigns. A book is born into a puddle of treacle; the brine of hostile criticism is only a memory."[4] Book reviewers used to evaluate and critique. Now, under pressure from the big publishers, they offered inoffensive, obsequious takes in order to keep the machinery of book promotion intact. Reviews had become propaganda.

Much of the Sturm und Drang that surrounds book reviews exists as a function of their ultimately ambiguous actual effects. People might read reviews, and people often will talk about reviews, but whether a good or bad review will directly hurt or help one's career and reputation or remotely affect sales is unclear. In the 1980s, several empirical studies revealed a set of contradictory findings. One editor pointed out that a front-page *New York Times* book review dramatically increased sales, while sociologists found no relationship between bestsellers and book reviews.[5] The only consensus reached is that *some* books benefited from reviews while others did not, but the array of confounding variables is so numerous that any posited relationship is dubious. Ironically, this ambiguity of effect has only intensified the contentious chatter around reviews. If one gets a bad review, one could say: *well it doesn't matter.* If one gets a good review, one can say: *this really matters!* The data supports both interpretations, and as with any debate of ideas, the debate will be endless when participants deeply care about its stakes but no amount of polemic or evidence can ever resolve it. As John Hollander remarked: "the defects of the *New York Times Book Review* are the table talk even among those who write for it."[6]

Insights into the effects of book reviews took a more sophisticated turn in the 1980s, when a group of cultural sociologists, inspired by the work of Pierre Bourdieu, began to study reviewing as a "social practice."[7] Rather than determine whether book reviews were becoming "worse" or "better" or whether they affected book sales or the careers of authors, scholars such as Wendy Griswold and C. J. van Rees were more interested in how book reviews produce value and enable specific types of meanings for specific types of texts and how book reviewing, not unlike the field of literature itself, operates through a set of discernable rules and relations. Griswold has studied how American and British critics talk about race when reviewing novels by authors explicitly marked as nonwhite (she finds American reviewers are relatively more obsessed with foregrounding the racial background of novelists).[8] And van Rees has analyzed how extremely sensitive book reviewers are to the judgments of their peers and how they often adjust their final take on a book based on what others have already said via a process of "orchestration."[9] Critics, it turns out, are just as fixated on "taking positions" in the literary field as novelists. A book reviewer for the *New Yorker* writes for a set of expectations and readers that differs wildly from a book reviewer for, say, *Publisher's Weekly*—a difference that echoes the difference in how John Updike and Sue Grafton write their novels. How a novel is ultimately received depends upon this dynamic as much, if not more, than its content.

This scholarship represents an improvement over the more vernacular ways of talking (and kvetching) about book reviews. But there is something about the latter that still has value and significance. Implicit in the feelings of resentment that authors express toward book reviews and book reviewers is a sense of *inequality* and lack of *fairness*. That behind closed doors at the *New Yorker* or the all-powerful *New York Times Book Review* a cabal of snooty editors is laughing at one's work and merrily conspiring to sabotage or simply ignore one's hard-earned efforts. There is the feeling that this process of "orchestration" is stacked against certain types of writers. And that when one gets a bad review in the *Times*, or no review at all, one has been victimized. After all, Hardwick wrote her screed against book reviews not only because she felt that book reviewing was "on the decline" but also because she felt that this system is unfair to novelists like herself, and she wanted to do something about it. This is a fairly paranoid reading of the literary field. But there can be inequality without conspiracy. And these are questions not yet fully addressed by the current scholarship. Sociologists ask and answer questions like "what makes a literary masterpiece?" But we still don't know whether reviewers, for example, will only review novels by women if they write on certain themes. These are valid questions, and they are motivated by the frustration expressed by Hardwick about the felt *inequality* of reviews.

Toni Morrison intuited as much after writing a string of well-received and widely reviewed novels. During an interview, she says: "I've always had a secret desire to write reviews of white people's books from that point of view, and make all these observations. I think that would be a scream. I'd say, this is a better book because that's the way white people *really are*. I mean what does that mean?"[10] Black writers like Morrison have long guessed that reviewers treat white and black authors differently when evaluating how and how well they write.

Armed with a bit of data, a simple counting exercise confirms this view. For example, I built a large dataset that recorded information (or metadata) about where every English-language book published in America between 1965 and 2000 was reviewed: which magazine or newspaper reviewed which book, and when. This trove of data is vast—about nine million entries. Next, to make this dataset more manageable, I only kept the books written by American authors and written in English. This naturally greatly reduced the dataset. But it's still vast. Next, I only kept the *most reviewed novels in the dataset*—that is, I only kept the top 1 percent of the most reviewed books in this period. Why the top 1 percent? Novels in this select corpus, of course, do not represent the full breadth of the literary field, but it represents, I argue, the perceived "significant" novels of the time—as judged by critics. These are the novels that commanded the greatest amount of "literary attention," and as such, they signal what I refer to as the "literary elite" or "1 percent of literary culture." This further compressed our list of books to 1,776 unique novels. Finally, to learn more about these novels, I identified the race and gender of the author of each novel, as well as the publisher of each book, through a rigorous manual process of research and tagging.[11]

What does this exercise tell us, exactly? It tells us that when we look at the top 1 percent most-reviewed English-language novels written by U.S. authors between 1965 and 2000, we learn that the authors are 90 percent white, 5.9 percent black, and 4 percent "person of color" (POC)—a category I use to describe nonblack racial minorities such as Asian Americans, Latinx, and Native Americans. It also tells us, perhaps surprisingly, that these numbers are relatively stable over time. Visually, the results are shown in figure 2.1. What do we make of these results? The numbers are *bad* insofar as they reveal a distinct racial inequality in reviews. If book reviewing is a field of attention, white writers get most of that attention, at least at its high end, its "elite." So, for example, the most reviewed novel of the 1960s is William Styron's *The Confessions of Nat Turner*; the most reviewed novel of the 1970s is Thomas Pynchon's *Gravity's Rainbow*; the most reviewed novel of the 1980s is Saul Bellow's *The Dean's December*; and the most reviewed novel of the 1990s is Cormac McCarthy's *All the Pretty Horses*. Ninety percent is a staggering figure—in most workplaces, it would signal a gross inequality (as a baseline, it is worth recalling that in 2000, 75 percent of the U.S. population was identified as "white"). One might look at this graph and say: well, that top line looks to be decreasing. In statistical terms, though, the "effect size" is trivial, and in any case, it declines only because we see a slight

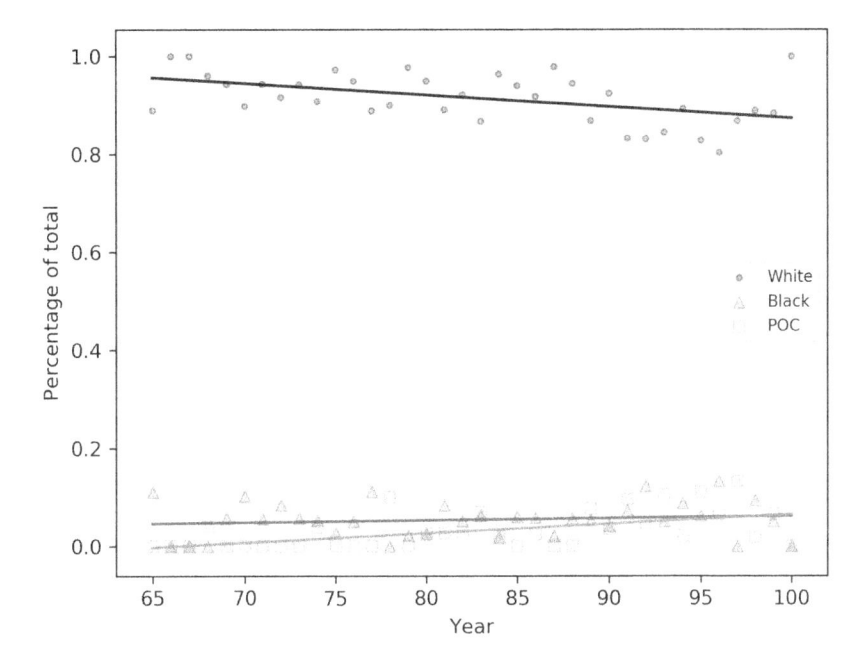

FIGURE 2.1 The percentage of identified white, black, and POC (Asian American, Latinx, and Native American) novelists in the top 1 percent most reviewed titles as indexed by the *Book Review Index*, 1965 to 2000.

uptick in the number of POC authors in our dataset.[12] The representation of black authors in this data is unchanging. Racial inequality is resilient.

This chapter will argue that what drives the field of postwar U.S. literary attention, the social practice of book reviewing, is not only a sense of gathering anger about the "decline" of literary criticism but also a deep and enduring racial inequality as to who gets into the 1 percent of the literary field and who is kept out. Using a mixture of qualitative and quantitative methods—close reading and social network analysis in particular—I show that there exists a discrete set of rules that articulate what kinds of stories can be told and how they should be told. And I will argue that these "rules" weigh especially heavily on nonwhite, minority novelists. In particular, I demonstrate that the literary elite conjures an image of "multiculturalism" that elevates a very specific type of minority novelist at the expense of other types of nonwhite authors. Ultimately, this elevation simply reinscribes racial inequality in new, if less blatant, ways.

In the end, we should be hardly surprised that book reviews offer just a soft improvement in racial inequality compared to book publishers, barely scaling down its whiteness from a daunting 97 percent to an only slightly less daunting 90 percent. Publishing and reviews are a part of the same literary establishment; reviews, as the next phase in the life of a novel, do not represent a separate or autonomous entity. In their sociological study of publishing, Coser, Kadushin, and Powell refer to their relationship as a "systematic social and commercial circle":[13] top editors at trade houses like Viking and Random House regularly communicate and trade opinions with top reviewers at magazines like the *New Yorker* and newspapers like the *New York Times*, and so on. Editors decide which books get promoted and, to a certain text, get into the hands of reviewers. We should be hardly surprised then that the same decision-making apparatus that creates a publisher's list 97 percent white would also help create a book-review field 90 percent white.

BOOK REVIEWS AS DATA

Here, I describe the data in further detail. The first step to constructing this corpus was consulting the *Book Review Index*. The *Book Review Index* is a resource project that is owned by Gale and was started in 1965 to record information about book reviews published in North America and the United Kingdom. It focuses on English-language reviews. The *Index* publishes its information in monthly (now bimonthly) installments, targeted for library and university audiences. The project indexes hundreds of publications that span academic journals, literary magazines, newspapers, and periodicals. A very small sample includes the *American Journal of Education*, *Children's Book News*, *Essence*, the *New York Times Book Review*, *Publisher's Weekly*, the *Yale Review*, and the *Village Voice*.[14] The *Index* continues to publish, but for the sake of the current analysis, I limited my data curation for the period between 1965 and 2000.[15]

The amount of information in this dataset is enormous: over nine million entries. I am interested in the most influential texts and writers in this corpus, so I kept only the top 1 percent most-reviewed American texts in the dataset, using a principled process that I describe in this chapter's notes.[16] After this filtering, 1,776 unique titles and 1,003 unique authors were left.

Next, we can perform some simple numerical analyses to understand this data in terms of dynamics of race and gender. First, let's look at race. Let's specifically look at the racial breakdown of authors in this corpus of the literary "1 percent." I'll compute these figures in two ways. I'll first calculate percentages based on the number of novels that appear in this corpus by authorial race;

then I'll calculate percentages based on the number of reviews that each novel in this corpus has received, also by race. The results indicate that both are the same. White authors receive 90 percent of book attention, while black and POC (again, Asian American, Latinx, and Native American) authors respectively get 6 percent and 4 percent. Whether we're looking at the racial breakdown of the top 1 percent of reviews by how many novels appear in that top 1 percent or by how many book reviews each novel in that top 1 percent has received, the racial breakdown is identical.

But this second analysis is useful insofar as we can refine it. Not all book reviews are equal. A book review in the *New Yorker* carries more or a different type of weight than a review in *Kirkus Reviews* or, for that matter, an academic journal or genre magazine. In my initial calculations, I put all book reviews into the same category, but we can break them down into subcategories. I divided the reviews into two categories: "mainstream" reviews, which include magazines like *Time* and *Publisher's Weekly* and represent a middlebrow readership, and "elite" reviews, which include the *New Republic* and the *Nation* and represent a highbrow readership. When we break down race through these subcategories, the results shift slightly. The percentage of reviews accorded to nonwhite authors increase. Black and POC authors now receive, respectively, 8 percent and 7 percent of this share. Here the results tell a useful if predictable story: that more "serious" and literary journals like *Harper's* or *The Atlantic* aspire to greater racial inclusiveness in whom they decide to bestow book-review attention onto, at least compared to more popular magazines like *Time* or *Newsweek*, which speak to a less culturally rarefied reader.

Gender has been the missing piece of this analysis so far. If we perform a gender-based breakdown, we get the following: novels by men are 59 percent of the literary 1 percent, and novels by women are 41 percent of the literary 1 percent. And we can combine our two types of analysis to get further traction. With a bit more handling of the data, we can explore the interaction of race and gender. What are the breakdowns of the 1 percent if we look at these two variables together (table 2.1)? This is a lot of data to absorb at once, but it tells a fairly clear story. Take a look at the difference between white men and women; the reviews favor white men. But take a look at the difference between black men and women, as well as POC men and women. The dynamic reverses. Black women and POC women get more reviews than their male counterparts. In sum, men tend to get more review attention than women, but only if the author is a white man. The dynamic is the opposite for writers who have been identified as black, Asian American, Latinx, or Native American.

74 RECEPTION

TABLE 2.1

AUTHOR TYPE	ALL REVIEWS (%)	ELITE REVIEWS (%)	MAINSTREAM REVIEWS (%)
White men	64	70	68
White women	36	30	32
Black men	39	42	42
Black women	61	58	58
POC men	38	40	39
POC women	62	60	61

The percentage of novelists in the top 1 percent most reviewed titles as indexed by the *Book Review Index*, 1965 to 2000, broken down by race and gender, across categories of all book reviews and identified subcategories of "mainstream" and "elite" review venues.

We can do some additional analysis. The results just described treat the data as locked into one monolithic time period: 1965 to 2000. But what about temporal dynamics? Do these distinctions of race and gender change over time? Using a statistical method called linear regression, we can identify chronological patterns in the data and determine whether any patterns are statistically significant (or just "noise") and, if so, how significant. Earlier, I produced a graph that visualizes the breakdown of reviews by race. What we see is that nothing changes; white authors on top and nonwhite writers far below. I did the same analysis looking only at "mainstream" and "elite" book reviews and found the same pattern. But what stands out in the data is that when I perform this analysis using gender as my variable of interest, we see a *massive* effect (fig. 2.2).[17] The story here is unambiguous: over time, male and female authors reach parity in terms of the number of book reviews they receive in magazines and journals. I also performed the same analysis, this time only looking at mainstream and elite reviews, and found the same results. Across the field of literary evaluation, women have reached "equality" by the year 2000, whereas black and POC writers continue to face a grave and unchanging racial inequality (which, to recall our previous chapter, entirely tracks with what we see at mainstream publishers like Random House).

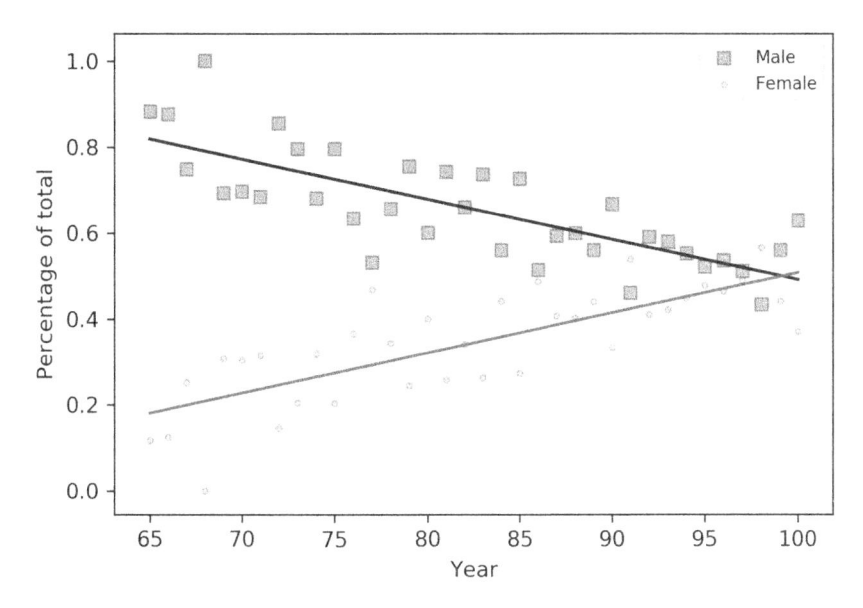

FIGURE 2.2 The percentage of identified male versus female novelists in the top 1 percent most reviewed titles as indexed by the *Book Review Index*, 1965 to 2000.

NETWORKS OF LITERARY ATTENTION

The data so far tells an interesting and potentially important story. But that story is ultimately limited and coarse because it aggregates texts and authors into monolithic, reified categories, such as "novels written by black women." The data perhaps are useful from a sociological perspective in uncovering basic trends of inequality and comparisons between and among different categories of writers based on gender or race. In thinking about the history of book reviews in postwar America, this information is not trivial. It points to fundamental patterns of inequality that confirm, among other things, that white male writers receive special treatment in the American literary field. Yet this space of interpretation is highly constrained in its ability to tell us other things. It doesn't tell us much about individual texts or how specific writers relate to one another. It gives us no leverage to disaggregate our categories of "white male writers" or "POC female writers" and therefore present a story that is not just a list of numbers.

Implicit in our data, however, is a more robust conceptual structure. Novels and novelists relate to one another not just on the basis of their nominal identity categories, like man or woman or white or black. They relate to one another by virtue of a third mediating figure: the magazine or journal that reviewed their book. For example, Toni Morrison's *Beloved* and John Updike's *Rabbit Run* were both reviewed by the *New Yorker*. But while *Beloved* was reviewed by *Essence*, Updike's novel was not. What we have is a very simple network structure in which two novels are connected to each other through a mutually received token of attention by a major literary magazine but disconnected or not connected through the lack of a shared received token of attention by another magazine, one relatively more focused on topics or works of interest to black readers. While, again, this is a highly simple network, if we added into this structure our other 1,774 novels, the network would grow immense. *Beloved* and *Rabbit Run* would become connected by dozens of other magazines and connected to hundreds of other unique novels.

In other words, we can imagine the conceptual space of postwar U.S. reviews as a "literary network" that links authors and texts to one another through a vast and cascading array of properties and dynamics. Network analysis has become a large and important field of research in the social sciences and sciences. In the 1960s and 1970s, sociologists like Stanley Milgram and Mark Granovetter used this method to study simple communities, such as a karate club, to understand how individuals relate to one another and form structures of interaction based on some core underlying dimension of affiliation such as friendship or simply talking to each other. Since then, the field has rapidly and quickly expanded. The increasing availability of large troves of behavioral data largely enabled by the rise of the internet has made network science a privileged mode of analysis to understand the structure of relations of millions of people—say, networks of Facebook users based on what types of posts or comments they "like." In particular, the field has become interested in understanding networks as the basis for not only human interactions but interactions across nearly all types of systems: biological, transportation, cosmological, and so forth. In the 1990s and early 2000s, the method caught the eye of scientists in particular, such as Albert-László Barabási and Duncan Watts, who became keen to uncover "universal" laws and rules that seemingly different types of networks—for instance, neural networks and transportation networks—all shared, thereby making them analyzable using the same basic mathematical tools.[18]

Very recently, network analysis has attracted the interest of literary scholars. The method has been used to study the relationship of Anglo-American modernist poets in the 1910s based on which poets published what poems in what journals and to chart British religious epistolary networks in the sixteenth century.[19] What compels this work is the possibility of producing a "bird's-eye view" of a vast field of cultural interaction based on a large and complex set of relations (however measured) that form structures otherwise invisible or opaque to the human eye but that constitute important forms of power and/or resistance. Cultural networks, of course, have long been inferred by critics and historians. However, an empirical approach allows researchers to view such networks as concrete and discernable entities, facilitating both new macro-scale readings of the network as a totalizing structure and more local readings of specific effects. Still, there are two important caveats. First, literary critics must avoid the allure of reading into one's network grand "universal laws" of behavior not subject to the contingency of the specific things constituting that network. Novels are different from Facebook likes. Second, network science for literary studies must not erase close reading. Rather, as Ruth and Sebastian Ahnert have argued, "network analysis can work in tandem with the equally necessary and more established approaches that operate closer to the ground—or in this case, closer to the text—thus providing both a more comprehensive overview of a field of research as well as specific suggestions for further avenues of research."[20]

Last, I describe the basic mechanics of network analysis as applied to our specific dataset of book-review information. Network graphs consist of "nodes" and "edges." In visual terms, the "nodes" are represented by circles or dots and "edges" by the lines that connect them. The nodes and edges can be of varying size and thickness, respectively, signaling how important the node is or the strength of the edge. Thus, for our data, we can imagine a network graph that describes the relations between writers based on where they get reviewed. Nodes are authors; edges are whether two authors have been reviewed by the same publication. Visually, the network will consist of 1,003 nodes, each representing a writer, and lines between them, the thickness of which is based upon how many times the two writers have been reviewed by the same publication. Two novelists who have never been reviewed by the same venue will not be connected by an edge. Two novelists who have been often reviewed in the same periodical will be connected by a thick line. Overall, the network graph will tell us something about patterns of book-review attention in this period. We might find that authors break down into two or three large clusters or groups. Or that black writers tend not to be reviewed in the same places as white writers.

Finally, we come to the all-important question of "operationalization." What concept or idea is our model attempting to quantify? I argue that the model seeks to quantify the concept of "literary attention." When a magazine or newspaper chooses to review a novel, that decision encodes a form of attention, and that attention corresponds to power and prestige. When the *New Yorker* reviews a new novel by John Updike, it is also implicitly deciding not to review hundreds if not thousands of other novels. Again, deeply encoded in that decision—the decision to bestow attention on a specific literary text—are dynamics of power. Each moment of attention marks a moment of inclusion, yet at the same time it also marks a moment of exclusion. The model of the social network allows us to understand each moment of inclusion/exclusion at scale. That is, the network produces precise *measurements* of inclusion and exclusion for authors and texts, and using such measurements as a foundation, it *models* the relations between authors and texts, including, for example, the relations instantiated by their identities, such as race. What is being quantified or operationalized is the concept of "literary attention and reception." My premise is that book reviews act as proxies for literary attention, and as such, they enact a bridge between crude numerical data (how many book reviews when and where) and higher-level concepts, such as inequality. With this bridge in place, we can expose how *fairly* or *equally* literary attention and reception is distributed across different categories of writers in the literary field.

THE TONI MORRISON EFFECT

Let's start by making a network. As a first pass, we'll explore the relationship between all of the authors in our corpus based on book reviews. Our network consists of 1,003 unique authors (represented as nodes) and 28,261 unique connections between them (represented as lines or "edges"). A line exists between two writers if they have been reviewed by the same magazine, newspaper, or journal. Now, if we were to visualize this network, we wouldn't see much—we'd merely see a large mass of white authors with a few nodes, here and there, representing black and POC authors. We wouldn't see much of a pattern, and as network scientists have long warned, network visualizations can be deceptive and should not be relied on for analysis. A more reliable and precise approach is to compute a series of statistics to identify underlying structures in our network graph. For example, we can measure which nodes represent the graph's "center"—the authors that occupy a central position in our network based on how often they are reviewed (and conversely, the nodes that are not at the center can be thought of as falling at the network's margins).[21] We can then discern whether white versus nonwhite authors are more likely to be at the center. The results were null: there is no "white" center to the graph, and there is no explicit "margin" populated by racial minority writers. Based on this measurement, black and POC authors are not more likely to be found at the network's margins than white novelists.

The results here would suggest a positive story. Of course, the field of the literary elite, as defined by book-review attention, is highly unequal. It is 90 percent white. However, *when* this field of the literary elite "allows" a racial minority writer to join its ranks, it does not appear to put any constraints on that writer's participation. It does not force that author to the corners of literary attention. *Once* a minority author is able to crack the literary elite and break through to the top 1 percent, he or she will apparently *not* be subjected to any further slights or discrimination. He or she will not be cast to the edges of literary attention or put into some far outer niche.

This would be a nice story if it were true, but of course it is not. One way we can get more traction in discerning structure in our network is to think about attention. Not all nodes/authors are equally important. Obviously, some authors, for example John Updike, get reviewed more often than others, say, Mary Gordon. But how do we measure "recognition" in our network? One way to do this is to compute a metric called *eigenvector centrality*. A naïve way to measure the importance of a single node is to count how many other nodes it's connected to. But not all connections are equal. Some links are more important than others. For example, a link to Updike carries more weight than a link to Gordon because Updike himself is connected to many other authors, whereas, we imagine, Gordon is connected to fewer other authors. The eigenvector centrality thesis says that a node is important if it is linked to by other important nodes. We can compute this value (EC) for every node in our network. And once we have these values for every author in our dataset, we can get a better sense of which authors represent the most important individual figures in our network and which authors are marginalized, even though all belong to the broader field of the literary 1 percent. Then we can judge if literary attention is equally distributed across the field in terms of race, and if not, how implicit "rules" of inclusion dictate latent patterns of inequality.

If we ranked all of the novelists in our dataset by eigenvector centrality score, would we see a pattern? We can first rank novelists by the novels they wrote; this means constructing a network graph in which novels (rather than authors, as just described) represent nodes and book reviews instantiate edges. We then compute EC scores for each novel (table 2.2).[22] So far, nothing terribly surprising. A lot of famous white men: Saul Bellow, John Updike (a few times), William Styron. One surprise, of course, is that Lorrie Moore's novel makes it to the very top. And Anne Tyler—a writer who has yet to make it into the academic firmament—also cracks the pantheon. But for the most part, our list reflects critical

TABLE 2.2

RANK	NOVEL TITLE	AUTHOR	EC SCORE
1	Birds of America	Lorrie Moore	0.0455
2	Humboldt's Gift	Saul Bellow	0.0425
3	Ragtime	E.L. Doctorow	0.0420
4	Rabbit Redux	John Updike	0.0419
5	A Month of Sundays	John Updike	0.0418
6	Breathing Lessons	Anne Tyler	0.0412
7	The Coup	John Updike	0.0411
8	Sophie's Choice	William Styron	0.0410
9	Falconer	John Cheever	0.0408
10	The Dean's December	Saul Bellow	0.0407

The top ten novels in the top 1 percent most reviewed titles as indexed by the *Book Review Index*, 1965 to 2000, based on calculated eigenvector centrality (EC) scores.

anticipation. Bellow, Updike. And another perhaps nontrivial surprise: no black or POC authors. The list is all white. But we can also rank authors as authors. That is, we can again treat authors as nodes in order to identify the individual effects that authors have in this network. Some have written many books. We see this already in our results—Moore beats out Updike for the top spot, but Updike has three novels in the top ten alone. Surely, if we treat authors as our unit of interest, Updike would display a greater impact or force in the field, and he indeed does (table 2.3). This list, perhaps more than our first list, even better accords with scholarly expectation. No single Roth novel rules the field, but "Philip Roth," the author who has created a veritable microcanon of literature, does.

Yet what perhaps most stands out about this second ranking is the appearance and high position of a black female author: Toni Morrison. "Toni Morrison"—the literary institution, not unlike "Philip Roth" or "Joyce Carol Oates"—exercises great power and authority in the mental attentions of literary gatekeepers. But

TABLE 2.3

RANK	AUTHOR	EC SCORE
1	Philip Roth	0.0697
2	Toni Morrison	0.0692
3	John Updike	0.0689
4	Anne Tyler	0.0673
5	Joyce Carol Oates	0.0670
6	William Styron	0.0655
7	Thomas Pynchon	0.0646
7	Norman Mailer	0.0646
9	Bernard Malamud	0.0645
10	Gore Vidal	0.0636

The top ten authors in the top 1 percent most reviewed titles as indexed by the *Book Review Index*, 1965 to 2000, based on calculated eigenvector centrality (EC) scores.

if we look harder at our list of top authors, a disturbing trend appears. There are no other black authors anywhere near the top ten of most influential writers. The next closest author is Alice Walker, who comes in just inside of the top fifty. The space between numbers 2 and 47 is filled with nonblack authors, a flood of white novelists. Vidal, Mailer. And after Walker, we find a relatively random distribution of black authors, from Ralph Ellison to Ossie Davis, fanning out across the rankings, number 47 to number 997. (As a sidebar, it is worth noting the high number of Jewish writers on this list; however, for this analysis, I bracket out the question of how Jewishness articulates a specific type of "whiteness," even though I acknowledge the complicated history by which Jews became "white" in this period.)

Here we come to the following observation: the literary gatekeepers as represented by book reviewers appear *very* interested in *certain* black authors. Toni

Morrison signals an "outlier" of great consequence, a figure of extraordinary distinction in this field. But what does her status as an outlier truly signify? Why does she in particular get to the top of the list?

I will make the following argument: *when* the literary gatekeepers admit black authors into the literary 1 percent, they do so with very specific rules of inclusion. They will only distribute their attention in highly unequal terms, favoring specific single authors, like Morrison. This has the effect of producing a severe inequality within the field of black writers whereby a tiny minority of black authors rises to the top and the rest fall to the margins. I refer to this as the "Toni Morrison effect": the literary 1 percent will only admit very specific types of authors and books while simultaneously excluding and devaluing other types of stories deemed unimportant.

We can quantify this effect using a statistic called the Gini coefficient. This metric is typically used by economists to measure the amount of economic inequality that exists within a nation. If the wealth in a country was distributed equally among all of its citizens, then the Gini coefficient for that country would be zero. The distance of one's score from zero thus indexes the amount of income inequality that exists relative to a posited baseline of total equality. We can adapt this model to discern how much inequality exists in the field of literary attention for black writers. If, say, all black writers received the same number of book reviews—their share of literary attention was completely equal—then their Gini coefficient would be zero. And their distance from zero would indicate how much inequality exists among them. The bigger the score, the more that single black writers are getting all of the attention and the rest, by comparison, are being ignored by reviewers. Last, to get a sense of how bad or good this score is, we need a point of reference. We can also compute this same score for white writers. This will allow us to see how severe inequality is for black writers compared to another group of writers. The Gini score for white authors is 0.256, and the score for black novelists is 0.329.[23] Again, this tells us that when reviewers look at novels by white authors, they tend to look at a broad range of white authors. But when they look at novels by black authors, they tend to look at only a very, very few.

Literary critics and ordinary readers might defend this situation on the basis that Morrison rightfully deserves all this attention because her novels are so outstanding. I would not disagree: Morrison's work is extraordinary and of singular quality. I am not interested in downgrading the importance or superiority of Morrison's literature or in deciding whether she is deserving of her unique status in this network. Rather, I seek to track and understand the effects of Morrison's dominance within the literary field of attention. The valorization of a single black author in the field means that a number of less distinguished black authors get pushed to the margins of attention. In a system where recognition is finite, there can be no other way. Every time the gatekeepers decide to push someone up, they must, however invisibly, push someone else down. In 1990, Charles Johnson directly criticized Morrison's dominance. Her success has meant nothing but "a triumph of political correctness." Morrison, perhaps more than any other living writer, has been "the beneficiary of goodwill."[24] The goodwill of the literary elite.

Who, then, are the nonbeneficiaries? Who gets left out? To get a better sense of how Morrison's dominance works, I explored her status in different types of journals. I recomputed EC scores for black authors, this time only looking at journals identified as "elite" (the *New Yorker*, *New York Times*, and so forth), and found that Morrison ranks first on that list. And then I did the same but only looking at journals identified as "the black press" (*Essence*, *Callaloo*, and so forth) and found that Morrison ranks first on that list, too. And I found that Gini scores for both cases were roughly the same when we look at all journals and magazines. At first blush, it appears that the black press does not distribute its attention to black authors all that differently than the elite or overall press, particularly at the "top." Morrison, again and again.

However, one aspect of these results did surprise me. When we compare these two lists, there is one author who stands out by appearing in the top five of our black press list (falling between Alice Walker and Ralph Ellison) but is *completely absent* in our elite press list. This author—Brent Wade—is distinctive because the black press finds his work very interesting and significant, yet the elite press does not find it interesting at all, so much so as to ignore him completely. Wade does not receive a single review in magazines like the *New Yorker*. Overall, when we compare the top ten authors on both lists, we find important moments of divergence, such as the elite press's elevation of, for example, Jamaica Kincaid (who got her break at the *New Yorker*) and the black press's promotion of, for example, Octavia Butler (table 2.4). Yet Wade articulates precisely a more explicit fault line between these two groups. One group has decided to pay strong attention to his work, while another group has decided to neglect him totally. A gaping hole of attention in one becomes a vibrant space of conversation in another.

This raises a new set of questions. Why does this second group care about Wade's *Company Man*? Why is it interesting or at least worthy of review? And vice versa, what qualities make it unattractive or at least not worthy of review by the elite literary press? In a space of review attention largely organized by Toni Morrison, why do some specific novelists, like Brent Wade, and more

84 RECEPTION

TABLE 2.4

RANK	ELITE PRESS-AUTHOR	ELITE PRESS-EC SCORE	BLACK PRESS-AUTHOR	BLACK PRESS-EC SCORE
1	Toni Morrison	0.283	Toni Morrison	0.287
2	James Baldwin	0.243	Ishmael Reed	0.267
3	Alice Walker	0.238	Alice Walker	0.264
4	Ishmael Reed	0.212	Brent Wade	0.245
5	Darryl Pinckney	0.203	Ralph Ellison	0.231
6	Claude Brown	0.198	Sherley A. Williams	0.222
7	Jamaica Kincaid	0.198	Edward P. Jones	0.211
8	Ralph Ellison	0.194	A. J. Verdelle	0.211
9	Terry McMillan	0.163	Octavia Butler	0.211
10	W. M. Kelley	0.161	Louis Edwards	0.160

The top ten identified black authors in the top 1 percent most reviewed titles as indexed by the *Book Review Index*, 1965 to 2000, based on calculated eigenvector centrality (EC) scores, when only looking at black authors, across "elite" and "black" review venues.

particularly, why do some specific novels, like *Company Man* (the only novel he published during this period and thus his only text in our dataset), totally vanish from view?

COMPANY MAN VERSUS *SONG OF SOLOMON*

Company Man is a novel about the black upper middle class in the late 1980s. Its protagonist is William Covington, a thirty-eight-year-old electronics executive who has rapidly climbed the corporate ladder. Covington, by the standards of white America, has made it: he is an executive; he is very wealthy; he lives in a large house in the suburbs; he has a beautiful, black trophy wife, whose father is a physician; he owns a Lamborghini. Yet, as the story unfolds, a series of racially driven crises unravel his state of domestic and professional happiness. William's white boss, who sees William as a "white ally," pits him against the firm's black workers, who demand better wages. He also finds himself unable to perform sexually for his wife, which prompts him to have an affair with his white secretary, who then accuses William of sexual harassment. Both of these crises emanate from a larger sense of identity crisis in which William is unable to live up to the expectations of white America for "good black men" as well as black America and what it expects from its "talented tenth." William cannot shed racially motivated feelings of social inadequacy—what he calls feeling "niggerish." He is alienated from both of these sets of expectations. By the end of the novel, he is overwhelmed by these feelings and attempts suicide. However, through a mishap, he fails to kill himself, and his accidental survival allows him to escape his crisis at work and reconnect with his wife. William Covington begins his life anew in the novel's final pages.

Wade's novel appeared at a good historical moment for black literature. As Michael Hill observes, "by the late 1980s, the African American novel had transformed from a brooding genre to a space of confident executions and unqualified critical and commercial successes." The decade had brought important works by Ernest Gaines and John Edgar Wideman, Alice Walker's *The Color Purple*, and *Beloved*, by Toni Morrison. In the next decade, black novelists would gain further traction in both commercial and critical spheres. But virtually no one thought *Company Man* had anything significant to contribute. The *New York Times* didn't review it. Part of this neglect is sociological. When we look at what scholars have identified as a list of the major black writers from this period, we can place many of them in a professional genealogical chart. For example, David Bradley studied with John Edgar Wideman at the University of Pennsylvania; Gayl Jones's creative writing professor at Brown University introduced her to Morrison at Random House, who published her first novel.[25] East Coast private universities and New York City publishing houses are very important to this genealogical tree. You're in or you're out.

Wade, like William Covington, was an executive at a large electronics company and generally avoided the Manhattan-based academic-media-publishing complex. He fell out of what Coser, Kadushin, and Powell call the "social and commercial circle" so necessary to getting one's book reviewed and noticed by the press. Unlike Toni Morrison, he didn't have a powerful publisher and social network to promote his book (*Company Man* was published by Algonquin Books, an independent publisher based in Chapel Hill, North Carolina). Again, publishers and book reviews are a part of the same literary establishment, and the latter merely amplifies the former's inequality. Still, the institutional explanation only gets us so far; when we more directly compare this novel with the period's most influential novel by a black author, the results both confirm and challenge our intuition as to why Wade gets sidelined by the literary 1 percent.

Based on our EC score calculations, the most important novel by a black author between 1965 and 2000 is *Song of Solomon*, by Toni Morrison, published in 1977. Scholars have long intuited the novel's pivotal status. Its "publication catapulted Morrison into the ranks of the most highly acclaimed contemporary writers," winning National Book Critics and American Academy of Arts and Letters awards.[26] Morrison's third novel after *The Bluest Eye* and *Sula*, it is perhaps most distinctive in widening her aesthetic range to include both male and female protagonists, focusing particular attention on a lone male character, Macon "Milkman" Dead III. The novel unfolds in the early 1960s, at the onset of the U.S. civil rights movement. Geographically, it takes place primarily in Michigan but meaningfully shifts location to the American South (Virginia) by its second half. The main characters include Milkman, the son of a financially successful black man; Ruth, his mother; his two sisters Magdalen called Lena, and First Corinthians; his aunt Pilate; and his friend Guitar. The narrative is nonlinear and features intense dilations of time and memory. But broadly it functions as a mythic quest story in which Milkman seeks to discover an authentic identity. His father was an upwardly mobile businessman who instilled in him materialist and acquisitive values. While Milkman at first embraces these values, he gradually seeks to free himself of his father's influence by returning to his "roots" in the U.S. South. Pilate, his mother's sister, serves as his guide. She reveals the truth of his family's troubled history and helps him locate and enjoy a nonmaterialistic notion of personal fulfillment. At the same time, Milkman also struggles against his best friend from childhood—Guitar, a political radical. This conflict similarly pushes Milkman to abandon notions of the individualistic self and in its place accept a more expansive and collective sense of identity.

The differences between *Company Man* and *Song of Solomon* are not hard to spot. Even the most casual reader will instantly detect massive distinctions in how the books are written: their *style*. Morrison is famous for constructing complex semantic webs of meaning built piece by piece through image, symbol, and archetype. She draws heavily on a folkloric, oral-composition tradition. Book reviewers in the 1970s were most quick to pick up on this aspect of *Song of Solomon*, praising its "verbal richness."[27] *Song of Solomon* is also distinct in its narratological complexity. The text rapidly shifts between realist and mythic registers, pivoting seamlessly between places and times. The novel is, in the words of one reviewer, defined by its "negotiations with fantasy, fable, song, and allegory."[28] For most readers, the novel is rather *difficult*.

I'm most interested in how *Song*'s style engages its reader. In several interviews, Morrison emphasizes that she writes (what she calls) "village literature, fiction that is really for the village, for the tribe."[29] She takes as central to her work the construction of a bridge between the black novelist and her community, a forging of identification. Critics have elaborated on this point. Gay Wilentz identifies *Song* as an "interrogative text" that invites "participation from the reader,"[30] while Judylyn Ryan similarly remarks that Morrison's novels "inscribe a reader who is neither a consumer nor a decoder, but a co-creator of the text."[31] Yes, Morrison's writing style is difficult. Yet it is meant to draw the reader closer rather than alienate her. In working through the text's dense semantic and allusive web, the reader joins the author in building the text's overall meaning. Take the novel's famous concluding scene:

> Milkman was shouting now. "You need it? Here." Without wiping away the tears, taking a deep breath, or even bending his knees—he leaped. As fleet and bright as a lodestar he wheeled toward Guitar and it did not matter which one of them would give up his ghost in the killing arms of his brother. For now he knew what Shalimar knew: If you surrender to the air, you could *ride* it.[32]

By the time the reader encounters this passage, she has already been trained effectively to read it as a "co-creator" of meaning. There is the rapid pivot into mythical register—the "lodestar" allusion—that jostles against the realist stakes of the scene—imminent conflict and violence between Milkman and Guitar. There is the allusion to "Shalimar," one that seamlessly moves between the biblical and geographical. And there is the ambiguity to what really happens at the novel's end. What does it mean for Milkman to fly? Does he die? Does he kill Guitar? The reader has learned to juggle and sustain all possible textual interpretations, and through this work, the gap between the artist and her community, the author and reader, becomes attenuated.

Compare this to Wade's novel. *Company Man* is also a text explicitly interested in engaging its imagined reader. It does so through its very first page: "Thank you for your letters. Yes, I have been reading them, to answer one of your questions, I'm sorry I've taken so long to reply, but I've been engrossed in a project. Nothing you should know about just yet. I've abandoned it for now anyway. But for the longest time it required every spare moment I could steal."[33]

The novel, of course, is written in the epistolary form. It uses a sequence of letters that the novel's protagonist, William, has written in order to structure the narrative. Each letter is a chapter, and the story unfolds through the temporality of how Will writes and then presents to the reader each letter. What stands out about this passage, compared to *Song of Solomon*, is that it frames reader interpellation as seduction rather than work. The reader is the literal addressee of the text's narrator. Meaning is not oblique, a thing to be worked for, finally attained through participation. It is directly presented, given transparently to the reader, who is called upon as "you." Both novels are imagined as dialogues, as dialogic in form. But while one is mediated through a series of complex and opaque discursive elements, the other offers itself more plainly.

The epistolary form of the novel constrains its capacity for literary figuration. For example, while the text often invokes symbols and archetypes, those various literary figures are shown to emanate from the diegetic space of William's own mind (rather than, say, from the narrative itself), and the text is therefore symbolically and rhetorically limited to what William can invent with such symbols and archetypes. William begins one letter with a striking image and obvious symbol: "One of the starlings stopped by to say hello this morning. I saw him perch on my windowsill and glare in at me with his mocking inky eyes, bobbing convulsively as he cackled. They're strangely handsome birds." But what starts as an evocative symbol of blackness or identity quickly devolves into a tedious or mundane set of mental associations: "I called them Heckle and Jeckle at first, not realizing they were building a home and a family together. I think Heckle and Jeckle were magpies anyway."[34] The trouble is that there is no lever to push William's thought process to levels that exist outside of his own mind. This makes for compelling reading at the level of plot and story. It intensifies the reader's suspense in figuring out why William has tried to kill himself and how he will resolve his problems. But it limits the production of imaginative registers that go beyond William's mind, which is, by deliberate design, blunt and ordinary. One reviewer celebrates Wade for "mastering the ritual language of business, the lexicon of shifting responsibility, of keeping oneself safe . . . strategic silences, whispered reassurances . . . pleasant puppet smiles."[35]

The constraints of this form become even more evident if we take Morrison's text as a counterpoint. Consider the following passage and scene:

"Well let's see now." Guitar stopped to scratch his back on a telephone pole. He closed his eyes, in either the ecstasy of relief or the rigors of concentration. Milkman stared off into the sky for inspiration, and while glancing toward the rooftops of the used-car places, he saw a white peacock poised on the roof of a long low building that served as headquarters for Nelson Buick. He was about to accept the presence of the bird as one of those waking dreams he was subject to whenever indecisiveness was confronted with reality, when Guitar opened his eyes and said, "Goddam! Where'd that come from?"[36]

The appearance of the white peacock, a symbol, contrasts sharply with the appearance of the starling in *Company Man*. Whereas the starling appears merely to encourage William to conjure a set of free associations that increasingly drifts toward the ordinary, the white peacock troubles the boundary between the real and imagined. The peacock marks the text's interest in pivoting between different minds and perspectives—here, the different types of minds instantiated by Milkman versus Guitar. Ultimately, their different ways of looking at the world cannot be entirely reconciled, but the white peacock, as a generative, open-ended symbol, allows the narrative to represent both worldviews at the same time, holding taut the tension that this coevality produces. And naturally the white peacock is itself very striking. The figure that works to ground the dialogic tension between our two main characters is unreal and fantastical—the exact opposite of William's imagined starling or blackbird, with its more obvious suggestions of racial identity. This is what reviewers loved the most about *Song of Solomon*: "fantastic events and symbolic embellishments."[37] As one book reviewer gushes, "Morrison dazzles like a daydream."[38]

The stylistic and narratological differences between *Company Man* and *Song of Solomon* are fairly obvious and straightforward. These differences, it seems, only intensify when we look at their actual story content. *Company Man* takes place in the late 1980s and narrates the story of a wealthy black executive who struggles to handle both the professional and personal expectations placed upon him by white liberals as well as by fellow upwardly mobile, upper-middle-class blacks. *Song* takes place in the late 1960s and narrates the story of a confused young black man who goes on a quest to discover his true identity and shed the troubled bourgeois legacy of his father by returning to his roots in the American South, just as the civil rights movement takes off. I could list a number of other important distinctions. The black women in *Company Man* are one-dimensional and prop-like, and the story prominently features a white woman who merely serves the function of generating illicit desire for the protagonist. By contrast, *Song* features a rich cast of complex and multifaceted black women, one of whom doubles as a co-protagonist and enables the unfolding of the story's submerged history. And most strikingly, homosexuality appears in *Company Man* as one of the central sites of identity tension for the main character. William writes his letter to his best friend from youth, a homosexual man. He rejects his friend when he declares his sexual identity. By the end of the novel, William, it is revealed, in part writes these letters to reach out to his long-lost friend and to restore a part of his identity that has become suppressed. It is unclear and unlikely that William is gay. But it becomes clear that accepting his friend's sexual identity represents a key part of accepting his own identity as a black man. By contrast, same-sex male desire is essentially absent in *Song*, although black masculinity is a central theme.

Yet despite such obvious differences, the two novels share key thematic concerns. The most crucial is their common theme of social alienation. As Susan Willis argues, Milkman's "quest" is a struggle to break free from his father's overbearing, bourgeois worldview: "For Macon Dead, Milkman's father, all human relationships have become fetishized by their being made equivalent to money. His wife is an acquisition; his son, an investment in the future; and his renters, dollar signs in the bank." Milkman's trip to the South, which doubles as a journey to his family's past, signifies his liberation from "reified and fetishized relationships." If Morrison writes with a "theme" in mind, it is to condemn the "horror of bourgeois society."[39]

This protest against the reifications of middle-class life anticipates the central concerns of *Company Man*. In an interview, Wade states that his core theme is socioeconomic "alienation."[40] William's existential struggle is a struggle against the accumulation of *stuff*. His wife is an acquisition; his son, an investment; and his (mostly black) workers, dollar signs. For most of his life, not unlike Milkman, he has accepted the reifications of social life as a necessary and even pleasurable part of achieving upward mobility. It's only at mid-life that he starts asking questions. William can't enjoy intimacy with his wife because he objectifies her; he struggles to find pleasure in having a child because he sees reproduction as more than just an "investment"; and he can't fire his black coworkers because he views them as more than just "dollar signs." *Company Man* is, in many ways, the story of a man's liberation from the "horrors of bourgeois society."

But the two novels diverge in how they specifically articulate the terms of such reification. For *Song*, Macon's valorization of bourgeois norms assumes form as the "bag of gold" that he, as a younger man, had discovered in a cave and murdered a man to keep (and subsequently left in the cave). At the start of the novel, Milkman is determined to return to the cave and find the bag of gold. Yet as the story unwinds, Milkman learns that the bag in fact does not contain gold but instead carries the secret to the history of his family's history. The "bag of gold" acts as the story's mechanism to allegorize Milkman's final rejection of bourgeois values and his discovery of a fulfilling, nonreified idea of relationships. What's striking is that Morrison grounds this story of personal transformation in a symbol or image that could only be interpreted as a symbol or image. The "bag of gold" that sits in a cave for decades is clearly not meant to signal a form of verisimilitude. It drifts outside the narrative's realist register in order to be woven into its more mythopoetic plane. By contrast, social and economic alienation takes form in *Company Man* as William's "Lambo." His car provides a literal index of his economic success. He loves it.

Critics (both book reviewers and literary scholars) generally recognize the validity and effectiveness of Morrison's "bag of gold" as the basis for a critique of reification while largely writing off Wade's focalization of critique in "the Lambo" as "pretentious" or silly.[41] Ironically, a symbol of reification rooted in actual contemporary forms of reification (rich men loving cars) earns the contempt and disinterest of critics, whereas a symbol of obvious anachronistic and nonrealist import wins their approval. The bag-of-gold symbol is so critically effective because it is a metonym, a figure the reader must parse in order to understand the thing it means to signify: capitalism. It demands *work*. It's not freighted by the mundanity of merely being the thing it means to be. By contrast, Wade's symbol of capitalism appears so uninteresting to critics because it doesn't require reading or interpretative mediation. It offers itself up in the vernacular of a world excessively familiar. William loves his Lambo. All of this is much too literal.

One could identify more differences between *Company Man* and *Song of Solomon*, but the point of this exercise has not just been to describe such differences or validate why one novel is more sophisticated than the other. Rather, it has been to mark a series of soft signals that help explain why one novel has been better received by an elite group of reviewers and, thus, also to suggest why certain styles and themes are relatively ignored by that group.

It would be, I think, an overinterpretation of the evidence to say that Morrison's success *directly causes* Wade to be marginalized in the literary world. Instead, it would be more appropriate to describe this literary attention as a strong preference that inflicts a range of unintended consequences upon other black writers. The danger of such preferences (which are not, I emphasize, inherently negative) is that they normalize a specific vision of black writing, and that vision inevitably crowds out other visions. This process takes the concrete form of excluding writers like Wade from the pages of the *New Yorker* and the *New York Times* and, more broadly, from the field of elite review attention that in part defines postwar American literature.

I also think it would be an overreach to say that the preference for a certain type of black writer evinced by the literary 1 percent, which serves to enact a hierarchy of aesthetic values, is innately racist. However, it is plausible that in valorizing a single, specific type of black fiction, the elite press shows a plain disregard for other types of black stories—for example, stories about the lives of middle-class black people or gay black men—that potentially point to a more latent form of antiblack racism or at least a pattern of racial stereotypes. Wade wrote a novel that spoke to the concerns of the black press. The elite press does not share those concerns and thus writes them out of its idea of black fiction. They enact an inequality. They say that one type of black writer and one type of black story has more value than the many others.

THE JOY LUCK CLUB REVOLUTION

What is perhaps most surprising about this dynamic is its resilience. This observation defies intuition or expectation: black studies scholars have drawn a great deal of attention to the ascent of black female writers in the literary field starting in the mid-1970s. Here, we might mention the cohort of writers recruited and published by Morrison herself at Random House: Toni Cade Bambara, Gayl Jones, Angela Davis. And in the next decade we have writers like Octavia Butler. This intuition is not entirely wrong. Review attention does rapidly intensify by the late 1970s. But it is not for *black female writers as a group* but, rather, for *a single black female novelist*. For example, here is a short list of black authors who get far less attention than Morrison by the elite press: Samuel Delany, Octavia Butler, and, rather surprisingly, Toni Cade Bambara—one of Morrison's own most valued authors as an editor at Random House![42]

However, this effect still raises the question of whether any racial dynamics of the literary 1 percent do change over time. Earlier, we found that the review attention paid to POC novelists (Asian Americans, Latinx, and Native Americans) gently increases over this period. To better understand this trend, we can first identify the highest-ranked POC authors in our corpus based on their eigenvector centrality scores (the same measure we used in the previous section). The POC authors that rank the highest are generally all women writers: Maxine Hong Kingston, Amy Tan, and Louise Erdrich. And if we compute the same scores but based on individual novels instead of authors, we find that the majority of the highest-ranked novels were published in the pivotal window of the late 1980s and early 1990s: *The Joy Luck Club* (1989), *Tripmaster Monkey* (1989), *The Beet Queen* (1986), and *Dreaming in Cuban* (1992). This handful of texts effectively disrupted the field of literary attention by breaking what had essentially been an unchanging, fixed ratio of attention paid to white versus minority novelists beginning in the mid-1960s. And perhaps most surprising, our single highest-ranking novel is Tan's *The Joy Luck Club*.

In the next few pages, I want to run a few statistical tests to better understand this trend and identify potentially significant patterns. The first obvious thing is to study our EC scores over time and break those scores down by racial category (white, black, POC) in order to determine whether the POC category follows any obvious trend. Overall, though, the trend lines for all three racial groups are relatively flat, and we don't have enough data to conduct a proper statistical test to determine meaningful time-based patterns.[43] We cannot reliably quantify an upward or downward increase for any of our three racial groups. At best, we can simply confirm that there are more black and POC novelists in our dataset as we approach the year 2000.

We can get some more traction if we approach the data in a slightly different way. So far, we've been thinking of literary review attention as a single phenomenon: when a magazine or journal reviews a single novel, that counts as an observation, and we have been tracking trends to see how such observations play out in terms of race. But we can extend this analysis. We can ask not only are magazines paying more, less, or the same amount of attention to white versus nonwhite racial authors but also, when they *do* pay attention, do they do so randomly, or is there a pattern? More specifically, when literary periodicals decide to recognize or notice nonwhite authors, do they imagine such writers as unique events, as special stars in a vast universe to be gazed upon one at a time, or do they tend to review nonwhite minority authors *together*, recognizing the emergence of say, an "Asian American" or "Latinx" literary movement?

We can build a statistical model to track this effect. We recall that in our network graph, two writers are connected if they have been reviewed by the same magazine. Thus, John Updike and Toni Morrison will have a thick line between them because they are often reviewed in the same places, like the *New Yorker*. We can then quantify the rate or likelihood of any two authors being "connected," and we would find, for example, that Updike and Morrison have a higher "connection rate" than Updike and Gayl Jones, than Morrison and Jones, and so forth. Now, we can scale up this measurement to determine the rates of connection not just by authors but groups of authors by race. We can ask: when magazines assign their book reviews, do they (consciously or not) tend to group white authors together, issue by issue and year by year? Or is it random? And the same question for black authors and POC authors. This is just another way to determine if book reviews follow a pattern over time regarding nonwhite writers (fig. 2.3).

This is how you read this graph: first, I broke up the data into five-year intervals: 1965 to 1970, 1971 to 1975, and so forth.[44] We recall that the data consists of information about each individual novel (race, gender, and publisher of the

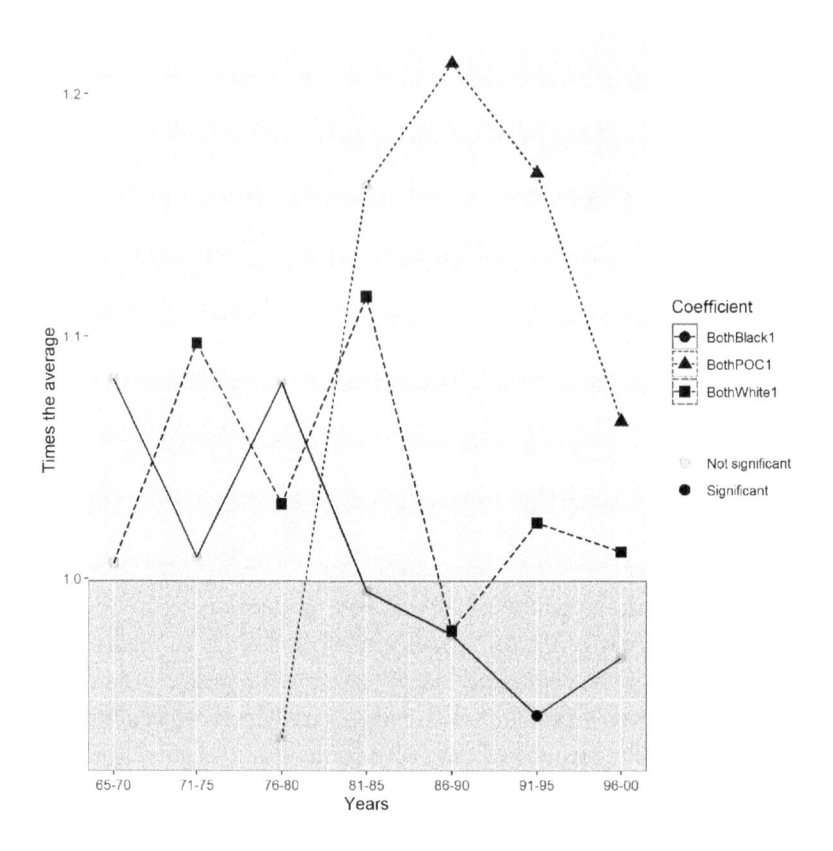

FIGURE 2.3 The graph indicates the odds (as represented on the y-axis) that two authors of the same identified race (white, black, or POC) are reviewed in the same newspaper or magazine.

text), represented as single "nodes" in our network, and information about which other novels each novel is linked to, based on where each novel was reviewed. A novel is connected to another novel if they were reviewed at the same magazine or journal, and the strength of their connection is weighted by the number of times they are reviewed at the same venue. Here we trace the likelihood that two types of novels—in the present case, we'll be interested in "race," but it could also be whether the two novels are published by the same press—have been reviewed by the same journal and, thus, are connected in our network. Again, this value is a proxy for how magazines think about race when they assign reviews. We computed this value for each racial group—white, black, and POC. Let's first look at the results for white authors, figured as the square line in figure 2.3. The value for 1971 to 1975, for instance, is 1.1. What does that mean? I calculated the average likelihood that any two novels in our corpus will be connected; you can think of this as the baseline. If we pick two novels at random and if categories of race and gender don't matter, they should more or less have that value. In a world where race or gender or publisher do matter, though, that value will be more or less than 1. It will be a factor larger or smaller than that baseline, which, again, represents a world where race doesn't matter. So, if we follow that line over time, we see that being white does matter in this world—authors identified as white tend to be reviewed together at the same places in each time interval, peaking between 1981 and 1985, and then dipping dramatically in the next interval, meaning that white authors suddenly tend *not to be* reviewed together. And then by 1991, white writers experience a very quick reversal and are yet again above the 1 value.[45]

Looking at this graph, the obviously visually compelling effect is the triangle line: the sudden explosion of interest paid to POC authors in the 1986 to 1990 interval. This finding, of course, mirrors our earlier, coarser analysis, which indicates that POC authors, particularly women, are getting reviewed more often. Here, we can use these results to sharpen that first-pass analysis. Two points: First, yes, POC authors in general are getting reviewed more often by the year 1986, but in particular, they are getting reviewed more as a *collective*. That is, *when* magazines pay attention to POC authors, they do so as a unit or grouping, recognizing their literature as a part of a movement. If Maxine Hong Kingston makes it into the *New York Times* or *Kirkus*, she does so in part because Amy Tan and Louise Erdrich also make it in. If you see a review of *Love Medicine* in the press, it's likely to appear before, after, or next to a review of *The Joy Luck Club*. Second, this effect comes at the expense of both white writers and black writers. What is so striking about the sudden rise of the triangle line is the simultaneous rapid drop of the square line and, indeed, the circle line, which represents the review fortunes of black novelists. One can and should think of these results in relational terms: starting in 1986, POC writers break the surface in getting the attention of reviewers, especially when imagined as a "movement." And this means that reviewers are less inclined to see writers of other races, such as white authors, as equally "movement" based. If before reviewers tended to review white writers together, implicitly regarding them as naturally cohering together (Roth and Updike, Bellow and Mailer), that tendency partly dissolves by 1986. POC authors are suddenly the thing to pay attention to as an imagined authorial cohort. But it's equally important to note that this trend is short lived and reverses course by 1991. By then, once again, the triangle line is falling, and falling fast, especially by the year 2000.

This result appears to tell a generative story about POC authors and book reviews. But it makes large assumptions about the reception of individual authors, like Amy Tan, when the model works at the scale of the entire category of "POC author." We need more granularity. Now that we have a general signal regarding book reviews and POC authors over time, I wanted to know more about the review attention ascribed to clusters of authors within that broader category; I wanted to break down the POC category into finer bands of individual writers.

One way to do this is to use a popular social network algorithm called "community detection." Community detection identifies clusters or "communities" in our network graph, where communities are groups of nodes in a network that are more densely connected to one another than to other nodes. The algorithm quantitatively determines how much denser a community will appear if such and such node is in that community than if it wasn't. It turns that computation into a value and then uses that value to place each node into a "community."

I implemented community detection on our social network graph, and the algorithm discovered three "communities" (labeled 0, 1, and 2).[46] Now, I am interested in how POC authors are partitioned into these various communities. Are any communities particularly flush with POC authors—is one of those communities a POC community? This is to answer the important question of whether POC authors are more likely to be segregated from white authors—put into their own segregated niches or corners. I ran a statistical test to see if any community was more likely to have POC authors than not, and I found that *community 2 is*. In statistical terms, the odds of appearing community 2 as opposed to community 1 is 3.2 times higher for POC authors compared to white novelists.[47] Community 2 is thus racially distinctive, at least when compared to community 1, being more likely to have POC authors than white authors.

Now here is the interesting puzzle: the community (community 1) that has the POC authors that I have flagged as significant to the network (high eigenvector centrality, or EC, scores and thus most recognized by book reviewers), such as Amy Tan and Maxine Hong Kingston, belong to the community that has lower odds of having POC authors than white authors (again, when compared to community 2 as a baseline). This is a community that happens to have POC (and black) authors in it, but in statistical terms, it is not a distinguishing aspect of that community. They just happen to be there. By contrast, the community (community 2) with greater odds of having POC authors tends to possess novelists that have been largely identified as less recognized or eminent than writers like Tan or Kingston. These writers include Susan Choi, Fae Myenne Ng, and

TABLE 2.5

COMMUNITY 1 AUTHOR (SAMPLE)	COMMUNITY 2 AUTHOR (SAMPLE)
Toni Morrison	Gish Jen
Philip Roth	Susan Choi
Amy Tan	Frank Chin
N. Scott Momaday	Jhumpa Lahiri
Jamaica Kincaid	Lan Cao
Salman Rushdie	Bharati Mukherjee
Don DeLillo	Edwidge Danticat
Cormac McCarthy	Brent Wade
Maxine Hong Kingston	Fae Myenne Ng
James Baldwin	Toni Cade Bambara

A sample of authors that appear in community 1 and community 2, based on a community detection algorithm run on the data.

Gish Jen (table 2.5). In other words, there *is* a community of authors in this network more likely to be constituted by POC authors, but that community is populated by novelists perceived to be relatively less distinguished and less well received.

What we find is a curious partitioning of nonwhite authors: in one group, we find a number of highly distinguished black and POC authors, such as James Baldwin and Maxine Hong Kingston—arguably, the most recognized nonwhite authors (as, for example, indexed by our EC scores) of the postwar period. In another group, we find a denser array of nonwhite authors—authors, without a doubt, widely read and celebrated, but relatively less celebrated by critics than Morrison or Kingston, such as Frank Chin or Susan Choi. Here, again, is the conundrum: book reviewers do appear to associate groups of POC authors when they evaluate novels. But the authors they seem most interested in writing about (again, as indexed by eigenvector centrality) are paradoxically held apart from that grouping. Despite a growing interest in recognizing POC authors as a kind of community, certain writers like Kingston are partitioned out.

By no coincidence, Toni Morrison falls into community 1, as do other widely reviewed and critically acclaimed black writers, such as Jamaica Kincaid and James Baldwin. And by no coincidence, Brent Wade is in community 2—the African American author we have identified as denied access to the literary elite in terms of book-review attention. To be clear, this pattern is not complete or perfect—a number of writers well regarded and often celebrated by the elite press, such as Jhumpa Lahiri, fall into community 2. But a general trend is apparent: the nonwhite authors in community 1 are, on balance, more celebrated and, I argue, are seen to be more representative of African American or "ethnic" minority literatures than the novelists who appear in community 2, although, again, that distinction is not without exceptions.

We can think of community 1 as the partition of our social network that welcomes a certain type of POC author (as well as black author) who has a perceived critical distinction. But we also need to think of that community as one that does not (at least as identified by our algorithm) include POC authors *in aggregate* as a statistically significant entity. It's very happy to associate with writers like Tan or Morrison. But it holds the line there. The real meaning of this effect becomes clearer when we inspect community 1 beyond just its list of nonwhite authors. This list now opens up to include a swath of critically acclaimed white writers: Philip Roth, Joan Didion, Don DeLillo, Cormac McCarthy, David Foster Wallace. This network community gathers the elite of the elite, the 1 percent of the 1 percent, the authors who over time have come to dominate critical and journalistic discussions of the postwar American novel (although again, I must register a caveat: this definition is not perfect—several nonelite authors, for example, Mario Puzo, appear in community 1; I simply argue that community 1, compared to the other communities identified by our algorithm, possesses a substantially higher number of celebrated novelists).[48] And it has a very specific relation to race: a strong interest in *certain* nonwhite authors, but at a volume that prohibits race from becoming a statistically significant factor in how that community is identified.

There is more to say about this community, but I want to draw attention to Amy Tan. Tan stands out in our results because she does not appear where she should be, based on scholarly expectations. Tan is the most recognized POC author in our data (based on EC scores), and similarly, she belongs to community 1, the "elite of the elite." Both metrics indicate that she is one of the most significant nonwhite authors in our network. However, unlike our other most highly ranked authors (POC or otherwise) and the other authors in community 1, Tan is not particularly revered or studied by literary scholars and critics. Compared to authors like Maxine Hong Kingston and certainly Toni Morrison and James Baldwin, Tan experienced just a very brief flicker of scholarly attention in the mid-1990s, and for the most part, as the new century has worn on, she has largely fallen out of the canon. Yet based on our statistical analysis, *The Joy Luck Club* was instrumental in affecting a revolution in review attention in the early 1990s. As an outlier in multiple senses—the most statistically impactful POC author in our data and also the only nonwhite author in community 1 who is not highly regarded by scholars—Tan enacts a form of *leverage* that can help us better understand the main puzzle of this chapter: why does the "literary 1 percent" embrace a very particular kind of nonwhite author at the expense of recognizing so many others and at a limited scale that keeps race from being a statistically significant factor?

The Joy Luck Club was immediately recognized as a major "event" in publishing when it appeared in 1989 by Putnam. The novel's instant success and its author's sudden rise from obscurity to massive literary fame is now the stuff of publishing legend. In its first year, more than two hundred thousand copies were sold in hardback. Paperback rights were sold for a remarkable 1.2 million dollars. It became a finalist for both the National Book Critics Circle Award and the National Book Award. Tan's novel was one of the most reviewed novels of the year (if not decade) and received glowing notices in major outlets like the *New York Times* and the *New Yorker* as well as in popular, glossy magazines like *Glamour*. One book reviewer noted in the *Washington Post*: "everyone loves Amy Tan. She's the flavor of the month, the hot young thing, the exotic new voice that is giving hope to a publishing industry weary of the old trends."[49]

Literary scholars, especially Asian Americanists, have held a vexed relationship to *The Joy Luck Club*. A fair amount of scholarship quickly followed in the wake of the novel's vast commercial uptake. Most of this work was critical in nature. Academic writing on Tan's novel has typically followed the following formula: (1) a general skepticism toward the book's broad public appeal and a framing of that appeal as a version of U.S. Orientalism. Sau-ling Wong argues that popular interest is driven by "an unusually keen appetite for mother-daughter stories by and about people of color,"[50] while Melanie McAlister argues that the story simply props up popular misconceptions of Asian Americans as "model minorities."[51] (2) A critique of specific textual elements in the novel that facilitate such consumable Orientalist representations for ordinary readers. For example, Wong: "Tan's fiction has apparently been able to hold in colloidal suspension two essential ingredients of quasi-ethnographic Orientalist discourse on China and the Chinese, which both have a long genealogy on this country. These ingredients are 'temporal distancing' and 'authenticity marking.'?"[52] And, finally, (3) reading against the novel's grain to construct new readings that defy the forms of reactionary Orientalism immanent within the text. McAlister: "As readers, we can and should develop a strategic counter to the crass Orientalism of the mainstream press; we can use the novel to read against the drive to construct exotic Asian women uniform in their difference."[53] Recent scholarship on *The Joy Luck Club* has been more nuanced and nimble than this initial work.[54] But for the most part, there is a general, acknowledged consensus: while Tan's novel is important because it was so widely read and talked about, it's also very "problematic" in how it represents Asian American people and China. But we can still recover latent textual features that support a program of racial empowerment and critical insight.

Reading the scholarship is thus an odd experience. Rarely has a group of scholars been so "disappointed" by their object of study ("disappointed" is a word that appears with striking frequency in the research).[55] Scholars lament that the text is not as interesting as it could be—a lament compounded by Tan's missed opportunity to write something truly radical—and aim to use criticism to "fix" its shortcomings by performing a series of contrarian or subversive readings, all in hopes of turning the book into a more resistant and progressive version of itself. As early as 1995, just six years after the novel's publication, Sau-ling Wong asked the interesting question of how literary scholars would reconcile this tension. Would *The Joy Luck Club* gain admission into the canon of English literary studies and/or ethnic studies?[56] The answer is now quite clear: *no*. As one astute book critic has pointed out: "Amy Tan has become the Rodney Dangerfield of contemporary novelists."[57] In the eyes of scholars, the list of offenses committed is long: Orientalism, supporting model-minority stereotypes, and pandering to white readers.

But, again, our data suggests Tan is important for a wholly different reason: for, in the eyes of the literary elite, leading an apparent paradigm shift in postwar American literature. Taking a close look at an exemplary review of *The Joy Luck Club* allows us to get some traction on this observation. Orville Schell's review of Tan's novel in the *New York Times* was likely its most important, and it encouraged a number of follow-up reviews in other major literary venues, like the *New Yorker*. It is also the most criticized by literary scholars. Melanie McAlister contends that articles like Schell's review have "insisted on interpreting Tan's text lyrically, passing over the individuality of the characters in order to more easily assimilate a uniform version of 'the Chinese American experience' into a vision of American inclusionism." Schell, in particular, "rewrites Tan's novel as an Orientalist dream world."[58]

However, it's worth taking a harder look at what exactly Schell and other reviewers specifically found so compelling about *The Joy Luck Club*. In Schell's very long review, he includes an extensive excerpt from the novel to offer a miniature summary:

> Even without makeup, I could never pass for true Chinese. I stand five-foot-six, and my head pokes above the crowd so that I am eye level only with other tourists. My mother once told me my height came from my grandfather, who was a northerner, and may have even had some Mongol blood. "This is what your grandmother once told me," explained my mother. "But now it is too late to ask her. They are all dead, your grandparents, your uncles, and their wives and children, all killed in the war, when a bomb fell on our house. So many generations in one instant."
>
> She had said this so matter-of-factly that I thought she had long since gotten over any grief she had. And then I wondered how she knew they were all dead.
>
> "Maybe they left the house before the bomb fell," I suggested.... "Some of them could have escaped."
>
> "Cannot be," said my mother, this time almost angrily.[59]

Based on their overall reading of the text, we can anticipate the kinds of critiques that McAlister and others would level at this scene: the author's self-reification of "Chinese-ness," the evasion of "Chinese-American" as a viable social identity, the elision of class. However, it is useful to parse what the passage does well. What stands out is how extremely literal and flat the writing is. The matter-of-fact delivery of the mother is the matter-of-fact narration of the text itself. Here, the passage does not wrap up China's traumatic wartime history (whether Japanese colonialism or the rise of the Chinese Communist Party) in a dynamic, reflexive postmodern sheen (what we see more clearly in Kingston's *The Woman Warrior*). Rather, it's effective in how it delivers information in a pithy and vivid form ("so many generations in one instant"). Further, it presents a rich landscape of compelling verisimilitude, such as the detail regarding Chinese northerners having Mongolian blood. For McAlister, such details read as examples of a kind of performative self-Orientalism, the sprinkling of pseudo-ethnography to entrance white readers. But for readers like Schell, such bits are precisely compelling and valuable because they are informative. They help explain a world otherwise largely unfathomable to white readers.

Again and again, scholars like McAlister will fault readers like Schell for being what Merve Emre has called a "bad reader" and, similarly, fault ordinary readers who follow Schell's approach as also failing to read adequately or thoughtfully.[60] And they will fault the novel itself for courting this bad reading, for not producing language that invites a critical disposition. Here, "bad reading" means vacating structural and historically determinant accounts of race, gender, and class in understanding experience. I do not disagree with McAlister and Wong's interpretations, and I obviously endorse a critical reading of Tan's novel. But to dismiss completely the print media's positive reception of *The Joy Luck Club* as a kind of reactionary Orientalism, something literary scholars must wash their hands of and move on from, obstructs our ability to grasp the transformative force the novel had on the American literary field, particularly in how it suddenly made the category of "Asian American" writing interesting for the mainstream and elite. As Schell writes in his review, Tan has initiated a "new genre of American fiction."[61]

Of course, most Asian Americanist scholars would dispute the idea that Amy Tan (rather than, say, Sui Sin Far or Frank Chin) created the "new genre" of Asian American literature. But our data analysis makes clear that it was, for better or for worse, *The Joy Luck Club* that most served to effect a revolution of review attention to POC literature and how the literary field came to understand and validate Asian American literature as a "new genre." And we need to reckon with the fact that this attention sometimes aligns with our scholarly habits, like recognizing the significance of writers like Morrison, Kingston, and Erdrich, while sometimes it does not, such as how our network's elite zone of review attention prefers Amy Tan to Fae Myenne Ng. Scholars will lament all of the bad readers that surround *The Joy Luck Club* and insist that we need more good ones to fix its various shortcomings. However, just by skimming a dozen or so reviews of the novel by lay readers on Goodreads.com, it is clear that indeed *The Joy Luck Club* was typically the very first novel that person had read by an Asian American author and that the novel, more than any other, instantiated the idea of an "Asian American literature." The discipline of literary studies would rather shed this unhappy effect. But we live in its long shadow.

Still, even as Tan's novel helped bring Asian American fiction to the mainstream, one wonders what potentially deleterious side effects it had. Do we see a kind of "*Joy Luck Club* effect" analogous to our earlier "Toni Morrison effect?" In general, no. No single Asian American author had the kind of effect that Morrison had on American literature. But the data reveal a few interesting Asian American authors and texts that do appear to get sidelined by Tan's success in the 1990s. For example, an author and text that ranks very low, based on eigenvector centrality scores, is Marie Myung-Ok Lee and her novel *Necessary Roughness*, published by HarperCollins in 1996—just seven years after *The Joy Luck Club*.[62]

The novel is about a Korean American family that moves from Los Angeles to Iron City, a fictional town in Minnesota, and the various forms of cultural clash and racial discrimination they face. Its most distinguishing feature is its genre: the novel is a work of young-adult (YA) fiction. It was released through the publisher's HarperTeen imprint. One wonders if this specific kind of experience gets in part written out of the idea of Asian American literature in the aftermath of Tan's novel: one focused on the American Midwest, rather than the coasts, and one voiced through the YA genre.

MIRAGES

The initial statistics reported in this chapter—book reviews as 90 percent white, 6 percent black, and 4 percent POC—offer up a mirage of postwar American literary history. They suggest that as we progress in the cycle of literary production and reception, the staggering racial inequality that we find in mainstream book publishing, Random House in particular, has attenuated, and that we can perhaps thank the enlightened journalists who are paid to write about books for a living for this improvement. One perhaps might feel that once we get outside of a more explicitly corporatized environment, one in which the bottom line figures centrally, literary professionals are freed to rectify what had gone terribly wrong at an earlier stage of literary production—the acquisition, editing, marketing, and publication of novels. The argument of this chapter, however, has been that such numbers present a mirage of progress or change. The attenuation of racial inequality in book reviews, especially at its most elite journals, simply enacts new forms of inequality. Specifically, it means the elevation of specific nonwhite writers at the expense of demoting or rendering invisible a majority of other nonwhite writers. This then has unintended consequences for what types of stories get naturalized as "minority literature," instantiating another form of inequality at the level of content and form. Racial inequality in postwar U.S. fiction means not only delimiting who gets to be heard but also what types of stories get recognized.

In the end, we shouldn't be too surprised that racial inequality persists as we move from publishers to book reviews within the life cycle of the novel. As I have already argued, there exist strong connections between publishers/editors and periodicals/reviewers. The two constitute what Coser, Kadushin, and Powell dub a "social and commercial circle" in which opinions and preferences about books get amplified and reproduced. What editors like and want to promote inevitably gets in part magnified by the reviewers they constantly talk to. However, we are perhaps surprised by the ways that racial inequality becomes more covert with reviews. Compared to their counterparts in publishing, book reviewers are, statistically speaking, promoting more minority writers. They are just finding more stealthy ways to impose a set of rules of inclusion that stratify and penalize the majority of nonwhite writers who do not fit a specific mold.

Indeed, our results should give literary scholars pause. English professors are in the business of producing enduring canons of literature, and we tend to think of ourselves as less responsive to the vicissitudes of literary fashion that reviews partly register and sometimes create. We tend to think of our literary judgments as a category apart from what happens in the pages of the *New York Times*, even as we might occasionally glance at them to get a sense of the "now." But when we look at what book reviewers have identified as the "elite of the elite," we find a striking symmetry with what scholars have largely recognized as the authors most worthy of criticism as well as with whom we tend to teach in the classroom: Thomas Pynchon, Toni Morrison, Philip Roth, James Baldwin, Maxine Hong Kingston, Don DeLillo, and so on.

The results of this chapter suggest that book reviewers perform a labor of filtering and sorting that affects the work of literary criticism in ways we perhaps haven't yet fully registered. Book reviews represent a powerful form of gatekeeping for the field, and they can powerfully determine what readers—both ordinary and expert (that is, college professors)—get to see and, therefore, get to read. It is a potent screening device. More research needs to be done to determine the degree to which reviews directly affect the choices of scholarship and syllabi. But even if only partly true, the circuit between not only publishers and book reviews but also between reviews and the university should provoke concern. How have scholarship and syllabi perhaps unconsciously reproduced the forms of racial inequality implemented by book reviews, namely, the creation of a set of rules that allow some nonwhite writers, under specific conditions, to join the elite, while denying that privilege to the majority of other minority authors? In my fourth chapter, I explore this effect in the context of postwar literature canon building. For now, I argue that the origins of this stratification reside at an earlier phase of the literary field: book reviews.

3

RECOGNITION

Literary Distinction and Blackness

98 PERCENT AND 91 PERCENT

One story frequently told about American culture after World War II regards the "Great Divide": the notion that there exists a fundamental distinction between elite and popular forms of art, such as literary prize winners and popular bestsellers, and that the first is inherently superior to the second. Much of this original narrative—initially asserted by cultural critics like Dwight MacDonald in the first two decades after the war—has been largely debunked by both sociologists and cultural historians on empirical and conceptual grounds.[1] Today, scholars are more interested in studying the porousness and interchangeability of these categories, rather than their imagined difference or hierarchy. But the question remains a live one, even if the major terms of the debate have become challenged or inverted. The categories of "high" and "low" art are still important to cultural scholars; it's just that the imagined space between them has contracted or at least has become altered, shaping the way works of literature are judged and received.

Another important story often told about American culture after World War II concerns the "emergence" of minority literatures: the efflorescence of writing by African American, Asian American, and Latinx authors, particularly novelists, in the postwar period. Here, some familiar landmarks might include the Black Arts Movement in the 1960s and 1970s, the popular and critical success of Maxine Hong Kingston's *The Woman Warrior* in 1976, and Toni Morrison winning the Nobel Prize in Literature in 1993. This is a story told largely in sanguine terms. For example, Asian American authors team up with political organizations, such as CARP (Combined Asian Resources Project), in minority demographic hotspots, such as Berkeley, to produce transformative works of literature such as *Aiiieeeee!* Breakout minority novelists like Morrison, with the help of scholarly allies, defy the white literary establishment to win major literary prizes, such as the Pulitzer, forever changing the broader criteria by which "great novels" are judged. After a near fifty-year drought since Richard Wright's *Native Son*, books written by black authors, for example Terry McMillan, once again become fixtures on the *New York Times* bestseller list.[2]

It would be impossible to think about postwar American literature without taking into account both of these stories, but rarely are these two narratives thought about together, as mutually constitutive. The two stories are clearly adjacent. For example, we might recall the scandal surrounding the 1988 book-award season, in which forty-eight black critics and writers wrote an op-ed for the *New York Times* protesting the fact that Toni Morrison had yet to win either the National Book Award or the Pulitzer Prize.[3] But for various reasons, it's difficult to think about one through the lens of the other. One possible explanation is that scholars have assumed a mutually affirming symmetry of interest in these stories: as the "Great Divide" between high and low culture attenuates, racial minority authors, particularly black writers, increasingly receive both financial and critical recognition. Darryl Dickson-Carr has argued that the "three decades between 1970 and 2000 constituted the most productive and successful period in African American literary history." Black writers could be expected to sell "hundreds of thousands" of books as well as win "some of the top literary prizes in the United States and in the world, including the Nobel."[4] One might assume that the erasure of "high" and "low" reflects a growing democratization of U.S. culture and that this process has directly benefited minority authors.

But a more likely reason for this avoidance of direct contact is that the study of high and low in the postwar American literary field and the study of the emergence of minority literatures represent an awkward or inappropriate analytical match. Drawing from a framework inspired by Pierre Bourdieu, scholars generally understand elite versus popular culture as categories that have historically formed in reaction or relation to each other. A simple example would be graffiti art, which in part first emerged as an alternative or subversion of traditional fine art. By contrast, one might find it problematic to think of "African American literature" as a category purely formed in opposition to whiteness. This thinking negatively evokes the disturbing history of racial classification in America. Scholars of African American literature, rightfully I believe, have focused instead on the formation of black writing as possessing autonomous aesthetic features, as not simply the structural *other* to books written by white people.[5] A Bourdieu-inspired analysis often means putting things into bins, even as it admits that those bins are contingent and arbitrary, and asserting "scientific" rules for how the things in those bins interact. A model that stresses classification and rules is not an ideal one for thinking about race and literature.

The wager of this chapter, however, is that bringing these two stories directly into contact with each other will reveal some important yet still unnoticed patterns of distinction in the U.S. literary field. Consider a simple counting exercise. What are the demographics of American fictional bestsellers and literary prize winners published between 1950 and 2000 (table 3.1)? (I describe in greater detail how I define these categories in my next section.) The gender ratio for both bestsellers and prizewinners is bad (worse than 2/3 male), but the figure that most starkly jumps out is the "white" ratio: of the 620 bestselling novels published between 1950 and 2000, a mere *three* were novels written by black authors (*Paradise*, by Toni Morrison, and two novels by Terry McMillan). The figures associated with "prizewinners" are slightly better, but they are still bad: women are slightly better represented, and nonwhite authors also are slightly more represented, but white writers still account for 91 percent of the total. One might also be curious about a possible "white man effect" in these categories of literary distinction. But here the results suggest that the inequality of the postwar American literary field is driven primarily by race: white male authors represent 74 percent of bestsellers and 64 percent of literary prize winners. These figures are, of course, hardly signs of progress, but they are still an order of magnitude less than the social inequality suggested by the ratio of whiteness alone.

While it is difficult to find a happy story in these numbers, we can identify one ostensibly positive trend that scholars have long intuited: the category of

TABLE 3.1 AMERICAN AUTHORS WHO HAVE WON A MAJOR U.S. LITERARY PRIZE OR APPEARED ON THE *PUBLISHER'S WEEKLY* BESTSELLER LIST (%)

TYPE	MALE	FEMALE	WHITE	BLACK	POC
Bestseller	76	24	98	0.5	1.3
Prizewinner	80	20	91	5	4

The percentage of American authors who have won a major U.S. literary prize or appeared on the *Publisher's Weekly* bestseller list between 1950 and 2000, broken down by race and gender.

the literary prize winner in the United States is increasingly a mechanism to promote multiculturalism, and thus we would expect to see greater racial diversity in prizewinning selections than in examples of bestsellers, especially as the century wears on. There is, we know, an insidious story we can tell about this trend—that it merely marks the commodification of racial and ethnic difference by cultural elites and that when minority authors win prizes, they are merely being prized for their racial "otherness."[6] But putting aside the polemical debate, the numbers indicate an undeniable distinction: the category of the prizewinner is far more interested in rewarding forms of identity diversity than the bestseller, which appears to value, by sharp contrast, a marked commitment to whiteness. Figure 3.1, which plots the percentage of American authors who have won a major literary prize between 1950 and 2000 by identified race, helps us visualize this pattern.

So far, we have one very bad story about bestsellers and one not-so-bad story about literary prize winners. First, the very bad story: the overwhelming whiteness of the bestseller category—so much so that one could posit an equivalence between bestsellerdom and whiteness—is striking. The bestseller lists I am using do not include grassroots black bestselling novels, such as Teri Woods's *True to the Game* (1994), and these lists themselves in part encode racial bias. But if we take seriously these lists as indexing a nontrivial form of financial success and recognition, the simple statistics I report are disturbing. And they put

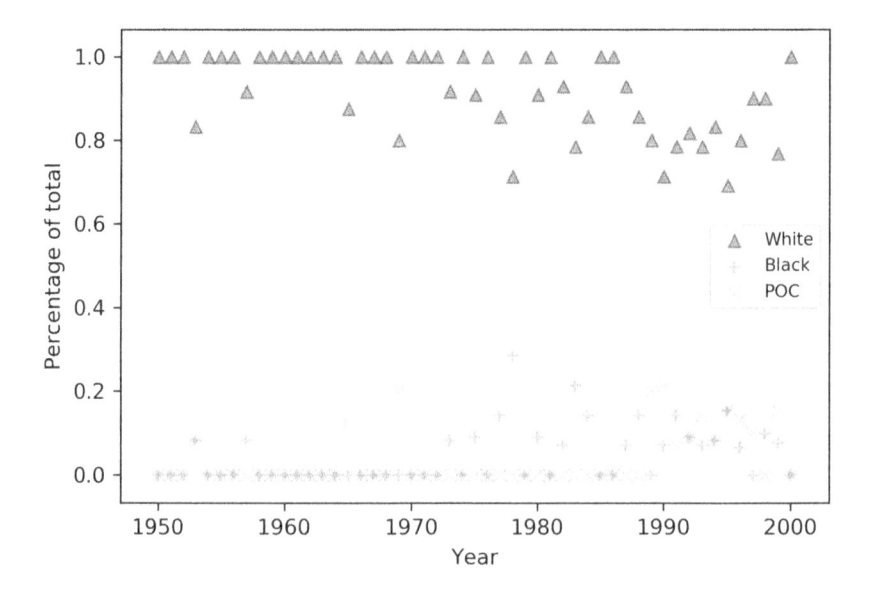

FIGURE 3.1 The percentage of American authors who have won a major U.S. literary prize between 1950 and 2000 by year, broken down by race.

pressure on claims made by Dickson-Carr and others who contend that there came a rising tide of sales for black novelists after the war. Black authors are, for sure, experiencing greater literary market penetration, but make no mistake—there is still a massive white hegemony that has ceded little ground to minorities.

And second, the apparently not-so-bad story regarding prizewinners: here, the data seems to support a largely consensus view of postwar American literature, race, and prizes, which is that novels like Morrison's *Beloved* started winning major book prizes like the Pulitzer in the 1980s, which helped effect a broader transformation in the literary-prize economy that benefited nonwhite racial minority authors.[7] But that story also seems a bit dubious once we look at the details of our results. The trendline of decreasing whiteness and rising blackness is deceptive if you peer closely at the points on the graph. After a jump in prizewinning novels by black writers in the 1980s and early 1990s (correlating with Morrison's rise to dominance in the literary field), by 1999, that trend partly regresses to the mean of the period's overall ratio: 91 percent white (a trend that echoes the pattern of racial authorship we find at Random House after Morrison leaves as editor). And while the headline number of 91 percent is better than 98 percent, it's still bad. The category of the prizewinner is not *totally* white, as we see with the bestseller category, but it remains relentlessly and discernibly white, and by the year 2000, that whiteness is not fully fading.

I produce this graph and report these statistics not because I think they alone are especially meaningful or convincing as arguments; rather, I am interested in how they help set up a set of further investigations into the relationship between race and literary distinction in the postwar American novel. My statistics are what we might refer to as (merely) "sociological"—as simply describing a relation that exists between the racial identity of an author and the type of literary reception that author's books have received in the post-1950 era. It is a counting exercise. And as such, it doesn't tell us much about the features of American literary history we tend to care about: language, form, style, and narrative, that is, things that cannot be so easily counted and added up. But even these coarse results, I suggest, reveal a potentially important story—that the story of American literary distinction after the war, how books get identified as either prestigious and/or popular, is inextricably tied to the question of race and identity. That is, racial difference represents a primary axis upon which the categories of both the popular and the prestigious rotate. The coherence and meaning of these categories is underwritten by a vast and unchanging racial inequality: 98 percent white and 91 percent white.

In the rest of this chapter, I move away from coarse empirical description and toward reading and analyzing literary texts. This work is animated by a desire to bridge the gap between my initial quantitative results and what literary scholars have said about race and the postwar novel. This gap—this interpretative dissonance—troubled me, and I assumed the texts themselves would reveal some key oversight to the rough statistical results reported in this chapter's introduction. But the story stays troubling. Bestsellers and prizewinners not only tend to exclude black writers. They also tend to exclude literary forms and contents representative of novels by black authors. In the rest of this chapter, I use a mix of close reading and text-mining methods—machine classification in particular—to show that the defining feature of distinction in the postwar American literary field is not so much an interplay—diverging or converging—between "high" and "low" categories of the novel but rather an unchanging aversion of both categories to novels written by black authors in terms of language, style, and narrative. The central, organizing logic of postwar American literary distinction is a denial of blackness.

This chapter thus also continues the story told in the first two chapters of this book. The story so far has been that whether looking at the literary field through the lens of production (publishers) or its aftermath of reception (reviews), what most defines this field is an exclusion or tokenization of nonwhite authorship. We perhaps are not terribly surprised that the next phase of the field—sales and prizes—sustains this racial inequality. Publishers pick which books to promote, and those tend to sell well; book reviewers often sit on prize juries. We are perhaps surprised, though, that both exhibit such a similar aversion to literary blackness. After all, the forces that work to make a book a bestseller and/or prizewinner are very different, yet computation helps show how both simultaneously tend to deny a set of tropes and themes common to novels by black authors.

THE DATA OF DISTINCTION

My list of American bestselling novels for 1950 to 2000 is based on the records of *Publisher's Weekly*, which has kept lists of bestselling American novels for this period. This is an imperfect list. For example, why not use the *New York Times* bestseller lists? Based on existing research into the history of American bestsellers, there appears to be a scholarly consensus that the *Publisher's Weekly* list is the most transparently gathered and the least animated by a specific ideology, as we might see with the *New York Times*. So I have followed that scholarly consensus.[8] Also, why not use or include alternative bestseller lists that provide more diverse coverage of interests, such as "Urban" bestsellers? Without a doubt, such a list would have less of a racial skew toward whiteness. But my goal for this research is to first study the category of the "bestseller" in its most traditional form to see how this normative category exercises racial inequality. Once we have this baseline understanding of the bestseller, I hope that future scholars will study other modes of the category to see how they resist the normative bestseller class.

I have already mentioned several basic demographic statistics of this corpus, but I provide a more thorough accounting here. We have a total of 620 American bestselling novels written by 239 unique individual authors for 1950 to 2000. Seventy-six percent of the titles are written by men and 24 percent are written by women. Ninety-eight percent are written by identified white authors, 0.5 percent by identified black authors, and 1.3 percent by identified POC authors. As with my other chapters, the process of identifying the gender and race of an author was completed through a rigorous process.[9] Likewise, I drew a sample of texts that were digitally available to facilitate automated text analysis.[10]

My list of American prizewinning novels is derived from a curated process. I asked a group of colleagues in American literary studies and creative writers to provide a list of "important" and "recognized" literary awards for novels. The list consists of both highly canonical awards, such as the Pulitzer, National Book Award, and PEN/Faulkner, as well as several awards that are more niche, such as the Drue Heinz Literature Prize. I should be clear that our list of awards is deliberately mainstream: it noticeably is missing awards that target works written by sexual minorities (such as the Lambda Literary Award), American racial minorities (such as the Premio Quinto Sol prize), and awards for genre fiction, such as the Hugo and Nebula prizes for science fiction.[11] Again, my goal for this chapter is first to understand the normative operation of the category of the prestigious prizewinning novel, and my hope is that other scholars will take up the challenge to examine how other types of literary prizes, which define themselves in part in resistance to this canon, deform and critique this baseline articulation of what it means to be worthy of a prize.

Here I produce a full account of the demographics of this corpus. We have a total of 508 prizewinning American novels written by 353 unique individual authors from 1950 to 2000. Seventy percent are written by men, 30 percent by women. Ninety-one percent are written by white authors, 5 percent by black authors, and 4 percent by POC authors. I used the same process for bestsellers described earlier to manually tag each author for categories of gender and race. And as with my bestseller corpus, I created a sample of digitally available texts.[12]

Finally, I needed to create a corpus of novels written by black authors published from 1950 to 2000. This corpus would enable an analysis of how bestselling and prizewinning novels stand in relation to novels written by black authors in terms of textual dynamics, such as language, form, and narrative. Here, I collaborated with the Project on the History of Black Writing, based at the University of Kansas, to acquire such a corpus. For the past thirty years, African Americanist scholars and librarians at the project have assembled a definitive list of novels written by black authors from 1850 to 1990, totaling 1,200 titles, of which so far a random sample of 162 texts published from 1950 to 1990 have been digitized. To make this corpus reach the year 2000 and be equivalent in size to our bestseller and prizewinner digital corpora, I added sixty-seven more novels by black authors. I chose these novels based on library records, identifying texts commonly held by libraries across the world, and thus they signal a mix of popular and prestigious.[13]

Still, two clarifications: while scholars at Kansas have produced a sound representation of "novels by black authors," I *emphasize* that this category is a contested one and that our corpus presents just one version of this category, not a definitive one. And second: I refer to this corpus as "novels by black authors" rather than "African American literature" because I recognize that this designation represents a contested scholarly construction, and I am most interested in studying the effects of blackness on the field.

Finally, one more significant clarification. The process by which we identify writers as "black," "white," or "POC" is based on the body of academic scholarship surrounding each author, yet this process still risks reifying racial identity as a category. The racial ontology of an author is not stable; what it means to be "white" or "black" changes over time and place. For example, most literary scholars today identify the mixed-race writer Nella Larsen as "black." But this categorization has evolved since the 1920s, when she first wrote. At the same time, labeling authors "white" or "black" risks erasing dynamics of intersectionality. A novelist like Samuel Delany is labeled "black" in our corpus, but Delany also identifies as a gay man. One cannot understand one form of social identity without the other. Once again, my hope is that future researchers will enrich this data to account for a broader range of social identities, such as sexuality.

MACHINE CLASSIFICATION

My goal in this chapter is to understand the relations between three recognized categories of American fiction: American bestselling novels, American prizewinning novels, and "novels written by identified black authors." Pierre Bourdieu has asserted a theory of how bestsellers and prizewinners emerge in the literary field and structure the field by articulating its two opposite poles. On the one hand, we have authors who aim to sell books, accruing as much financial capital as possible. They represent the commercial side of the field. On the other, we have authors who seek to win prizes, accruing as much symbolic capital as possible. Such writers represent the prestigious corner of the field and are largely defined by their desire to achieve autonomy from the economic marketplace. The story of how a novel is received in the literary field is one of how that novel positions itself ("position taking") between these two poles and what forms of capital (economic or symbolic) it accrues. Along the way, each novel attains "marks of distinction" that index its particular place in the literary field, between or among such poles.[14]

Bourdieu's model is ubiquitous in sociological approaches to literature. For example, scholars juxtapose materialist readings of institutions or statistical information about book sales with close readings of individual texts.[15] And for this current chapter, we could certainly proceed by analyzing several novels from our various bestseller and prizewinner corpora. But I've assembled these corpora to identify *patterns* of language, form, and narrative that correspond to Bourdieu's notion of literary "marks of distinction." I am interested in revealing consistent textual features *at scale*. What we will inevitably lose in granularity in detail at the level of the page, we gain in our ability to generalize at the level of the corpus. These features, I will show, illustrate an empirical systematicity to the forms of textual distinction that engender these three literary categories.

New methods in artificial intelligence and machine learning allow us to precisely compare large corpora of texts and identify textual features that distinguish them at scale. Let me walk through an example of how a machine learning algorithm—a *classification* algorithm—performs this task. We'll focus on bestsellers versus novels by black authors as an example. First, we'll give both of these two corpora to the machine, and we will tell the machine the categorical identity of each text. Next, we'll ask the machine to study the qualities of these texts and try to identify consistent differences that distinguish our two classes of writing. To help it, we'll give the machine a list of textual features that we think are important to distinguishing bestsellers from novels by black authors. These include diction, syntax, literary style, and narrative form (in my next section, I specify more precisely what these features are). Now, the computer will create a kind of grid or chart—what we call a "language model"—that will identify textual properties more common or specific to each corpus, and it will quantify those distinctions. It will find that bestsellers are far more likely to use the word "enormous" than novels by black authors, for example, and that novels by black authors have a higher rate of dialogue. These features get weighted more heavily in the machine's language model because they significantly help its ability to distinguish or classify one type of text from another.

Once we have our language model, we can move on to the classification or prediction stage of the process. Now, we of course know which texts belong to which category. But we also want to know how powerfully our textual features determine each category. Based on these features, how truly different are bestsellers from novels by black authors? This is what we can do: we give the machine each novel in both of our corpora, one by one. But *we don't tell the machine which category the text belongs to.* It goes in blind. We ask the machine *to guess or predict* which category the text is based on its language model, which it computed earlier by looking at all of the texts. If the machine can guess or predict correctly at a very high rate—say, 90 percent of the time—we can say that there exists a very strong distinction in our categories based on our textual features. If the machine guesses wrong very often—say, 66 percent of the time or worse—we can say that our two categories are not very distinct, at least based on the textual features we've looked at. In the end, machine classification can tell us two important things: (1) how different our two corpora are based on how accurately it can predict their difference, which comes in the form of a percentage, and (2) a set of textual features that the machine has identified as significant to the process of classifying or distinguishing our two categories of literary texts.

Machine classification is typically used for commercial purposes, like separating real email from spam email in your inbox. When applied to literary criticism, scholars need to be careful in how we use it. The goal of criticism is not just to separate types; the goal is to understand better what constitutes those different literary types and make sense of what distinguishes them. Moreover, the analysis of types of creative writing will need to account for a more sophisticated sense (historical, critical) of the ontology of those categories. In trying to figure out what's spam and what's not, few will care about the historicity of the spam category. But in trying to make strong claims about the difference between X and Y genres of literature, literary scholars care deeply about the historical constitution of these categories. They will reflexively ask whether those categories even represent coherent and realistic entities and, if so, how and why. Cultural analytics scholars like Ted Underwood and Katherine Bode have used this approach to track the historical development of literary genres in Anglo-American and Australian contexts.[16] For example, in his analysis of popular literary genres, Underwood finds that the genre of English-language "science fiction" has been far more coherent and stable over the past one hundred years than literary critics and historians have claimed.[17]

Yet the issue becomes far more vexed when we introduce the category of novels written by black authors into this framework. As already alluded to, just the simple mention of race and "classification" is enough to give one pause: one need only utter "eugenics" or "the bell curve" to recall that, historically speaking, most attempts to use a quantitative mechanism to measure race, particularly the ostensible features that constitute racial identity, have also usually enabled racial stratification and racial inequality. While we might be on safer ground in using quantitative methods to classify a book as a bestseller or prizewinner, the category of "novels by black authors" inhabits the very idea of a "category" differently than those first two. A fundamentally different set of social factors animate the constitution of this category. These factors perhaps are adjacent or in part overlapping with the literary market, but they are more often askance to it. The use of machine classification to discern features that differentiate, say, novels by identified "black" authors from bestsellers would then be at best naïve and at worst reproduce a set of stereotypes about black people that merely amplify "common sense"—normative assumptions about race, not unlike the dubious positivist claims made by eugenics.

The challenges are obvious, so I should be clear about what I intend to do. I do *not* use the method of classification to identify features immanent to black versus nonblack writers in order to announce natural differences that inhere between them or use such observations to impose or strengthen the belief in a natural "order" in the literary field based on racial difference. Rather, my interest in the classification method is to focus upon the *boundary line* between socially constructed categories of "novels by black authors" and American bestsellers and prizewinners: to analyze the integrity or erasure of that boundary, to parse how that boundary transforms over time, and to discuss the consequences of such transformations for the categories of writing that exist on each side. In particular, I am interested in the features that enable that boundary line—again, *not* as measurements or qualities innate to authors of specific racial identities but as markers of the relation between socially constructed categories. By now it should be obvious that I do not treat "black" (or "nonblack") as ontologically coherent. They are mere socially constructed categories, and I study their relation. The machine is a relational, not ontological, thinker.

By studying this line, we can also begin to understand what makes it tenuous or contingent. The machine can tell us how different categories of literature, such as bestsellers and novels by black authors, are. And it can tell us what exactly constitutes the line that separates them, such as words like "enormous" and the frequency of dialogue. However, it can also tell us what makes that line tenuous. Here I make a final and important methodological point. Even if our classifier is "good"—that is, if it can predict the difference of our categories at a rate of 90 percent or greater—it still sometimes gets it wrong. It occasionally *misclassifies* texts. For instance, it will mistake Harper Lee's *To Kill a Mockingbird* as written by a black author and Octavia Butler's *Parable of the Sower* as a U.S. prizewinner. When we look at these works in particular—"misclassified texts"—we can get a sense of what types of texts and, specifically, what types of specific textual features, such as syntax, tend to confound the machine's color line. In other words, we can use our classifier not only to demonstrate the reliability of categories such as "the bestseller" and "novels by black writers." We can also use it to deconstruct the very integrity of those categories.[18]

RACE AND LITERARY DISTINCTION

Let me begin with a simple hypothesis: based on an analysis of textual features of novels—namely, *diction*, *syntax*, *style*, and *narrative*—there exists measurable differences between literary categories of U.S. bestselling novels, U.S. prizewinning novels, and novels written by black authors published between 1950 and 2000. And if this is true, let me add a brief corollary: the difference that exists is greater between novels by black authors and both bestselling and prizewinning novels than that between bestselling and prizewinning novels. And if this is true, one final corollary: this difference—what we might think of as a boundary line that divides our three categories—is unchanging over time.

To test this hypothesis, we'll need a language model. Our model includes four types of features. First, diction: my model simply counts the frequencies by which different words appear in a text. Word frequencies can only tell so much, and they cannot capture things like metaphor or irony, but they provide a baseline to glimpsing the content or story of a novel. Second, syntax: my model also counts the frequencies by which certain parts of speech, such as "nouns" or "adverbs," appear in a text. Here, too, simply counting the frequency of parts of speech in a text can only tell us so much and cannot tell us about paragraph-level syntactical ambitions, but it can still tell us much about the sentence-level syntactical habits of the text.[19] Third, style: my language model computes the amount of repetition and the lexical density of the text. How often does a text repeat the same words per sentence or paragraph? How difficult is the text to read based on a measurement of lexical diversity per sentence or paragraph?

Again, this approach will not be able to pick up on such finely defined tendencies like a "Jamesian style," but it provides a useful report on the broader stylistic habits of the author. Last, narrative: the model will compute statistics relevant to the represented world of the story. These include the ratio of dialogue to narration, the number of characters that appear in the story, the average amount of attention paid to each character, the number of manmade and natural objects that appear in the story on average, the number of locations or settings that appear in the story on average. In total, I refer to these features as "narration." Once more, these narrative features cannot capture the full complexity of the concept of narrative as asserted by literary theorists. But they are useful, albeit coarse, accounts of how novels employ the building blocks of narration: characters, dialogue, setting, objects, and so on.[20]

The value of the language model is that it allows us to identify concretely and specifically, at the level of words, style, form, and narrative, how two corpora of literary texts are similar or different. Traditional close reading, of course, can spot such differences in single texts, but the machine can tell us how consistent and regular these differences or similarities are across a large number of literary works. It can identify systematic patterns of textual distinction between different literary corpora at scale.

Table 3.2 summarizes our features and their qualities. Now that we have a language model to characterize each text in our corpora, we can proceed to the classification stage, using the method I described earlier. As a first pass, I classify in pairs, such as bestsellers versus prizewinners.[21] I do so because I want to understand how each category of text is distinguished from each other one, within a binary frame. Table 3.3 is a report of each pairwise classification

TABLE 3.2 TYPES OF TEXTUAL FEATURES

FEATURE NAME	EXAMPLE
Diction	Frequency of words, like "dog" or "they"
Syntax	Frequency of parts of speech, like "noun" or "adverb"
Style	Average amount of repetition of words per sentence
Narrative	Average rate of characters or locations per text

A list of the types of textual features that will be used for our machine classification exercise with examples of each type of feature.

TABLE 3.3 RESULTS OF MACHINE CLASSIFICATION

PAIRWISE COMPARISON	ACCURACY SCORE (%)
Bestsellers versus prizewinners	74
Bestsellers versus novels by black authors	93
Prizewinners versus novels by black authors	89

Results of machine classification comparing novels by black authors to American bestsellers and prizewinning novels, along with their reported classification accuracy rates.

performed by the machine. What immediately stands out is the discrepancy between the first classification result—bestsellers versus prize winners—and the second set of results, where we compare novels by black authors to bestsellers and prizewinners, respectively.[22] But what is most important about these scores is not their autonomous value but the magnitude of their difference. The machine is *far better* at discerning the difference between novels by black authors and bestsellers/prizewinners than the difference between bestsellers and prizewinners. Both of the latter are nearly equally distinct from novels by black writers.

The major takeaway from these results is that the primary axis of distinction in the postwar American literary field between 1950 and 2000 is race. If anything, our computational textual analysis simply intensifies our initial counting study: black authors are underrepresented in both the bestseller and prizewinning categories, the degree of that underrepresentation is severe, and that severity is not attenuating or changing over time. Here, when we turn our attention to the content, style, and literary form of these categories, we find similar levels of exclusion. While bestselling and prizewinning novels indeed use things like diction and syntax differently, this difference pales in comparison to the difference marked by the use of these features by black authors. The bestseller and the prizewinner are distinct from novels by black authors in simply not including black authors. But they are also distinct in simply excluding textual features common to novels by black writers. The *way* that black writers write is also failing to break in.

These results are suggestive but still coarse; there are two ways we can sharpen them. The first is straightforward: we can track the strength of the distinction between our literary categories over time. When the machine guesses or predicts the categorical identity of each text, it also assigns a probability to each text—the likelihood of that text belonging to X or Y class, such as bestseller or prizewinner. This value tells us how confidently the machine believes each text to be one or the other. And importantly, that value exists on an infinite spectrum between 0 and 1. It's not binary. For example, it believes quite confidently— with 99 percent confidence—that John Updike's *Rabbit Redux* is a prizewinner and not written by a black author, but with Saul Bellow's *Seize the Day*, it's only 95 percent sure. We can plot these values over time.[23] Such a graph will tell us how strongly the machine believes each novel belongs to each category and, in aggregate, how strongly it believes each category of text to be distinct from the others. We can also use this graph to infer temporal trends: are these distinctions changing over time?

The story these two graphs presents is clear (fig. 3.2, fig. 3.3). This is how you interpret them: each dot on each graph represents a text. The text's x-axis position indicates which year the text was published, and the text's y-axis position indicates the odds of the text being identified by the machine as a bestseller, prizewinner, or a novel by a black author. In the first graph, if a text has a probability score above 0.5, the machine believes it is a bestseller; if it is below 0.5, the machine believes it is a novel by a black author. The same for

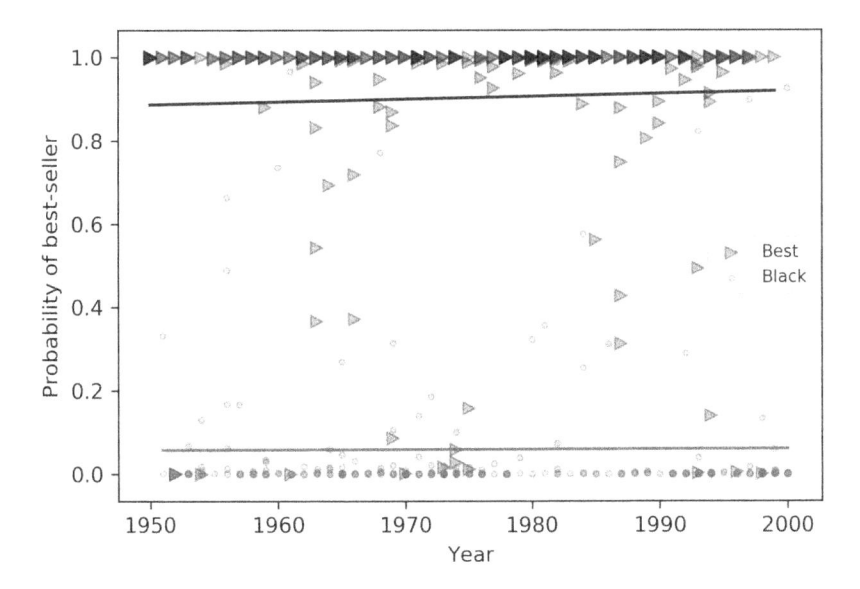

FIGURE 3.2 The predicted probability of American bestseller novels and novels written by black writers of being an American bestseller novel, based on our machine classification, 1950 to 2000.

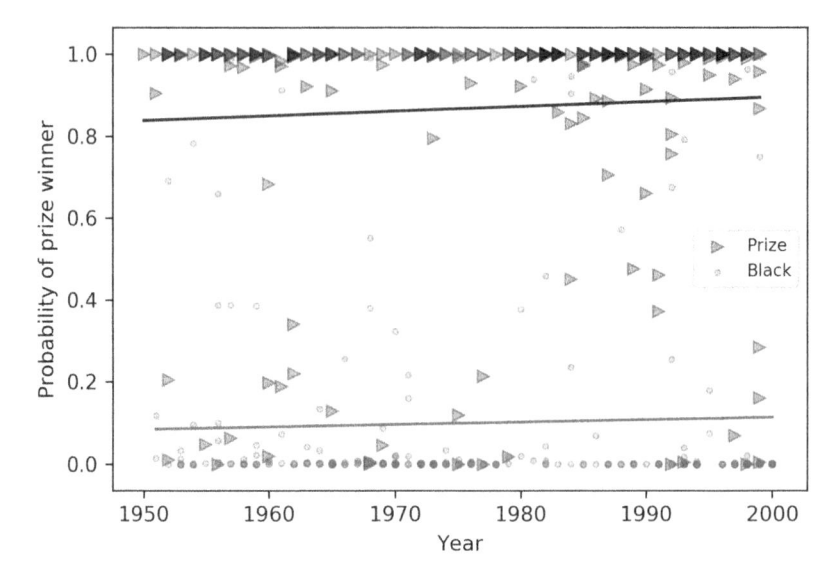

FIGURE 3.3 The predicted probability of American prizewinning novels and novels written by black writers of being an American prizewinning novel, based on our machine classification, 1950 to 2000.

the second graph, but with bestsellers now replaced by prizewinners. Finally, I mark each dot based on the text's true identity, and I add a line to indicate linear trends in the results. What we see for each comparison, whether bestsellers versus novels by black authors or prizewinners versus novels by black authors, is a steady level of distinction. If the categories were becoming less distinct, the lines would converge. Here, we see a yawning gap in both graphs, indicating a persistent distinction in the types of language, syntax, style, and narrative used by American bestsellers and prizewinners compared to novels by black writers, across the entire length of the second half of the century.

This approach allows us to attain some granularity at the level of the text; an even finer form of analysis, though, is to look at the specific textual features that animate this process of classification. I've already described how the machine will use a large set of features, provided by the researcher, to learn the differences between classes of text, and then based on that learning, it predicts whether a new and unlabeled text belongs to X or Y category of text.[24] I also explained how the machine assigns "weights" to each feature based on how important that feature is to distinguishing our classes of texts. We can then use

TABLE 3.4 DISTINCTIVE FEATURES OF AMERICAN BESTSELLERS

	DICTION	SYNTAX	STYLE	NARRATIVE
Bestsellers	enormous, divorced, airport, delicately, fiercely, champagne, afternoon, hours, worst	adverbs	none	none
Novels by black authors	white, colored, black, bus, skin, jazz, music, neighborhood, woman, brown	nouns	lexical diversity	dialogue, rate of objects, rate of people

A sample of the most distinctive features that distinguish American bestsellers from novels by black authors, across our four feature types: diction, syntax, style, and narrative.

TABLE 3.5 DISTINCTIVE FEATURES OF AMERICAN PRIZEWINNING NOVELS

	DICTION	SYNTAX	STYLE	NARRATIVE
Prizewinners	bristles, imagine, peaks, shaving, sunburned, delicately, afternoon, tennis, enormous	adverbs	none	none
Novels by black authors	brown, colored, frown, laugh, white, tears, lips, snatched, scream, anger, folks, smiled	verbs, nouns	none	dialogue, rate of people

A sample of the most distinctive features that distinguish American prizewinners from novels by black authors, across our four feature types: diction, syntax, style, and narrative.

these weights to produce a list of the most important features for each type of classification—bestsellers and prizewinners versus novels by black writers.

Tables 3.4 and 3.5 present a sample of the textual features that drive the work of distinguishing our three classes of novels at such high rates. This analysis helps flesh out the story of distinction so far limned by our initial set of classification results. If those initial results say that bestsellers and prizewinners are more distinct from novels by black authors than they are from each other, our feature analysis specifies the exact textual qualities that animate that distinction. Across the board, diction is a primary site of distinction (all three classes of novels talk about different things), and in my next section, I dig deeper into those results. But there are other important trends to observe. For example, if we compare American bestsellers to texts by black writers, what makes bestsellers distinctive compared to novels by black authors—how the former pulls away from the latter—is an attention to adverbs, or qualification. By contrast, novels by black writers are rendered distinct from bestsellers by their attention to objects and people. The overall narrative space of novels by black authors is markedly different from that of bestsellers. Similarly, American prizewinners pull away from novels by black writers with their focus on adverbial qualification, while again, novels by black authors, by contrast, are more attentive to people and the things that people say, as measured by the relative frequency of dialogue. In my next section, I look at examples of these features in individual texts to analyze what they actually mean and what they can teach us about how bestsellers and prizewinners both draw a bright red line between themselves and literary blackness.

READING THE MACHINE COLOR LINE

As I wrote about in chapter 1, one dramatic consequence of the corporatization of American book publishing after the war was a growing focus on identifying and publishing "bestsellers." Publishers like Random House increasingly took on a winner-takes-all mentality: rather than support a broad midlist of titles, they fixated on a very small number of books that were likely to become bestsellers. These were books not only likely to sell in large quantities but also have tie-ins or adaptations with film and TV. Large publishers adopted a "blockbuster" strategy in which editors prioritized signing up established "stars" or "name authors" in order to control the risk of failure, while maximizing the potential for profit, with their books.[25] This strategy and effect had become so obvious and ubiquitous, that in 1981 Thomas Whiteside wrote an exposé of the publishing industry, *The Blockbuster Complex*, in which he criticized book publishers for losing touch with the world of creativity and intellect.[26]

Some examples of American bestsellers, from each decade between 1950 and 2000, to give a sense of the rise of this complex, are: *Lolita*, by Vladimir Nabokov (1958); *The Fixer*, by Bernard Malamud (1966); *Fools Die*, by Mario Puzo (1978); *I'll Take Manhattan*, by Judith Krantz (1986); and *Malice*, by Danielle Steel (1996).

Editors were given the difficult task of finding the next big thing. As they did this work, and as we think about the historical category of "the postwar bestseller," we inevitably ask: do American bestselling novels have a discernable style? Do all of the novels on the bestselling list share any notable ideas, themes, or literary forms? What makes a bestseller is often a large institutional apparatus, the publisher, which mobilizes vast resources, such as promotion and marketing, to help a book succeed. But that insight doesn't answer the question of what makes an editor think a book will be a bestseller in the first place. There has to be something in the text itself to make her think that.

Literary scholars have offered some thoughts about what distinguishes an American bestseller. For the most part, they've been most interested in exploring the bestseller's relationship to a massively expanding U.S. reading public after the war. For example, John Sutherland has argued that the postwar bestseller's primary function is ideological: "the best-seller expresses and feeds certain needs in the reading public. It consolidates prejudice, provides comfort, is therapy, offers vicarious reward and stimulus."[27] And if the bestseller is designed chiefly to impart an accessible public message, Gordon Hutner and Elizabeth Long have argued that this "message" has been reliably a middle-class one: the valorization and exploration of a postwar, financial "American Dream." Long has offered evidence that bestselling American novelists arose largely, if not exclusively, from the "environing culture of the American middle classes."[28] Bestselling authors therefore tended to write about what they knew best—themselves—and the struggles and joy of achieving the best version of what they were born to do: strive for upward economic mobility. Hutner adds: "Taken as a group, these books create a whole storehouse of evidence for determining the history of American middle-class taste and cultural anxieties."[29]

Literary scholars have given us a general, thematic sense of what books editors might have been looking for, perhaps unconsciously, when trying to spot the next big bestselling novel: middle-class ennui, class mobility, and so on. Our model specifies this argument in two ways. First, it tells us that the existence of a bestseller style in part relies on its distinction from novels by black authors, and second, it shows us what precisely constitutes that style at the level of language, syntax, style, and narrative.

Our results first offer confirmation of the scholarly view (table 3.4). If we skim the words that tend to appear in bestsellers (as compared to novels by black writers), a signal arises: "divorced, "airport," and "hour." "Divorced" supports the claim that bestsellers turned toward stories of private life versus the public sphere by the 1970s; "airport" echoes the argument that bestsellers were chiefly interested in postwar affluence and class mobility; and "hour" suggests a deepening focus on psychological interiority, a claim also advanced by both Long and

Hutner.[30] Bestselling American novels after the war are full of characters who have family problems, are focused on work/travel, and fixate on the mundane and psychologically driven aspects of social life. Here I have included only a sample of the full list of most distinctive features. On the longer list, there are additional words to support this interpretation, such as "champagne" and "telephone."

But the model also tells us something we likely didn't see before: bestsellers are distinguished from novels by black authors based on syntax, not just content. Bestselling authors use the language of modification—*adverbs*—at a far higher rate than novels by black writers. Adverbs and adjectives dominate: "delicately," "fiercely," "enormous," and many others not reported in our table. Here, we begin to sketch the outlines of a bestseller style. If the narrated world of bestsellers is populated primarily by middle-class men and women drinking champagne, on the phone, worrying about divorce and, more existentially, the passing of hours, the form in which this narrative information is conveyed is distinct compared to novels by black authors. That information tends to be transmitted in qualified terms: a constant deferral of signification as what is meant to be said needs to be held up for just a moment as that thing is slightly modified. The voice of the American bestseller (whether it is the narrator or the characters speaking) is an overthinking one, a voice that needs to be just a bit more sure before it can speak.

At the same time, this feature is distinct in terms of what it makes less likely. In contrast to novels by black authors, the bestseller's focus on qualification lessens the possibility of a fully described world of people and things. If we turn our view to the distinctive features of texts by black writers, much of what we see lines up with criticism and scholarship. Lexical diversity: the frequent use of slang and nonstandard English necessarily creates a more diverse vocabulary compared to books written for a broad and mainstream American audience. Whether invoking a practice of "signifying" (Henry Louis Gates) or a "Blues aesthetic" (Houston Baker), black writers manipulate both the English language as well as how that language looks on the page to create a multiplicity of linguistic effects that are less common in mainstream novels.[31] Dialogue: the "plurality of voices" present in novels by black writers has been well documented by scholars like Mae Henderson; here, dialogism is a mechanism to "speak to and engage both hegemonic and ambiguously (non)hegemonic discourse."[32] And characters: Alice Walker argues that a signal achievement of the African American novel is the creation of vivid characters, characters "so intensified that I become involved with them, so exaggerated that they seem to exact human proportions, and I struggle and suffer with them."[33] Even our specific finding regarding adverbs has been confirmed by novelists like Toni Morrison, who claimed in an interview that she explicitly avoids using "adverbs" in her writing.[34]

Much of this is pushed out of the American bestselling novel. This is not to say that nonstandard English, dialogue, or the use of characters doesn't happen or happen very regularly in the bestseller. This is simply to say that *in comparison* to postwar novels by black writers, these aspects of the novel are highly deprioritized. The amount of things that can happen in a novel is finite. Bestselling authors prioritize, on average, the use of a particular kind of diction and the syntax of qualification compared to black authors writing in the same period. But the implications of this seemingly innocuous decision, likely taken on unconsciously by actual writers, are meaningful. A nontrivial attention to the vocabulary of the middle-class suburb ("champagne," "airport") and to adverbial modification crowds out a diction and literary style that would potentially force the text to assume a different overall discursive orientation. In crudest terms, the bestseller's frequent use of words like "delicately" forces out words like "jazz" or "snatched" and, more broadly, a literary style that thrives on lexical diversity. In other words, one form of semantic and syntactical attention makes very unlikely another type. Again, the machine cannot determine what is *innate* to the bestseller or novels by black authors in terms of language, style, or narrative. It can only tell us if there exists a dividing line between the two, and if there is a line, what constitutes that line. Here we see that line clearly.

The story I've told so far about the postwar American literary marketplace is that mainstream book publishers are incredibly white—97 percent white—in terms of whom they publish, and the books that become bestsellers are also very white—98 percent. These numbers basically line up, and they indicate a clear relationship: if nonwhite authors can't get published by big publishers, which have the resources to help produce "blockbusters," then they don't stand much of a chance of getting on bestseller lists.

But the results of our model enrich this analysis. That exclusion is not random or based solely on institutional dynamics. Our model can reliably tell the difference between bestsellers and novels by black writers at a rate of 93 percent, another number that closely lines up with our first two numbers: 97 percent and 98 percent. That means that bestselling novels emit a textual signal that makes it different from other kinds of novels, novels by black authors in particular. There is something inside these books that in part make them bestsellers, beyond the machinations that go on behind the scenes at big publishers with promotion, marketing, etc. Most likely, the institutional and textual dynamics exist within a feedback loop. Each day, an editor reads dozens of submissions in search of the next blockbuster or bestselling novel. Our analysis says that this editor, consciously or unconsciously, does this work in part by noticing a set of textual features that are simultaneously very common in previous bestsellers and very uncommon in novels written by black writers.

Indeed, these features are things that most readers can see on the page. Take, for instance, Judith Krantz's massively bestselling 1978 novel *Scruples*. Random House purchased the novel and offered a massive advance. Its paperback-right auction, conducted shortly after its initial purchase, set a record of $3.2 million. Before *Scruples* was even published, Krantz got a $400,000 advance for the hardcover rights for her next book.[35] And when it was published, it was an immediate bestseller. Editors at a large publishing house believed that *Scruples* would be the next big thing—that it had "it"—and they were right. At the same time, the novel possesses a clear "bestseller style" when compared to novels by black authors. The machine believes with total confidence—99.9 percent confidence—that *Scruples* belongs to the category of the bestseller. It also believes it is unambiguously distinct from novels by black authors. Whatever editors (and, later, readers) saw in the novel, they likely saw that distinction—a distinct aversion to words, styles, themes, and narrative elements often found in novels by black writers.

Scruples follows the life and times of a young white woman, "Billy" Winthrop. Billy is born into a wealthy Boston family, but after her mother's death, she is forced to work for a living and becomes relatively poor. The story narrates her upward mobility as she leaves the stuffy American East Coast for the West Coast and makes her way into the world of wealth and Hollywood, marrying a famous film director. There is drama and scenes of adventure, as well as a good deal of saccharine romance.

The following passage, selected nearly at random, instantiates seemingly self-parodically what the machine has identified as an "American bestseller style":

> Valentine boarded the polar flight one day ahead of Josh. His wife and, unfailingly, some of his children always met him at the airport after any business trip, a fact that caused Los Angeles to become a reality again. Even then, in the departure lounge, she did not speak of the next week or the next month. What, after all, was there for her to say? Only as the future unfolded itself would she see the shape of it.[36]

Here we see the importance of specific things and places, like airports and lounges, to establishing the parameters of life for a particular kind of person.

In the narrative voice, we hear the voice of a probing and wondering interior mind, the constant drift toward mental representation over the material world. And in its language, we see—again, nearly comically—the fixation on *adverbs* to render this world and its way of thought as literature: "unfailingly," "again," "even then," "after all," and "only." Nearly every sentence includes an overdrawn adverb. What we need to remember is that not only does the American bestseller care about and represent a specific social world but also that it is less interested in other social worlds. That is, in this case, it draws a bright red line between itself and the kind of world common to novels by black authors—both in terms of what exists in that world and how it is depicted.

American literary prizes have also had a complex, if not vexed, relationship to race, blackness in particular. But here, unlike with bestsellers, because prizes are selected by a visible and discrete group of designated literary experts, they've been held more accountable in terms of promoting racial diversity and multiculturalism. For example, the National Book Award (NBA) was reconstituted into its modern form in 1950 as an alternative to the perceived more reactionary Pulitzer Prize. The NBA in part gave its book award in 1953 to Ralph Ellison's *Invisible Man* to mark its distinction from the Pulitzer. This choice was implicitly a gesture toward racial inclusion.[37] That year, the Pulitzer Prize for fiction went to Ernest Hemingway's *The Old Man and the Sea*.

By the late 1980s, with the rise of a growing number of racial minority novelists, such as Alice Walker, Scott Momaday, Maxine Hong Kingston, and Toni Morrison in particular, literary prizes once again became scrutinized and criticized for failing to recognize nonwhite authors, particularly women of color. When the NBA decided to award its fiction prize to Larry Heinemann's *Paco's Story* in 1987 over Morrison's *Beloved*, a major literary scandal erupted, in which forty-eight distinguished African American scholars and writers published an op-ed in the *New York Times* to protest. This public outcry no doubt put pressure on the Pulitzer, which awarded its prize to Morrison later that year. In an ironic reversal of our 1953 example, the Pulitzer Prize now positioned itself as the more progressive alternative to the perceived backward National Book Award.[38]

Literary historians generally see the NBA book prize scandal as marking a turning point in the history of the literary prize. Morrison and her allies forced powerful cultural institutions like the NBA (and Pulitzer) to acknowledge a long-standing racial bias in how it understands "cultural value." In James English's account, their victory helped expedite the "rising prestige" of

African American literature, now increasingly recognized for its potential symbolic capital.[39] If anything, English gently admonishes Morrison and her allies: in demanding recognition from literary institutions like the NBA, they ultimately reaffirm their cultural authority and legitimacy.

Yet English and other literary historians largely seem to agree that something happened. But did something really change? Figure 3.1 does in fact indicate that by the late 1980s and into the early 1990s more major literary prizes are being given to racial minority authors, black authors in particular. Morrison alone won several prizes. However, the graph also indicates an apparent regression to the mean: by the late 1990s, we see that the number of nonwhite prize winners starts approaching 1970 levels. Echoing our analysis of Random House and its representation of nonwhite authors, we see a clear spike in the number of nonwhite prize winners, but that effect is quite ephemeral. Once the 1987 NBA book scandal apparently fades from memory or, at least, visibility, literary awards revert to what they have previously been—90 percent white.

Further, the data indicates that the distinction between prizewinners and novels by black writers is also unchanging over time in terms of content. Take another look at figure 3.3. The height of that line tells us how different prizewinners and novels by black authors are, and we observed that the line is very high, indicating a sharp difference. But that line is also statistically flat and unmoving.[40] The likelihood of being a prizewinner versus a novel by a black author, based on our model, does not change or improve whether we're looking at the 1950s and 1960s or the 1980s and 1990s. In other words, literary prize committees are willing to give a few more book awards to racial minorities, but the kinds of stories they like and tend to valorize are not changing in a way visible at scale. Despite the impact of the *Beloved* scandal in the late 1980s, we have no evidence that literary prize committees suddenly have changed what types of books they value.

What does that distinction specifically look like? The results of our language model (table 3.5) reveal a set of patterns. As with bestsellers compared to novels by black writers, we find a clear pattern in how prizewinners distinguish themselves from novels by black writers in terms of diction. The language of middle-class desire and anxiety comes to the fore: "tennis," "sunburned," and "lawn" (as far as things go), supplemented by more abstract language that points to a bourgeoisie psychology—"confiding" and "sentimental."[41] What is striking is the use of a similar vocabulary to the bestseller. Populating the world of the postwar American prizewinner is a set of things (tennis instead of champagne) and affective concerns (sentiment instead of the hours) not much different from the bestseller. And indeed, a number of words overlap in the list, such as "enormous."

Of course, it's possible—likely, even—that the prizewinning novel, as an imagined more nuanced and sophisticated literary version or subversion of the popular bestseller, is ironizing the semantic and narrative world of the latter. But even in that case, what largely happens in that world at the level of semantics is the same. Compared to novels by black authors, both genres are constrained to a set of things that can be talked about.

This claim gathers additional force when we look at the prizewinner's distinctive syntax: again, adverbs.[42] Bestsellers and prizewinners share a syntactical preference, at least when compared to novels by black writers. So much of what fills the pages of the prizewinner, as with the bestseller, is endless linguistic qualification and modification. Houses cannot just be houses; they must be "enormous" houses. Matters of the heart are never just talked about; they need to be talked about "delicately."

We can also again examine what this textual orientation excludes. Looking at the list of textual features that mark novels by black authors in comparison to the U.S. prizewinner, we see much of the same when novels by black writers are compared to the U.S. bestseller: for example, we find a list of words that are specifically about race or identity ("brown," "colored," and "white"). Again, I will argue that the prizewinner's emphasis on a specific diction and heavy use of adverbs essentially crowds out words tied more specifically to race. And at the narratological level, we find a similar set of features, dialogue in particular. Dialogue, of course, represents a major location in the expression of racial identity and racial difference in novels. A text will often signal that a character is racially marked based on how he or she speaks or is represented to speak. It is, for instance, more often than not the place where racialized slang materializes.

Individual novels that exhibit this pattern with particular intensity include John Updike's *Rabbit Is Rich*, John Cheever's *The Wapshot Chronicle*, and Saul Bellow's *The Adventures of Augie March*.[43] This group of texts confirms the sense that what in part animates the semantics of the prizewinner is a concern with the white middle class. Literary scholars have argued that novelists like Updike and Cheever, with their interest in narrating the lives of suburban career strivers and disaffected outsiders, helped instantiate a postwar conception of "whiteness" as rooted in middle-class ennui.[44] What my analysis suggests is that what also makes them "prizeworthy" in this period is partly animated by a specific textual disposition that, as I show with bestsellers, brackets out a semantics and literary form representative of books by written by black authors.

A closer look at a single novel helps show this disposition at work. Consider a specific scene from *Rabbit Is Rich* (1981), by John Updike. The novel continues the story of Harry "Rabbit" Angstrom—an upwardly mobile white man from a working-class suburb of Pennsylvania—as he now approaches middle age with a family and an affluent life. One major tension is that despite his growing affluence, he continues to live in his relatively lower-middle-class town of origin, and this has various psychological effects. In one scene, after a long outing, Rabbit reflects on the course of his life:

> In his memory of these outings they always seem to be climbing toward the ocean as toward a huge blue mountain. Sometimes at night before falling to sleep he hears his mother say with a hiss, "Hassy." He sees now that he is rich that these were the outings of the poor, ending in sunburn and stomach upset. Pop liked crab-cakes and baked oysters but could never eat them without throwing up. When the Model A was tucked into the garage and little Mim tucked into bed Harry could hear his father vomiting in a far corner of the yard. He never complained about the vomiting or about work, they were just things you had to do, one more regularly than the other.[45]

Rabbit's long mental meandering enacts the kinds of ennui that literary scholars like Catherine Jurca mark as definitive of postwar suburban whiteness.[46] But we can also now see how this ennui and anxiety get marked by specific and discrete semantic markers. What triggers this reflection is the image of his parents getting "sunburned." And this recollection triggers a larger imagined world that includes things like crab cakes, Model A cars, and suburban yards. Further, we notice the frequent use of adverbs such as "never complained" and "more regularly," which intensifies the feeling that the main character is an overthinking one. And last, we notice that this litany of things and qualifications drives out the possibility of dialogue. Dialogue can only exist through the prism of Rabbit's mind, not in the world. As with our reading of *Scruples*, what becomes evident is how this specific semantic and narratological space—a set of objects and things to think about, and how to think about them—makes impossible a different physical apprehension of the world and way of talking about that world.

Here, we arrive at perhaps the most important aspect of our results. A good deal of scholarly work still focuses on the distinction between bestsellers and prizewinners and how that distinction sets up the two major poles of the literary marketplace.[47] I do not deny that they are markedly different—after all, our model can tell them apart with 74 percent accuracy. And I do not deny that *Scruples* and *Rabbit Is Rich* are also very different. But I argue that when we compare these two texts and, more broadly, the literary categories they represent (bestsellers and prizewinners, respectively), what makes them distinct is less how they are different from each other and more how they are both different from novels written by black authors, at least the novels that constitute our corpus. Again, I emphasize that it is possible, if not likely, that there are aspects of our texts that our model cannot pick up, nuances and subtleties of affect, figurative language, and so forth. But when we look at their core building blocks, such as diction and syntax—the things readers are most likely to notice—and we look at how they relate to literary blackness, American bestsellers and prizewinners appear far more similar than we have previously noticed, despite the fundamentally different institutional mechanisms that drive them.

CONTINGENCIES: *PARABLE OF THE SOWER*

The line that separates novels by black authors from prizewinners and bestsellers is hard, fast, and unchanging. The things that in part make a bestseller or prizewinner—the things that help a novelist to be one or the other or both—exclude novels by black writers at the level of literary form and content. The question I want to ask now is: what would it take to subvert this system? Is there anything a black writer can do to cut through this red line in terms of how she writes? In the end, how stable and rigid is this red line? Does it have vulnerabilities or contingencies? How does a black writer become an effective outlier, and what would being such an outlier mean to the bigger system?

Our language model indicates that prizewinners and bestsellers, when compared to novels by black authors, have a number of textual features that reliably distinguish one from the other. The reliability of these features allows it to relatively easily—with an accuracy of 93 percent and 89 percent, respectively—tell our categories apart. But it doesn't always get it right. Sometimes it misclassifies texts, as I described earlier.[48] That means that it looks at a novel like Harper Lee's *To Kill a Mockingbird*, which belongs to our prizewinner's corpus, studies all of its textual features, and incorrectly predicts that the novel belongs to the category of novels by black writers based on those features. In table 3.6, I provide several more examples of these misclassifications.

Misclassified texts are important because they tell us that the dividing line between bestsellers/prizewinners and novels by black authors is not always complete. They tell us that some specific authors are doing things in their novels, at the level of content and form, that are subverting the otherwise hard distinctions that separate our categories. Even if, in the end, that black author was not successful—that is, her novel never became an actual bestseller or prizewinning

TABLE 3.6 NOVELS MISCLASSIFIED BY THE LANGUAGE MODEL

TITLE	AUTHOR	TYPE OF MISCLASSIFICATION
To Kill a Mockingbird	Harper Lee	Bestseller → novel by black author
The Old Man and the Sea	Ernest Hemingway	Bestseller → novel by black author
Something Happened	Joseph Heller	Bestseller → novel by black author
The Seven League Boots	Albert Murray	Novel by black author → bestseller
The Parable of the Sower	Octavia Butler	Novel by black author → bestseller
The Confessions of Nat Turner	William Styron	Prizewinner → novel by black author
The Catcher in the Rye	J. D. Salinger	Prizewinner → novel by black author
The Age of Wire and String	Ben Marcus	Prizewinner → novel by black author
The Salt Eaters	Toni Cade Bambara	Novel by black author → prizewinner
The Farming of Bones	Edwidge Danticat	Novel by black author → prizewinner

A sample of novels that have been misclassified by our language model, spanning our three categories of the American bestseller, the American prizewinner, and novels written by black authors. The "Type of Misclassification" column indicates the novel's "correct" class (the first term) and the novel's predicted "incorrect" class (the second term).

book—our model tells us that she is nonetheless doing things that are undermining those distinctions, pulling apart that red line.

One black author in our corpus that our language model consistently is confused by is Octavia Butler. Most of her novels are correctly classified, such as *Kindred* and *Patternmaster*, which the model identifies as a novel by a black author, but two others, *Parable of the Sower* and *Clay's Ark*, the model incorrectly predicts to be a prizewinner and/or bestseller. Butler, in other words, exists on both sides of the machine's color line. She is doing something in her writing that subverts that line.[49] Of all the black authors in our corpora, Butler gives us an idea of what one needs to do to break the system.

Octavia Butler never wrote a bestseller, and she never won a major literary prize. While she won several science-fiction awards for her fiction, such as the

Nebula, she never won one of the major mainstream book prizes that confer total prestige, such as the National Book Award or the Pulitzer Prize (and that's why she is not in our corpus of prizewinning texts). She always wanted to do both, though. In 1981, she submitted a copy of *Clay's Ark* to Toni Morrison at Random House, hoping to break free from the science-fiction label in order to reach a "wider audience."[50] And in 1988, she wrote in her journal: "I shall be it. Bestselling author. So be it!" which is followed by a similar wish to win a major U.S. literary prize.[51] Butler, in other words, tried very hard to be both a bestselling and prizewinning author, and while this wish would go unfulfilled within her lifetime, our language model seems to hear in its pattern recognition the echo of that wish. We hear in its hearing a set of tactics Butler undertook that, again, while not ultimately successful, indicates a broader strategy of subversion. In the end, she didn't break the system, but our model sheds light on how she still tried and what it looked like.

What does this subversion look like at the scale of a single novel? In this final section of the chapter, I offer a close reading of Butler's *Parable of the Sower*, published by Four Walls Eight Windows in 1993. Along with *Clay's Ark*, published in 1984 by St. Martin's, this text especially confounds our machine's color line. It's here, at a very local level—at the scale of the page, the paragraph, the sentence, the word—that we can discern the contingency and tenuousness of our three categories and what it might take to undo them. Both novels would make for a productive close reading, but I have chosen to focus on *Parable of the Sower* both because the novel is longer and more substantial than *Clay's Ark* and because the former represents (what many argue to be) a more mature example of Butler's work (it was written nine years after *Clay's Ark*).

Parable of the Sower is a work of dystopian fiction that takes place in California in the near future. American society has largely fallen apart because of worsening climate change and massive state corruption. The rich have fled to protected enclaves, guarded by private militaries, while the poor are forced to survive amid an increasing lawless, anarchic state of bare life. The novel is told through the first-person perspective of Lauren Olamina, a young black woman and daughter of a preacher. After her gated community is destroyed by desperate, impoverished outsiders and her entire family killed by a roving band of drug-addled scavengers, she joins with a group of strangers to travel north to find sanctuary beyond the American West Coast. The narrative is composed of a sequence of journal entries written by Lauren. Interspersed are quotations from a religious text that Lauren has begun to compose— *Earthseed: The Books of the Living*. Lauren is what the novel describes as a "sharer," an individual able to experience near-supernatural levels of empathy with other nearby humans. She uses this capacity to begin imagining a new form of human behavior and belief—a religion, essentially—adequate to meet the current challenges of a world in profound crisis. Her religion emphasizes change, and over the course of the story her various companions begin to accept its tenets.

From this very brief plot overview of *Parable of the Sower* we can already begin to intuit explanations for why this novel is misclassified. The novel is not a "typical" or traditional work of black or African American literary fiction insofar as its social concerns are refracted through the conventions of science fiction. Of course, the novel features black characters, and racial tension is a primary feature of its described dystopian world. For example, the narrative emphasizes that "mixed race couples" are particularly vulnerable to violence in this world. But much of what the reader might understand as "racial identity" and "race relations" in our current, nonspeculative world is displaced along other futuristic vectors. It is for this reason that the novel, if partly ignored by conventional African American literary studies, has received considerable recent uptake by researchers in Afrofuturism studies. This subfield, first developed in the late 1990s by scholars such as Tricia Rose, Mark Dery, Kodwo Eshun, and Greg Tate, can be described as "Speculative fiction that treats African American themes and addresses African American concerns within the context of twentieth century technoculture—and more generally, black signification that appropriates images of technology and a prosthetically enhanced future."[52] Few would deny that *Parable of the Sower* is a novel in part about "race." But the form by which this concern is articulated is oblique to its ostensible referent in "our world." Eshun describes this form as "the proleptic, the virtual, the future conditional."[53]

Here we seem to have a plausible explanation for Butler's misclassification: *Parable of the Sower*, as a work of black science fiction or Afrofuturism, eschews tropes of racial realism associated with more traditional works of black fiction, tending to displace race or render it in semiabstracted terms. Thus, the machine gets a bit confused as to its membership within a larger corpus of novels that includes *Beloved* and *Middle Passage*. Yet this still doesn't explain why the machine believes that the novel sounds more like a bestseller and prizewinner than a novel by a black writer. We recall how sharply these two categories veer away from novels by black authors; the space that divides them in our earlier graphs is vast. That Butler's novel is cast so far in the opposite direction of black fiction, or at least our corpus of novels by black authors, is striking.

We can get some traction on this question by investigating precisely why *Parable of the Sower* confuses the machine in terms of its prediction. That is, we can determine which specific features contribute the most to that act of misclassification. Again, we can think of all the features as constituting the dividing line that separates novels by black authors from bestsellers and prizewinners. *Parable of the Sower* offers an example of when that line doesn't quite work or grows tenuous, and a close reading of the features that animate that failure can tell us something about the overall contingency and ontological nonintegrity of all three categories, that is, the field of literary distinction.

Table 3.7 summarizes the textual features that play the most important role in creating that failure of classification, the machine's inability to uphold its color line.[54] Here is how you read this chart. We're interested in whether each feature has a positive or negative sign and whether that sign is positive or negative for *Parable of the Sower* compared to its value for novels by black authors. If the sign is different than its value for novels by black authors (and thus the same

TABLE 3.7 DISTINCTIVE FEATURES OF *PARABLE OF THE SOWER*

FEATURE	*PARABLE OF THE SOWER*	BESTSELLER/ PRIZEWINNER	NOVELS BY BLACK AUTHORS
white	0.15	−0.30	0.58
colored	0.12	−0.28	0.56
music	0.11	−0.12	0.23
airport	0.08	0.13	−0.26
carefully	0.05	0.12	−0.23
obviously	0.04	0.13	−0.25
adverbs	0.13	0.09	−0.17
modal verbs	0.28	0.09	−0.19
conjunctions	0.14	0.14	−0.27
dialogue	0.03	−0.34	0.67

A sample of most distinctive features as they appear in *Parable of the Sower*, ranked by their frequency in the text, compared to how these features appear, on average, in bestselling/prizewinning novels and novels by black authors.

for bestsellers/prizewinners), that means that it is expressing this feature in a way statistically opposite to how "novels by black authors," on average, enact that feature. In that case, that feature is directly causing the machine to confuse the "true" categorical identity of Butler's text. So, for example, Butler uses the word "carefully" often, which is used infrequently in novels by black authors but frequently in novels by prizewinners and bestsellers. That single word in *Parable of the Sower* is doing a lot of work in destabilizing our categories.

This table thus provides a guide for close reading to help us understand why this misclassification happens at the level of the page. Here is an example. In this scene, the novel's protagonist Lauren is traveling with her new allies, including an older African American man, Bankole, and they stop by a store to purchase supplies:

> It was an antique—a bolt action Winchester, empty, **of course**, with a five-round capacity. **It would be**, as Bankole admitted, slow. **But** he liked it. He inspected it with eyes and fingers **and** bargained with the **well-armed** old man and woman who were offering it for sale. They had one of the cleaner tables with merchandise laid out in a neat pattern—a **small**, manual typewriter; a stack of books; a **few** hand tools, worn, **but** clean; two knives in worn leather sheaths; a couple of pots, **and** the rifle with sling and scope.[55]

This passage materializes the main syntactical features that confuse the machine as to the novel's "correct" categorical membership: the frequent use of adverbs, such as "of course"; the use of modal verbs, such as "it would be"; and the heavy use of coordinating conjunctions, such as "and" and "but." What all of these syntactical features emphasize is a language of qualification and modification: with adverbs, the text must constantly answer the question of why and where and how; with modal verbs, the text must speculate as to why things might happen in such a way; and with coordinating conjunctions, the text must align and combine different descriptions to construct a coherent whole.

Passages like this are common and for good reason. The dystopian world of *Parable of the Sower* is utterly new—precisely because the world has and continues to be eviscerated by violence and climate change—to both the narrator (Lauren) and the reader. It is an alien, strange world that needs to be described in order to be understood. Again, this is both a diegetic (Lauren often simply cannot believe the madness happening in this world) and extradiegetic strategy (the author needs constantly to describe this world to achieve the appropriate estrangement effect upon the reader). Without the constant use of adverbs and other elaborative or speculative forms of language, this world would simply not make sense. For example, the gun is described as "of course" *empty* to explain why an old man and woman would have so readily at their disposal a violent weapon. The gun was never meant to be used to kill, and only within a speculative mode of thought ("it would be") can it be imagined as something that can be used to kill humans.

Overall, our chart tells us that the novel privileges syntax over an explicitly marked racialized diction. *Parable of the Sower* uses terms such as "white" or "colored" at a frequency significantly less, on average, than novels by black writers. This orientation thus also attenuates the text's "racial realism": the use of obvious signifiers of race to mark certain characters as black or white. For sure, the novel explicitly describes a handful of characters, such as Lauren, as "black," and the issue of racial difference comes up repeatedly in the novel. For example, Lauren remarks that the wealthy, protected enclaves prefer to admit only white people. But for the most part, the highly descriptive nature of this world foregrounds a different set of features necessary to mark identity. Individuals are "scavengers"; they are "friends" or "strangers." In other words, what identifies a person is their simple ability to survive and the means by which they have chosen to survive. *Parable of the Sower* is a story of how normative forms of settlement fail or are destroyed. Each place that Lauren and her people visit briefly promises some now obsolete notion of "home" or safety, only to be quickly wiped out by forces of barbarity. With each moment of destruction, the need for survival increases, and as that necessity grows, conventional identity markers attenuate. Such signifiers are replaced by more basic markers of social difference: killer, killed. By the story's end, racial signifiers have all but vanished.

The novel's attention to syntactical elaboration at the expense of racial realism is what seems to confuse the machine's color line. But the text does not simply erase racial signification; it reconstitutes it. For example, a word often used in the text that appears with increasing frequency is "slave." This is not entirely surprising. As Kodwo Eshun argues, works that belong to the Afrofuturist tradition often precisely "stage a series of enigmatic returns to the constitutive trauma of slavery in the light of science fiction."[56] In *Parable of the Sower*, Lauren and her group, many of whom are black, resist the possibility of joining a protected community because such communities are owned by large corporations, and those who live and work within them often exist in a kind of owner-slave relation. Implicit within this arrangement are echoes of American chattel slavery.

But the novel's use of the word "slave" does more than just generate a type of allegorical return of history. It performs what Phillip Brian Harper has called a "semantic mutation."[57] By the end of the novel, what is striking about the use of the words "slave" and "slavery" are their repetition. These terms are used to describe many different, not entirely commensurable things. Working for a factory in America is akin to slavery. Working for a factory in Canada is akin to slavery. People who are weak and are captured by roving bands of violent scavengers are "slaves." Going to jail and working for the state as cheap labor is a kind of "slavery." The term is a highly flexible signifier. And this is deliberate. The term's constant reiteration and incommensurability among its present invoked meanings, as well as its traditional historical signification, serves to reconstitute racial blackness through the lens of historical change. Blackness has not attenuated within this new world. It has simply become revised. What the novel argues is that more regular tropes of racial realism, as inherently presentist, will be inadequate to articulate the terms by which racial blackness appears within a world that is not "now."

With this in mind, we can further parse what syntax is doing in the text. Consider the following brief passage, which appears on the second-to-last page of the novel. Lauren and Bankole (now her lover) reflect on the catastrophic state of their world. The two disagree; Lauren believes that society has hit rock bottom, while Bankole believes the worst is yet to come, for both society and their group of friends: "He shook his shaggy head, his hair, beard, and serious expression making him look **more than a little like an old picture** I used to have of Frederick Douglass."[58] The phrase "more than a little like an old picture" stands out. The use of the words "more" and "a little" function as adverbs to express how certain (or uncertain) the speaker feels about the thing she is describing, a photograph of Douglass. Overall, despite the great deal of language used to describe Bankole's appearance, the text's use of syntax garbles our overall understanding of his identity. The text does make an explicit reference: the picture of "Frederick Douglass." Bankole can only be a black man. However, the sentence's piling on of adverbs qualifies this attribution of racial identity. Lauren says that he only looks "a little like" Douglass, not indelibly so, and he resembles the great orator not because of his skin color but because of his "beard." And the picture is "old"—the referent itself is not reliable. The text's use of syntax introduces discrepancy into its economy of racial signification, even at moments when a relation of literal equivalence (the photograph) is posited. Nothing, not even racial identity, can ever be just what it is.

This reading gives us a better sense of what drives the machine's misclassification of *Parable of the Sower* as an American bestseller/prizewinner. At a coarse scale, our analysis shows that the novel's heavy use of adverbs, modal verbs, coordinating conjunctions, and a relative lack of diction that signals black "racial realism" accounts for this mistake. But it would be an error in human interpretation to assume that the novel simply adopts the semantic and syntactical style of the bestseller or prizewinner, using its various distinctive textual features to drive out racial blackness. In fact, it does the opposite. The novel performs a series of deliberate semantic mutations. It uses syntactical features—again, otherwise marked by the machine as *not* distinctive of novels by black authors—precisely to underscore the presence of race in its story frame, albeit in a radically transformed manner. Such textual features intensify, rather than eviscerate, racial difference as a primary problematic for both the content and form of the novel.

ANTICIPATIONS: *PARADISE*

In my book's introduction, I discuss the concept of *leverage*: the idea that quantitative models, like machine classification, reveal both broad patterns as well as outliers and that the outliers can often expose important contingencies to the patterns, including how those patterns might be subverted or undone from within. Throughout this book, I've looked at several examples of textual outliers that perform leverage. My analysis of Octavia Butler's *Parable of the Sower* presents one more within the context of literary distinction. This analysis says that *Parable of the Sower* produces a series of textual effects—effects largely associated with Afrofuturism—that destabilize the red line that separates, if not segregates, bestsellers and prizewinners from novels by black authors. It is possible that our best hope in potentially dismantling this system rests in works like Butler's novel and others like it. They anticipate a more equal literary world to come.

Indeed, I end this chapter with a further speculation. Between 1950 and 2000, the only black author to have won or been nominated for a major literary prize and written a bestseller is Toni Morrison. She more or less accomplished both in 1997 with *Paradise*, which became just the third novel by a black author to appear on the *Publisher's Weekly* bestseller list (the basis, again, for our bestseller corpus) in this period. It did not win a major U.S. literary prize, but it was shortlisted for a major European literary prize (the International Dublin Literary Award), and it represents the third and final installment of Morrison's Beloved trilogy, a trilogy that has won several major American literary prizes, including the Pulitzer Prize. The publication of *Paradise* represents a decisive moment in which a black author breaks through a literary system that has, historically, blocked black and nonwhite authors from the coveted benefits of distinction.

Morrison, of course, got there by writing a half-dozen remarkable and critically successful novels that earned the admiration of critics and by slowly building a devoted readership that expanded with each new publication. Further, *Paradise* was the first novel she wrote after winning the Nobel Prize in Literature in 1993, and her publisher, Knopf, threw all of its resources to promote and market it, in the expectation and hopes that it would indeed become a blockbuster hit. Its first print run was 400,000 copies. By 1997, prize committees knew Morrison's work and favorably anticipated this novel; similarly, her publisher did everything it could to help the novel become a bestseller. Institutional factors did a great deal to make this unique moment happen for *Paradise*.

Yet, again, institutional explanations only tell part of the story. There are also things going on inside of the novels—language, style, narrative, etc.—that make this system operate, the things that readers notice and like. And when we look at *Paradise* through the lens of *Parable of the Sower*—the latter as a potential anticipation for Morrison's novel—we find a number of striking similarities.

Scholars have already noted some obvious commonalities.[59] *Paradise* tells the story of a group of black families who establish an all-black town, Ruby, in Oklahoma after the war. The novel narrates the gradual decline and corruption of this town and how a group of women leave Ruby in order to provide an alternative and in many ways safe haven from the excesses and social hierarchies corrupting Ruby. They call this community the Convent. Over time, this alternative community threatens the stability of Ruby and produces anxiety in its citizens. Against the backdrop of a changing U.S. society after the war, particularly the rise of new social movements like Black Power, the novel describes a series of attempts by the men of Ruby to violently destroy the Convent. Based on this brief description alone, the thematic resonances between *Paradise* and *Parable of the Sower* should be evident: both tell the story of a group of sojourners who seek to create a utopian community to fend off the threat of an increasingly violent world, a world determined to create repressive hierarchies based on race, class, and gender.[60]

Our language model offers a more nuanced account, however. *Paradise* and *Parable of the Sower* not only tend to use the same types of textual features at a high frequency, but also *how* they use them in relation to prizewinners/bestsellers and novels by black authors tends to be similar too.[61] Like Butler's novel, *Paradise* is distinguished by its heavy use of adverbs and modal verbs such as "may" or "should." And in terms of diction, both converge on the word "neighborhood"—for *Parable of the Sower*, this is the term that is most significant in distinguishing it from every other text in the corpus. For *Paradise*, it is also important, ranking as one of its top fifty most important features.[62]

But indeed, what makes the two novels most similar at the textual level is how they employ these features in relation to bestsellers/prizewinners and novels by black authors. In terms of diction, the trope of "the neighborhood" is deeply important, and its use of the term draws them closer to novels by black authors, which also use the term frequently. But their use of syntax—specifically, the heavy use of adverbs and modal verbs, indicating a version of reality defined by qualification and conditionality—draws them away from novels by black authors. What seems to be a distinction shared by these two novels is how diction works in one direction and syntax works in another. That is, in terms of diction, both *Paradise* and *Parable of the Sower* look more like novels written by black authors, especially in how they evoke the literary theme or trope of "neighborhoods," but in terms of syntax, they look more like bestsellers and prizewinners. Compared to the novels in our "novels by black authors" corpus, *Paradise* and *Parable of the Sower* share a tension in how they think about people living together, a tension defined by how they use diction in relation to syntax to do that, which makes them distinct not only from other novels by black authors but also from bestsellers and prizewinners in this period.

I have no evidence that Morrison was at all inspired by *Parable of the Sower* or saw herself in dialogue with Butler, and it is impossible to infer any kind of direct relation or causality between these two novels based upon our current data. But there is a friendly resonance here, one that perhaps began when Butler wrote to Toni Morrison at Random House in 1981—a connection that is starting to get explored by literary historians.[63] Within the framework of literary distinction described in this chapter, Butler's text is doing something significant to destabilize the red lines that define its operation and maintenance. She never won a major book prize or wrote a bestseller. But the things that she is doing get echoed and repeated in a work of literature that finally does break through. *Parable of the Sower* seems to anticipate, however faintly, a future for how novels become bestsellers or win major literary prizes that is more equitable to nonwhite writers.

4

CONSECRATION

The Canon and Racial Inequality

THE PROBLEM WITH 61 PERCENT

Literary scholars will remember the 1980s as a period of intense disciplinary change and contestation in significant part defined by the so-called canon wars. The *canon wars* were a series of debates among literary and cultural scholars, as well as among university administrators and the general public, regarding the appropriate constitution of college literature syllabi in an increasingly multicultural society. What poems, plays, and novels should be taught to university students? At stake was the definition of a Western cultural "canon": the major texts we identify as representing "our" common heritage as a group of citizens. If the immediate postwar period's emphasis on social cohesion and political consensus lent itself to defining the canon as composed primarily of white male authors like Henry James and Mark Twain, the social movements of the 1960s and the sudden massive influx of women and racial minorities into U.S. colleges in the 1970s demanded a rethinking of the canon as the basis for reflecting society. Feminist scholars such as Elaine Showalter and Adrienne Munich critiqued the patriarchal, male bias of the existing canon; minority scholars such as Henry Louis Gates Jr. and Houston Baker challenged the elision of racial "difference" as a basis to understanding U.S. literature and its various aesthetic problems.[1] Broadly, English professors suddenly recognized literature as "an institution" and, as such, oriented toward the reproduction of specific values that favor specific groups. The goal was not to destroy literature's basis as an institution but to reform it to make it relevant for a new generation of students. "The canon" became the site upon which to debate this change.

Looking back, what one finds most striking about the canon wars is less its intensity (debates in academic journals and op-eds were often ferocious) and more its *brevity*. One might date the first mainstream awareness of "the canon" as a disciplinary problem to the English Institute session held in 1981 focused on "Literature as an Institution" and mark its conclusion to 1995, when David Palumbo-Liu declared: "the battles for the inclusion of ethnic literature in the curriculum of American literary studies have been fought and in many cases won."[2] It was not very hard, at least in the humanities, to dismantle the reactionary arguments of William Bennett and other conservatives, such as "black people can have no canon."[3] These ideas were already at odds with the general disposition of literary studies in the 1980s, and increasingly so by the end of the decade, with the rise of "theory." Fourteen years (1981 to 1995) is not a very long time, but it's likely just long enough for the old guard to give way to a new generation.

Indeed, debates over the canon take a curious turn in the early 1990s. The apparent and perhaps all too swift "victory" of multiculturalism (as Michael Bérubé writes: "we are all multiculturalists now")[4] merely induced a new set of concerns. John Guillory argued that we need to focus on the institution of the university—not just individual authors or subgroups of authors (for example, white men)—as the basis to understand why certain types of texts and authors get valorized and others do not; it's the university that assigns values to art and is therefore the real locus of power within these dynamics.[5] Cornel West worried that the otherwise salutary expansion of the Western literary canon to include women and minority writers has worked to "reinforce prevailing forms of cultural authority in our professionalized supervision of literary products" and that it only "serves the class interests of Afro-American literary academic critics," not actual readers or authors.[6] Ethnic studies scholars feared that the ascent of multiculturalism simply meant its institutional cooption. By the mid-1990s, few would doubt the gains made by "exploding the canon," but the terms and thus the actual value of such gains had become dubious. Perhaps what was always aspired to was not quick and easy victory but instead a long revolution.

In any case, the canon wars have become a distant memory as the critique of the canon has morphed into a broader critique of the university (what now goes by the name of "critical university studies"). But that morphing has indirectly enacted a blind spot in how we imagine the impact of such wars, for or against: how did they influence the actual *field of literature*? Of publishing? Book reviews? Sales? Prizes? In most writings on the canon in the 1980s and 1990s, the link between the university (what it values in terms of aesthetics) and literary production is underarticulated or glossed over. Occasionally, scholars invoke "the literary field" but only to loosely conflate what is read in universities with what is read by ordinary people. At best, the "world out there" of nonacademics writing and reading books is alluded to, as Guillory does in the final paragraph of *Cultural Capital*, but typically as a utopian horizon, the thing that might finally break the "game of culture."[7] In short, this elision has become a tacit assumption: the canon wars *did something* for the institution of the university, and *that thing* productively bore on the world outside of the university, what we might call "the literary field"—the world of book publishers, book reviews, book prizes, and bestseller lists. Feminist and critical race studies scholars rightfully worry that the nominal victory of multiculturalism simply enabled new forms of reactionaryism. But they accept that some type of victory in fact happened, however ambiguous.

And they are correct, at least in terms of college syllabi. If we are interested in the category of "American literature"—the American novel and prose writing in particular—and use the current 2016 edition of *The Norton Anthology of American Literature* as a proxy for what gets taught in college classrooms, the results of a simple counting exercise reveal a relatively positive picture. In terms of race, white authors represent 61 percent of all fiction/prose authors, while black authors represent 21 percent, and "person of color" authors (Asian American, Latinx, and Native American) constitute 18 percent.[8] The racial demographic numbers are particularly striking. Compare them to the numbers we have for the 1979 edition of *The Norton Anthology:*[9] white authors represent 81 percent of fiction/prose authors, while black writers are 19 percent and POC authors 0 percent.[10] One way to quantify the outcome of these wars is that they increased the percentage of black writers on college syllabi; made the category of Asian American, Native American, and Latinx fiction suddenly visible; and, perhaps most importantly, dramatically reduced the hegemony of white literary authorship from a rather daunting 81 percent to a relatively less dominant 61 percent. Again, my point is not to marshal these numbers as evidence of some clear "victory" of multiculturalism but rather to mark what we can consider the apparent impact of the canon wars on higher education.

Like Guillory and West, I am also skeptical as to what these numbers actually mean, but they are of a different critical sort. In chapter after chapter in this book, I have argued that what most defines the postwar U.S. literary field, particularly the novel, is an unrelenting dominance of white authors in terms of publishing, reception, and distinction and a corresponding marginalization of nonwhite authors. And, contrary to conventional wisdom, what most defines this dynamic is that it is largely unchanging through the second half of the century. A red line runs through the American novel after the war, and this red line deprives nonwhite authors from the coveted resources of book publishing, reviews, sales, and prizes. And this line directly shapes the content and form of this literature—the way that characters get represented, the way that social reality is portrayed, and the way that language appears on the page.

In this chapter, I will argue that one major, unintended consequence of the canon wars is that it caused literary scholars to overlook the problem of racial inequality in the American literary field *as it was happening* in the postwar period, especially the 1980s. Whether one is defending or deforming the canon, the canon always has a built-in selectivity. It needs to focus on a handful of texts to stand in for a broader literary tradition. It is this selectivity, I will show, that has enabled this scholarly neglect, an inability to see the true scale of racial inequality in postwar American literature, again, as it unfolded in real time. I will thus also argue that it is our commitment to a related set of methods and conceptual frameworks, such as close reading and critical theory, that contributed directly to this scholarly blindness. And if we want to rectify this blindness, we need to start valuing other methods of interpretation, such as quantitative analysis, or "counting," which have long been dismissed or devalued by scholars in literary and cultural studies. One irony of the aftermath of the canon wars is that while we would likely view the 1979 version of *The Norton Anthology of American Literature* as reactionary or deeply out of touch compared to its 2016 iteration, the 1979 anthology in fact offers a view of the postwar American literary field closer to how it actually was, in terms of race and authorial representation.

To be clear, the goal of this chapter is not to devalue or dismiss the work that feminist and critical race studies scholars accomplished in the 1980s and 1990s in expanding the Western literary canon to include a greater diversity of female and racial minority authors. This is essential work and has proven crucial in producing a version of English and American literature that reflects the needs and demographic orientation of a post-1960s American student body. Revising the canon represents real historical, social, and political work, and without it, the discipline of English risks irrelevance and complicity in reactionary norms. I acknowledge that the work of "canon busting" was not necessarily to reflect the literary field as it was but to reimagine it. My purpose here is not to "prove" that scholars who devoted their careers in the 1980s to this work were somehow misguided. I am not trying to discredit or trivialize their work. Rather, I seek to understand the reasons for a specific scholarly approach to the canon wars, the costs of this orientation, the oversights that resulted, and the consequences of such oversights.

Finally, in the last section of this chapter, I explore possible corrections to this elision, drawing directly from Toni Morrison's *Beloved*, which reminds scholars that the work of defeating racial oppression and inequality rests *equally* upon both "reading" and "counting" as tools of interpretation.

DISTANT READING THE CANON WARS

This chapter attempts to answer the questions just posed by reconstructing two key transformations in the English and literary studies discipline since 1950, particularly as they bear upon the study of American literature and race: critical theory and cultural studies. I perform this reconstruction through a combination of methods. Part of this reconstruction will look familiar as a form of intellectual history: I revisit and carefully reread several important statements and debates as they appear in the historical record in journals and monographs. But it will supplement this more intuitive and localist approach to historical reconstruction with a broader "distant reading" of the discipline's history. While the approach I have described has the advantage of identifying moments of intense rupture, thus illustrating the major fault lines that existed in the discipline at the time, it risks paying *too much* attention to such ruptures, perhaps mistaking disciplinary change as formed exclusively by explicit flashpoints of contention. We need another method that can track slow and gradual changes. My sense is that the discipline evolves and changes in ways both slow and fast, through moments of intense contention as well as through the almost imperceptible accretion of new ideas. Specifically, this approach will help us understand why and how literary scholars did not fully register the problem of racial inequality in postwar U.S. fiction.

Why focus on literary studies essays and articles in particular? The goal of this chapter is to understand the changing ways that scholars talked about race and literature in the postwar era, particularly how "race" itself emerges as a category of interest. Such a discourse indexes the process by which "experts" determine literary value and how specific texts become consecrated, invited to join the ranks of the Western canon. In short, I am most interested in this discourse as a way to trace what I view to be the endpoint of the cycle of literary production: consecration, or canon formation. There are, of course, other ways to index canon formation. We could look at Norton anthologies of literature and see how their tables of contents change or collect a large corpus of college syllabi and study their shifting reading lists. But neither corpus would be as *language rich* as a corpus of literary criticism. Neither would allow us to track the evolution of discourses of consecration, subtle and not-so-subtle shifts in how scholarly "experts" value different types of texts. Ultimately, it is professors, as recognized stewards of "culture," who determine the shape of the canon. And if we want to understand the underlying motivations for such a process, we would do well to go straight to the source: *their words.*

My corpus consists of 63,397 literary studies articles and essays published between 1950 and 2010. This corpus represents the entire holdings of literary studies articles fully digitized and currently held by JSTOR for this period.[11] The first question to be addressed is: how does JSTOR define "literary studies?" JSTOR consists of more than 1,900 journal titles, which it has divided into fifty or so "disciplines," such as political science and biology. Most of these disciplines map onto traditional categories of academic disciplines found at most American universities. Of these approximately 1,900 journals, sixty-three have been identified as belonging to "literary studies." Who made this decision? The process is somewhat opaque, but a group of librarians at a range of different universities, with the input of literary studies colleagues at those institutions, were responsible. What are some examples of those sixty-three journals? The titles fall into four categories: (1) English and American literatures (*English Literary History, American Literature, Shakespeare Quarterly*), (2) critical theory (*Critical Inquiry, Social Text, Signs*), (3) non-English and comparative literatures (*Yale French Studies, Comparative Literary Studies, Research in African Literatures*), and (4) cultural studies (*Journal of Popular Culture, Caribbean Quarterly*).

Naturally, this is not a perfect corpus. First, accepting JSTOR's arbitrary selection of journals under the designation of "literary studies" risks reproducing the biases of the cohort of librarians and scholars who created this category. Yet I believe the alternatives are far more problematic: I personally could select the list of journals based on what I think constitutes this field, but this form of bias would be even grosser than the previous; I could survey a group of colleagues at different institutions, but this selection would be biased toward my social networks; or I could online "crowd source" the selection of texts, but this would be biased toward those who happen to be motivated to participate in such a study and/or those who happen to use the internet regularly (a generational bias, most likely). In any case, I am not sure any of these options is superior to JSTOR's logic. JSTOR, of course, is an institution, and using their corpus means conceding to the logic of that institution, but that institution is composed of scholars and librarians in the field of literary studies, and its selection rationale represents more than three decades of accumulated knowledge. And it is worth acknowledging that much of that knowledge was formed through thoughtful discussion. The JSTOR corpus is the result of such discussions.

Still, a second question needs to be addressed: why specifically use articles? Our discipline is what many call a "book discipline." Why not use monographs or books? There are a few problems. First, there is a substantial number of arbitrary factors. For example, which publishers? Who determines which publishers are to be included in this corpus? Academic? Trade? Also, each academic publisher uses a different scheme to identify the disciplinary category of a book. How do we standardize these differences? And there is the question of professional status. Publishing favors those with tenure or tenure-track jobs. In limiting our account of scholarship writing to those who are able to publish a book, I worry that we will exclude a substantial part of the profession. Overall, again, while far from perfect, I find the JSTOR corpus to have far fewer complications than attempting to build a corpus based on book publication.

Regardless, as Amy Earhart and many other digital scholars point out, all datasets are limited by their construction, and the JSTOR corpus is no exception.[12] All of the data results that will follow must be taken with a grain of salt; the results do not represent a transparent account of "the literary studies discipline" but rather signal an account of *what JSTOR imagines to be the literary studies discipline*. Over time, we need to build bigger and more diverse and robust datasets. For now, we accept the inevitable tradeoffs of using the JSTOR data: an imperfect representation of the literary studies field, but one that is computationally exploitable and, thus, one that offers a new lens through which to view our field, however tinted.

Next, I describe our method. A simple approach would be to track the rate by which individual keywords, like "race," appear in our corpus. This approach has merits and can be convincing to a certain degree, but ultimately it offers no account of how *concepts* or *themes* appear in the corpus. It wouldn't help us understand, for example, how "race" arises in literary scholarship as a cluster of terms; we know that the single term appears, but we have no view of what words tend to co-occur with it and thus have no view of its wider conceptual force.

Recently, the computational method "topic modeling" has become popular among digital humanists and other scholars who study large corpora of texts with the aid of computers because it offers a way to identify themes or "topics," moving beyond the limits of tracking single-word semantic patterns.[13] Topic modeling is a statistical model of language. Its first assumption is that there exists in every collection of texts a set of topics. What are "topics"? Topics are latent entities. You can't see them. For example, if I receive an email from my department chairperson, I know what that message, more or less, is *about*. Its "topic" is likely "the department." There might be one major topic and/or other minor topics, like "teaching."

How does a machine identify topics? Rather than look at single documents and infer what topics or themes each is generally about, the algorithm analyzes a very large corpus at once, processing all of its texts, identifying a discrete number of topics (the researcher chooses this number), and finally assigning a set of topics to each document. This is in essence what a human implicitly does. When I read that email from my department chairperson, I decide what that message is about based on the tens of thousands of other emails I have read. From this experience, I know that the word "Renaissance" is likely to signify in a certain way, and when I see it co-occur with the word "search," I have a good idea what that email is about or at least what it is likely *not* to be about. The algorithm performs a similar task by formalizing this process. Instead of taking years, it will process and analyze the corpus quickly and develop its catalogue of what words tend to co-occur with other words through a mathematical model. And it will then take this catalogue and identify broader semantic patterns or topics. In the end, the topic-modeling algorithm can tell us what topics exist within our corpus, what individual words constitute which topics, and what topics, at what strength, exist within each document in our corpus.

Our present task is to analyze how literary scholars have understood race and its relationship to the books we tend to write about and how those attitudes have or have not changed dramatically in the past fifty years or so. Topic modeling is a useful method to track not only keywords such as "race"; it also allows us to track the evolution of broader conceptual edifices—that is, *discourses* of race and difference. Andrew Goldstone and Ted Underwood have used this method to reconstruct disciplinary trends in English literary studies in a large collection of 21,000 articles published over the last 120 years. Against commonly held views that our discipline is constituted chiefly by intense ruptures, such as the rise of theory in the 1980s, Goldstone and Underwood convincingly argue that the discipline is also composed by longer durational and subtle shifts in disciplinary rhetoric and language.[14] Literary and cultural studies scholars already have a good sense of the major ruptures that have marked our field, the ruptures that were violent and highly contested. Deconstruction. New Historicism. Cultural studies. But we have less of a good sense of what Goldstone and Underwood dub the "quiet transformations" of our discipline—the ones that happen over a long period of time and consist of muted rhetorical movements. Topic modeling, as they show well, is very good at revealing such gradual changes.

Topic modeling, however, is not a perfect tool. Several caveats are in order. First, as Benjamin Schmidt has argued, the model's assertion that its output indeed produces a coherent set of "topics" or "themes" needs to be carefully inspected.[15] The model will always generate a set number of topics determined by the researcher. And the model will always report a list of words most associated with that topic. However, whether the topic is coherent and significant (and not just noise) and whether the words most associated with that topic are also coherent and significant is up to the researcher and thus subjective. For example, I ran a topic model on our JSTOR data, and it reports the existence of a topic that is defined by terms such as "poem," "poet," "lines," "stanza," "lyric," "sonnet," and other similar words. By simply eyeballing this list, I decided that this topic is cogent and manifests a real topic, and I call it the "poetry" topic. The danger, of course, is that one may be tempted to read and define one's topics in a way that supports one's preexisting beliefs or intuitions. Further, topic models are what we call probabilistic or nondeterministic models; this means that each time we run the topic model algorithm, it may produce a different results. Two researchers can run the same topic model on the same data and get different output. Therefore it can be a challenge to replicate and validate its findings.[16]

In the rest of this chapter, I take measures to address each of these concerns. The key is to think of topic models as indeed *models*—as a tool to think with and, when necessary, deform and manipulate in order to better encode the humanist assumptions that guide one's experiment and respond to the complications that arise with each run of the algorithm.

LOOSE CANONS: BLACK STUDIES AND CRITICAL THEORY

Most scholars will remember the introduction of "critical theory" into the study of race, particularly African American literary studies, and the debates that ensued in the 1980s. (Critical theory, of course, is a vast field that spans the humanities and social sciences; in this chapter, I simply define it as a cohort of new interpretative methods, such as psychoanalysis and deconstruction, commonly associated with a group of European thinkers, such as Lacan, Foucault, Derrida, and Adorno, that became popular and had a large impact in literary studies in the 1970s–1980s.) But few will likely recall how fraught those debates were. The wider stakes of the debate concerned the interpretation of literary texts through the lens of racial difference. Yet the perceived applicability and appropriateness of theory to the study of black and other nonwhite literary traditions represented a major flashpoint. Looking back, it seems clear that debates over critical theory and race studies were closely connected, and the ascent of the former in part enabled a rethinking of the latter. And for at least one faction of scholars in Black studies, the field decidedly benefited from this encounter (and they would likely claim vice versa). As Jonathan Culler argues: "the effort of critics such as Houston Baker and Henry Louis Gates Jr. to bring contemporary theoretical concerns to the reading of Black literature effected an intervention of Black writing in contemporary theoretical debates."[17] It's easy now, with the canonical status of figures like Baker and Gates in Black studies and the normalization of critical theory approaches in the field, to accept a narrative of smooth and seamless evolution: Black studies, and critical race studies generally, had reached a threshold by the 1970s in terms of method, and the influx of theory energized the field by enabling new forms of reading, which in turn animated a rethinking of black literature's relationship to the canon, which in turn helped expand the canon itself.

But this transition, as with most paradigm shifts, was highly contentious. The history of this debate is valuable because it provides insight into how the topic of "race" became a dominant discourse in the discipline at large in the late 1980s, persisting well into the 1990s and 2000s. The abrupt and rapid importation of "critical theory" into the study of race (black literature in particular) transformed the terms by which race, racial difference, and racial identity was spoken of in the scholarship. Much of this history, I suspect, will be familiar or unsurprising to colleagues in the English literary studies discipline, especially those who lived through it. Yet I juxtapose this story of scholarly irruption and transformation with a second story—the story this book has spent the past three chapters reconstructing and parsing—about the postwar American literary field, one constituted by continuity rather than rupture. I put these two stories side by side to show that one apparent consequence of the assimilation of critical theory into literature and race studies was both an elision of "racial inequality" as a critical keyword and a basic awareness of the racial inequality of the contemporary American literary field. Of course, many other factors likely played a role in this elision, such as the changing status of the humanities in the university. In this chapter, I simply argue that the rise of critical theory represents one key factor.

A good place to start might be Houston Baker's "Generational Shifts and the Recent Criticism of Afro-American Literature," published in *Black American Literature Forum* in 1981. It's here that a relatively young scholar begins to work out the beginnings of a new critical movement in black literary studies. Baker finds (in what was then) the dominant mode of "Black aesthetic" criticism, animated by the Black Arts Movement, a set of limitations stemming from its belief that texts written by black writers immanently convey some black ethos, which then only the black critic can reveal. He finds in this logic an avoidance or evisceration of the aesthetic and, thus, an inability to articulate a theoretical program that studies black texts as a "mode of thought." Of note is that Baker engages the recent work of Gates and finds Gates's move to study black texts as "a system of signs" interesting. If anything, he only faults Gates for not knowing his "theory" well enough: "[Gates] seems misguided in his claims and only vaguely aware of recent developments in literary study."[18] In any case, this early invocation of theory marks a critical moment of recognition for two scholars who would transform the field by its import.

Indeed, much would happen in the next four years. Baker and Gates would speak with each other, sort out their differences, find common ground in their shared interest in critical theory, and start developing a theoretical program for African American studies based on the critical assimilation of new methods such as deconstruction. Together, they became the most assertive and visible proponents of this approach. A landmark in this collaboration appeared in 1985 as a special issue of *Critical Inquiry*, guest edited by Gates and Kwame Anthony Appiah, titled "Race, Writing, and Difference." Featuring essays by a mix of scholars invested in theory and race, such as Baker, Gayatri Spivak, and Barbara Johnson, Gates makes the case for the importance of "racial difference" as a lens to read literature. Yet while we may recall that the main goal of the issue was to foreground "race" as a keyword for literary studies, its more specific gambit was to demonstrate the utility of new paradigms in critical theory, such as psychoanalysis, for the study of race and writing.[19] "Difference" would be the mediating term. Gates leveraged Derrida's deconstruction of speech and writing to undo otherwise fixed binaries of racial identity.

The impact of this work was astonishingly fast. Within three years, a number of widely read responses appeared in prominent journals; likely the best known of these critiques is Barbara Christian's "The Race for Theory," published in 1988.[20] But I draw attention to an especially acrimonious encounter between Gates and Baker, on one side, and Joyce A. Joyce, on the other, in *New Literary History* to render vividly the debate as a direct meeting of adversaries. Joyce argues:

> The literary critical activity is not free of personality and history, as the deconstructionists would have us believe. Neither should literary critical involvement be free of commitment, especially in the case of the Black critic. The poststructuralist sensibility in its claim that to acquire knowledge is

impossible, its emphases on fragmentation, plurality of meaning, selflessness, and indeterminacy only exacerbate the Black critic's estrangement from the important social, political, economic . . . [the] forces that shape Black culture.[21]

Joyce's resistance to theory echoes earlier critiques of poststructuralism in the discipline more generally: that its foregrounding of concepts such as "indeterminacy" alienates the critic from her object, displacing the politics, emotion, and sociality of the text with an obscure and difficult field of semiotic tokens. Given black literature's prominent basis in social relations, this is particularly perilous. Gates, however, easily assembled a rejoinder. He had already frequently encountered such critiques in the early 1980s and had learned how to counter them:

> I have tried to utilize contemporary theory to *defamiliarize* the texts of the black tradition, to create a distance between this black reader and our black texts, so that I may more readily *see* the formal workings of those texts. . . . By learning to read a black text within a black formal cultural matrix, and explicating it with the principles of criticism at work in *both* the Euro-American and Afro-American traditions, I believe that we critics can produce richer structures of meaning than are possible otherwise.[22]

Gates presents a cogent response. Methods like deconstruction do not estrange the critic from the text; they provide a new lens to extract new forms of meaning, and this meeting of text and theory does not subjugate one to the other but instead produces a mutual transformation.

From the perspective of 2020, it would seem that scholars like Gates and Baker "won" the debate insofar as their work continued to gain followers and imitators in the 1990s and 2000s, and their various keywords, like "signifying," increasingly penetrated the mainstream of Black studies. It's important to register the critiques of Christian and Joyce as producing useful signs of caution to an otherwise unchecked expansion of critical theory in the field. But over time a consensus view has emerged, one already voiced by Culler: Gates and Baker, with the aid of allies such as Hortense Spillers and Michael Awkward, effected a major intervention by introducing methods from critical theory to estrange Black studies from previous assumptions over the ontology of its texts. We find a new disposition for the field by the early 1990s, one marked by a previously unfamiliar set of terms, such as "rupture" and "closure." By 1993, sentences like the following (which appears in Elizabeth Abel's

"Black Writing, White Reading") have become standard fare: "the text's heterogeneous inscriptions of race resist a totalizing reading."[23]

Quantitative evidence supports this more impressionistic reading. I fit a topic model to our corpus, setting the number of "topics" to fifty.[24] First, inspecting the topics and their associated words reveals a surprisingly coherent set of themes existing in our dataset. "Romanticism," "feminism," "Marxism," and other discrete topics emerge clearly in the model. As for our two matters of interest—"race" and "theory," we also find a clear clustering of terms that enact what appear to be coherent "topics" (table 4.1).[25] A quick reading of these lists indicates plausible results. For the "race" topic, we find a tight clustering of words that we would expect to signify scholarly discourses of "race," particularly in an American context. We have "black" and "white," of course, followed by historical markers of racial oppression, such as "slavery" and "racism." This is a

TABLE 4.1 "RACE" AND "THEORY" TOPICS COMPUTED BY TOPIC MODELING

RACE TOPIC	THEORY TOPIC
black	subject
white	self
African	desire
race	object
slaves	relation
Negro	difference
identity	discourse
freedom	Derrida
racism	Freud
South	writing

"Race" and "theory" topics as computed by the topic modeling algorithm; the chart reports a sample of the top ten terms most highly associated with each topic as computed by the model.

relatively tight constellation of terms. The same could said be for our "theory" topic. Keywords that define the critical theory project, such as "subject," "object," and "self," are prominent. And following such terms are other terms representing the branching subsets of theory, such as "Derrida," indicating deconstruction, and "discourse," indicating Foucault.

This chart offers a useful representation of our two topics in specifying the terms that constitute each topic. But the representation offers no diachronic insight; it represents the 1950-to-2010 span of our corpus as monolithic. However, we can understand the data temporally by tracking the yearly development of each topic. In statistical terms, this means computing the number of articles each year that enact race and theory topics at a certain numerical threshold and then plotting the sum of that value for each year over time.[26] Figure 4.1 is a graphical representation. A quick visual inspection of this graph suggests that race and theory topics are highly correlated, meaning that they follow directionally identical trends. In other words, in our corpus, when scholars start talking more about "theory," they also start talking more about "race," and vice versa. For example, both topics experience sharp upward trends as we move to the present, after a period of relative dormancy in the 1950s to 1970s. But what stands out is the role of theory as race's leading indicator. Race really only gets going in the late 1980s, a good ten years after theory's uptake. One cannot, of course, input causality with such data, but the shape of our curves suggests that the rise of theory at least *anticipated* the rise of "race." A simple statistical test provides further empirical proof: both trends are significantly correlated.[27]

That data thus seems to tell a story that we already know: that critical theory anticipates, if not also facilitates, the increasing presence of "race" in literary studies, and the latter jumps in intensity by the very early 1990s (say, a few

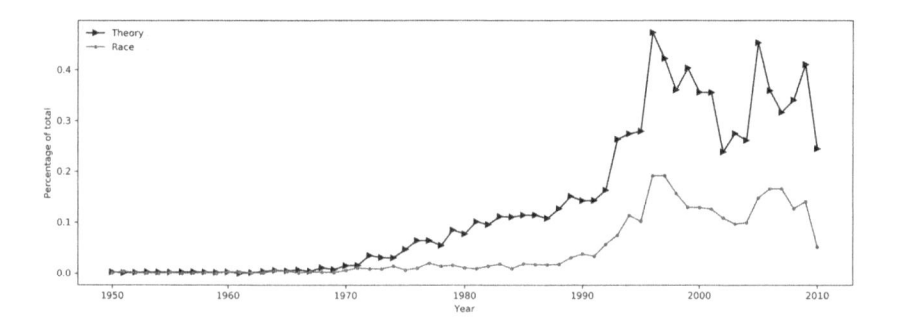

FIGURE 4.1 "Race" and "theory" topics as a percentage of all topics in all documents by year, 1950 to 2010.

years after Gates and Baker make their argumentative stand in *Critical Inquiry* and *New Literary History*), a pattern roughly congruent with the ascent of critical theory, if structurally "lagging" by ten or fifteen years. But the familiarity of what the data appears to speak about risks eliding a set of assumptions that motivated the more general project of "importing" critical theory into race and black studies. What in part animated the desire to reconstitute the contemporary study of African American and other racial minority literatures was not just the belief that new interpretative models such as psychoanalysis could productively defamiliarize one's objects, as Gates contends, but also that it was *justified* by the changing landscape of American literary production. No critic, Gates included, believed that the desires of the academy alone could provide a satisfactory warrant in reorienting how one reads minority literatures. Gates and many other scholars firmly believed that *something had changed in the state of U.S. literature* and that that change demanded new ways of reading as well as a new canon to support such new reading practices. In 1992, Gates makes this warrant explicit:

> What has happened with the profession of literature at the college level to elevate the status of African-American and other "minority" texts within the past decade and a half? It is difficult to be certain about the reasons for the heightened popularity of any area of study. Nevertheless, we can isolate several factors that, in retrospect, seem to bear directly both on the growth of student interests in these fields—an interest that has never been greater, if we can judge from the proliferation of titles being produced and the high sales figures.... One factor would seem to be the women's movement within the African-American and African literature. Since 1970, when Toni Morrison published *The Bluest Eye,* Alice Walker published *The Third Life of Grange Copeland*, and Toni Cade Bambara published her anthology, *The Black Woman*, black women writers have produced a remarkable number of novels and books of poetry. Morrison alone has published five novels, Walker four.[28]

What stands out about Gates's assertion is its emphasis on volume and success: literature by black authors, especially black woman writers, are producing a "remarkable" number of novels and books of poetry, and this "proliferation" corresponds to "high sales figures." Based on the evidence asserted in my previous three chapters, these claims are incorrect. For example, at the largest American publishing house in the postwar period, Random House, its percentage of white novelists steadily hovers around 97 percent and never drops below 91 percent, even at its best year. Random House, we will recall, stands out in this period as being particularly invested in black and minority literatures, having hired its first black editor, Toni Morrison, in the early 1970s. And similarly, the U.S. bestseller list remains resolutely 98 percent white throughout this period—no more than two different black authors (Toni Morrison and Terry McMillan) appear on that list.[29]

Yet if we juxtapose our "Race and Theory Topics Over Time" chart with our previous chapters' data, which describe the racial inequalities that exist through these vectors, we find that Gates's strong assertion is not necessarily based on an illusion. Rather, it is based on a highly ephemeral phase of the literary field. In terms of publishing, we'll recall the brief ten-year "blip" at Random House in which it publishes a higher volume of black authors, perfectly mapping onto Morrison's tenure as editor there; in terms of book prizes, we'll recall a similarly brief spike in novels by nonwhite minority authors winning major book prizes, which, unfortunately, largely recedes by the mid- to late 1990s, regressing near to its pre-1980 mean. It is beyond the scope of this study to impute causality, but there is a strong correlation between the former's spike in the use of critical theory to engage and discuss matters of "race" in literature and the passing late 1980s moment of increasing volume and recognition of minority literatures. If we were to gesture to a loose causality, we might say that Black and ethnic studies scholars like Gates respond to this ephemeral uptake, perceive that as a lasting new trend in the field, and that this in part provides the warrant (in addition to the other reasons for "doing theory") to rethink the analytical forms by which one makes sense of this literature as well as what are its essential texts. However, when one looks at the era as a whole, we find that this trend is largely passing and thus that the notion of an enduring transformation is largely illusory and not quite a warrant.[30]

The introduction of critical theory into Black and minority literary studies, of course, was compelled by a set of intellectual ambitions that far exceeded simply responding to the perception that contemporary American literature changed—for example, theory often provided a kind of leverage to reread canonical Western texts like *Jane Eyre* to locate otherwise suppressed traces of racial difference or to rediscover and valorize otherwise forgotten texts like Harriet Jacobs's *Incidents in the Life of a Slave Girl*.[31] But it is striking that that perception often is invoked as an alibi for the greater project. It is striking how that perception is often expressed through a language of crude "numbers" ("Morrison alone has published five books, Walker four"). However, it is not that Gates and others misread the field in terms of voicing a rich enthusiasm for the apparent influx of new black writers into the field, what appears to be a lasting trend in mainstream book publishing. It is that they do not see the broader structural inertia that frames such trends as passing blips. One cannot fault Gates or any other scholar in this period for not being able to see the entire literary field, from production to reception to sales to recognition, at once. But I argue that their mistaken belief that something changed about postwar American literature, and changed for the better, has in part become an alibi for a disciplinary change that has endured.

My main argument here supplements Kenneth Warren's critical account of the development of African American literary criticism from the 1950s to 1980s. In *What Was African American Literature?*, Warren describes the challenges faced by black critics to generate a viable category of "African American literature" worthy of academic study; during this period, there was intense pressure to demonstrate that black writers could in fact produce such a literature, in the eyes of both academics and the reading public. In identifying a canon of such works, scholars valorized novels, poems, and plays that manifested a specific kind of aesthetic excellence (or at least pointed to the prospect of such an excellence) and inevitably downgraded works that tended to be popular and oriented toward a mass audience. Warren argues that, as a final step in this process, scholars and professors such as Gates and Baker had to claim that these works of literature, "by evincing certain properties . . . expressed the identity of black people," even in the absence of evidence that those literary texts were at any time widely read.[32]

In this section, I argue that the work of constructing a canon of black literature is problematic twice over: it not only conflated popular and elite reading tastes, substituting the second for the first (*pace* Warren), but also erases or at least overlooks the forms of racial inequality that in part determine the very foundation of postwar American literature and, further, names a tragic precondition of what it means to be black and write fiction in this period.

CULTURAL STUDIES, 1983 (AND AFTER)

Still, our critical theory signal, while present, comes and goes relatively fast. It has a discernable peak (or peaks), one in the late 1990s and one about ten years later, likely some kind of aftershock. But those peaks quickly fade. This is a bit at odds with the felt intensity by which "theory" was debated within the field; for a good ten years, it seemed that *everything* in the field hinged on that debate. For sure, we find empirical signs that the debate mattered to the discipline, but it certainly did not completely consume its discourse, measured at scale as the sum aggregate of English literary studies articles published between 1950 and 2010.

This ambiguity takes on granular life when we explore specific essays. Our model allows us to rank articles by how strongly they express a topic or constellation of topics. To get a better sense of what "race meets critical theory" looks like on the page, we can identify the top essays ranked by their expressive intensity of race and critical theory "topics" (table 4.2).[33] This is just a brief list of the top five essays that match our criteria, but at least one major pattern starts to come into view: all but one of the essays were published after 1985, the apparent decisive year of intervention for critical theory in Black studies. This is a puzzle of sorts because if we look again at the first graph in our previous section, we recall that "critical theory," as a topic, no longer appears to be rising. After a steady climb to disciplinary prominence in the 1980s and early 1990s, the topic seems to reach its peak by 1996 or so. It experiences two very brief spikes in the 2000s, but the overall pattern or signal is noisy, with no clear upward direction.

When we look at the most highly ranked single essay in race and theory topics—Naomi Pabst's "Blackness/Mixedness: Contestation Over Crossing Signs," published in 2003 in *Cultural Critique*—we find more clues to understanding this effect. The subject of the article is mixed-race subjectivity. Pabst critiques attempts to produce empirical classifications of mixed-race persons relevant for,

TABLE 4.2 SCHOLARLY ARTICLES THAT EXPRESS "CULTURAL STUDIES" AND "RACE"

AUTHOR	ARTICLE TITLE	JOURNAL	YEAR
Naomi Pabst	"Blackness/Mixedness"	*Cultural Critique*	2003
Harryette Mullen	"Optic White"	*Diacritics*	1994
David Ikard	"Love Jones"	*African American Review*	2002
John Solomon Otto	"The Use of Race and Hillbilly Recordings"	*Journal of American Folklore*	1972
Sonnet H. Retman	"Black No More"	*PMLA*	2008

The top five scholarly articles that express "cultural studies" and "race" topics most highly as computed by the model.

for example, census taking. Instead, she reads the mixed-race subject as itself a useful problematization of the practice of classifying persons as racial types. She writes: "what is more interesting to me is the extent to which interracial subjects elide a classification that can be agreed on. I recommend that we abandon ongoing, pervasive and often aggressive attempts to determine, once and for all, the definitive social location, the true pigeon-hole for multi-racial subjects."[34] Pabst clearly draws from Gates and Hall in her attention to "difference."

But the essay has a discernable discursive drift that firmly sets it apart from Gates, Baker, and other examples of 1980s critical theory–influenced Black studies. The essay takes as its primary interlocutors black feminists like Angela Davis; while indirectly cited in the form of rhetoric, theory staples like Derrida and Lacan do not appear in Pabst's footnotes. Also, the essay has a fluency with sociological and legal material that extends its reach far beyond reading-aesthetic concerns. Readings of major African American literary texts, like *Passing*, are deeply situated within an interdisciplinary matrix of contexts, such as the legal history of the mixed-race person in America. Pabst's essay rose to the top of our list as highly expressive of "race" and "theory" topics, but her essay is better thought of as an example of "cultural studies."

Indeed, looking at all of the topics in our dataset, a topic even more highly correlated with "race" than "theory," and, indeed, even more than "gender" or "colonialism" topics, is a topic constituted by the following terms: "cultural," "culture," "social," "theory," "studies," "practices," "politics," "power," "critique," "identity," "contemporary," and "work."[35]

This topic appears to represent the interdisciplinary academic field known as "cultural studies," which first came to notice in the late 1960s and rose to prominence in both the United Kingdom and the United States in the 1980s and early 1990s. Compared to other recently new fields of inquiry like the New Historicism, cultural studies lacks a tight or cogent conceptual set of tenets and is far more diffuse in practice. One version of the history of this field might read: British scholars associated with the postwar New Left, including E. P. Thompson and Raymond Williams, retheorized Marxism to develop a more sophisticated understanding of the relationship between economics and culture such that this relationship does not signal a crude unidirectional dynamic in which the former fully determines the former. They were particularly interested in the new forms of culture emerging in the postwar era among the working classes and felt that existing theories of culture, whether Marxist or traditional, did not explain them well. Scholars like Stuart Hall and Richard Hoggart—who would form the "Birmingham School of Cultural Studies"—implemented this line of argument to explore a range of mass-cultural products that went beyond literature, such as advertising. They were inspired by the theoretical ideas of Althusser and Gramsci, who provided a conceptual framework to integrate culture into a wider study of the totality of society. Further, they embraced structuralism as a means to understand society as composed of various interacting "levels," whereby each level interacts via a complex chain of symbols and ideological forms. In 1983, Hall traveled to the United States to give a series of lectures that introduced "cultural studies" to American colleagues.[36] By the 1990s, a number of graduate students trained at Birmingham and other researchers inspired by the work of Hall and others had taken faculty positions at major U.S. universities, such as Yale. Academic units, such as Yale's Department of American Studies, in essence, were or had become departments of "cultural studies."

If we add our "cultural studies" topic to our previous analysis of race and critical theory topics, we get a sense of the full force of this new discipline's impact (fig. 4.2). The real story here is less the embattled relationship between critical theory and Black studies and the former's apparent "victory" and more the rise of "cultural studies" in the study of literature. By contrast, the ostensible "rise of theory" is more muted compared to the ascent of cultural studies. "Cultural studies" overtakes "theory" by the late 1990s. What we can infer from these curves—again, not on a causal basis, simply at a descriptive level—is that theory had a swift climb in the 1980s and had a seeming marked effect on race studies, particularly Black studies. But this rise was relatively brief, and its greater apparent purpose was to help broker the ascent and integration of cultural studies into literary studies, especially work focused on race, racial difference, and black culture. After all, of course, cultural studies is suffused with the language and thinking of critical theory: the work of Hall and others, like Hazel Carby and Michael Denning, is unimaginable without Foucault. But it is a mechanism, not the totality or focus of that work.

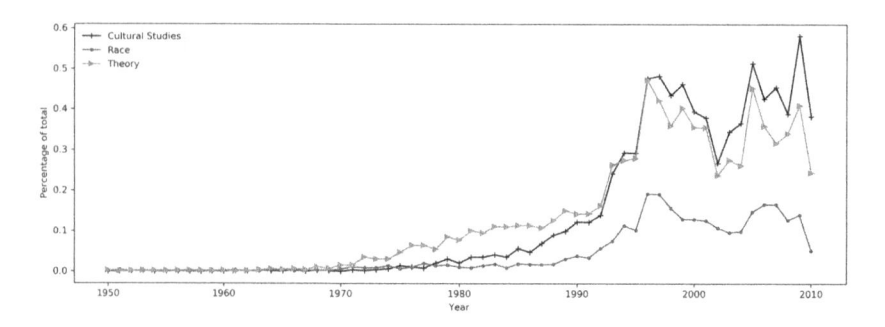

FIGURE 4.2 "Cultural studies," "race," and "theory" topics as a percentage of all topics in all documents by year, 1950 to 2010.

Consider Pabst's "Blackness/Mixedness," the essay that expresses race and theory topics most strongly in our dataset. The analytical story is there: the language of critical theory is ubiquitous in the essay ("power," "difference," "hybridity"), but the language itself is never the site of analysis or reflexive examination; that language is merely offered as a means to facilitate an analysis of a broader range of cultural materials or to embed an analysis of a "traditional" literary product, such as the novel, within a wider matrix of discursive texts, such as legal documents. All of this squares with Hall's description of the work of cultural studies in 1983. The institutional story is there as well: Pabst earned her PhD in the History of Consciousness at the University of California at Santa Cruz, an academic department that represented an important site in the diffusion of British cultural studies to the United States; her first academic position was at Yale University, in the Department of American Studies, working alongside scholars such as Carby and Denning, who had both studied at the University of Birmingham.[37]

Our results indicate that "cultural studies" and "theory" represented coextensive projects throughout the 1980s, 1990s, and 2000s. It is hardly surprising, then, that by 2003 we can see the full effect of this shift. Indeed, at a more granular level, our reading of Pabst's essay suggests that by the late 1990s to be highly "theoretical" really meant that one is likely just very "cultural studies." Again, the fallout of the late 1980s debates over race and critical theory was not necessarily the mainstreaming of critical theory within the literary studies discipline. Rather, it was the mainstreaming of cultural studies, with "theory" as its pivot. As Stuart Hall famously remarked: "theory is always a detour on the way to something more important."[38]

This encounter produced a very specific account of race, as well as an analytical framework to interpret it. Over time, this account would amount to an intellectual disposition, one that has largely become naturalized in the field. Much of this work bears strong traces of the 1980s race-meets-theory moment. Like Gates, Hall insists on the utility of critical theory as a lens to study black culture. In particular, he finds in the structuralist notion of "difference" a useful mechanism to understand "race" as not some entity that exists naturally in the world but, rather, as something that is invented in order to identify humans as different types of person. This approach then empowers the cultural analyst to unmask the range of identity categories imposed by top-down institutions, like the state, and return the power of naming to the subject.

I would describe Hall's cultural studies as an intensification of the project initially outlined by Baker and Gates. Hall makes plain his frustration with the excessive attention paid to textuality by critical theory and how this orientation shaped critical theory's first encounter with the study of race in the

American academy. As the 1980s came to a close, he very much began to worry that this trend would eviscerate what he saw as the field's main purpose:

> My fear ... was that if cultural studies gained an equivalent institutionalization in the American context, it would, in rather the same way, formalize out of existence the critical questions of power, history, and politics. Paradoxically, what I mean by theoretical fluency is exactly the reverse. There is no moment now, in American cultural studies, where we are not able ... to theorize power-politics, race, class, and gender.... There is hardly anything in cultural studies which isn't so theorized. And yet there is the nagging doubt that this overwhelming textualization of cultural studies' own discourses somehow constitutes power and politics as exclusively matters of language and textuality itself.[39]

Based on the results of our topic model and Pabst's essay, it looks like cultural studies after 1990 largely avoided Hall's worry that this new field would focus too much on problems of language. In the quantitative evidence, this turn manifests in our "cultural studies" topic's emphasis on keywords such as "social," "politics," and "practice," all of which indicate a decisive break from our theory topic's foregrounding of terms like "discourse" and "writing." And in the qualitative evidence, we see this shift in the types of nonliterary cultural material marshaled by literary scholars both directly and indirectly involved with Birmingham's legacy.

This is also likely a familiar story to literary studies scholars, especially those who lived and worked through the 1990s. But identifying 1994 as the precise flashpoint in which "cultural studies" overtakes "critical theory" in terms of the topical attention of literary scholars is useful in getting traction in understanding a potentially new motor for the articulation of "race" as a discourse or topic within the literary studies scholarship. However, what is largely missing from this discourse is the keyword "racial inequality." Did the apparent "handoff" of race studies from critical theory to cultural studies reverse what I have just argued was the latter's relative neglect or lack of awareness of "racial inequality" as a major feature of the contemporary form of the literary object it purports to study, or did it just continue or intensify that neglect, despite Hall's plea for a study of culture that is more materialist than purely textualist?

In this book's introduction, I marshaled evidence demonstrating the intense paucity of "inequality" and "racial inequality" in the discourse of literary scholars between 1950 and 2010. But if we look at the term on its own terms and look again at our data, we can track more precisely its behavior. If we plot the rate

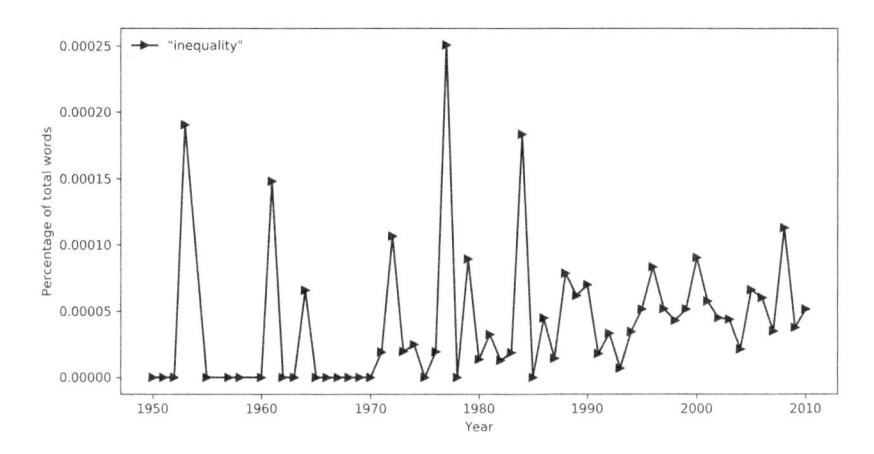

FIGURE 4.3 The term "inequality" as a percentage of all words in all documents that express the "race" topic at a threshold above 0.10, 1950 to 2010.

by which "inequality" appears in our current subcorpus of literary studies articles that express the "race" topic at a high rate, we see the pattern illustrated in figure 4.3.[40] A statistical test shows that literary scholars are not using this term any more or less over time.[41] But it is striking that the two spikes of attention that we do find—granted, fleeting and perhaps just an aberration in the corpus—occur in the late 1970s and early 1980s—well outside of the story of the rise of critical theory *or* cultural studies within the discipline. If there was a moment or moments that literary scholars, even if for just a passing second, were attracted to the analysis of race through the lens of "inequality," it was not prompted by the otherwise ostensibly transformative ruptures of critical theory or cultural studies in the decades to come. We find modest increases in the late 1990s onward but, again, not enough constitute a significant upward trend. And the brief spike we find in the late 2000s is likely a reaction to the financial crash in 2008 that occurred in the United States and galvanized an interest in income inequality.

The 1994 cultural studies handover did not assert inequality as a major keyword for the literary study of race. To get additional traction on this apparent elision, I divided our subcorpus of literary studies articles that exhibit the "race" topic at a high rate into articles published before and after 1994 and used a common text-mining method known as the "most distinctive words test" (MDW test) to determine what specific words most distinguish these two subcorpora when they are compared against each other.[42] The idea is that if 1994 signals the

166 CONSECRATION

moment in which "cultural studies" overtakes "critical theory" as the dominant methodological or conceptual mode guiding the study of race within literary studies, how did that transition induce a new set of terms or ideas and more or less create a new interpretative paradigm? If "inequality" is not a part of that new paradigm, what are the terms that do constitute that discursive shift?

What our results describe is less a transition from "critical theory" to "cultural studies," marked by perhaps a shift in more textualist theoretical language, like "discourse" to "context," and more simply the consolidation of a coherent analytical language of race that assimilates elements of both 1980s critical theory and early 1990s cultural studies (table 4.3). The "Before 1994" cluster of terms appears to represent the topic of race in a somewhat random or scattershot way. It seems to deploy a midcentury social scientific approach to understanding

TABLE 4.3 DISTINCTIVE WORDS FOR DOCUMENTS THAT EXPRESS "RACE"

BEFORE 1994	AFTER 1994
faculties	black
deviance	whiteness
evinced	identities
unambiguous	racialized
porters	discourse
baseball	representations
maids	1997
idioms	1995
pupils	1993
monsters	1996

A sample of ten most distinctive words for all documents that express the "race" topic at a threshold above 0.10 published before 1994 compared to documents published after 1994 as computed by the most distinctive words test.

racial identity, foregrounding terms like "deviance" and (mental) "faculties." And it conjures stereotypical images of nonwhite people as "porters" and "maids." Overall, the results are noisy, likely reflecting the lack of a scholarly consensus regarding how to write about race and literature. Our "After 1994" terms offer a sharp contrast: the scholarly discourse is tight and focused, emphasizing clear markers of racial identity ("black," "whiteness") and a set of linked analytical terms for their analysis, most or all stemming from critical theory: "discourse" and "representations."

My argument is that the ascent of cultural studies offered the discipline an opportunity to begin focusing on the contemporary field of literature as a material site of racial inequality—empirical questions of book production and reception and distinction—and indeed, "cultural production" would become a major subfield within cultural studies.[43] But the more obvious and pronounced effect of the 1994 handover moment was the intensification of critical theory as a lens to read race and literature, and with that continuity, there persists the relative erasure of the field of contemporary literary production as the object of interest or, at least, the field of production as constituted by measurable patterns of racial exclusion and inequality.[44]

Indeed, by the late 1980s, Hall had come to articulate an influential interpretative method known as "Black cultural politics," and this method rested upon a distinctly nonquantitative and nonempirical understanding of blackness and the black subject. Hall's readings in poststructuralism had liberated him to understand blackness as radically contingent:

> What is at issue here is the recognition of the extraordinary diversity of subjective position, social experiences, and cultural identities which compose the category of "black"; that is that black is essentially a politically and socially constructed category, which cannot be grounded in a set of fixed, trans-cultural or transcendental categories and which therefore has no guarantees in Nature. What this brings into play is the recognition of the immense diversity and differentiation of the historical and cultural experience of black subjects.[45]

This statement articulates well the primary, guiding understanding of the concept of race, particularly blackness, in the cultural studies project. Hall, along with his many students, such as Carby, would reaffirm this principle again and again in the years to come. The concept that comes under primary attack is *the category*. Racial categories, Hall argues, cannot contain the full diversity of the lived experience of black identity. Underlying this critique is a more general critique of quantification. The construction of categories relies upon the transformation of racial qualities into fixed quantities. What Hall calls for, in a sense, is the reverse engineering of quantitative racial categories, such as "black," to identify at each moment of numerical conversion some aspect of lived experience that has been erased by that quantitative moment; when the entire category has been unraveled, what we are left with is its original, "immense diversity."

Hall's intervention was extraordinarily influential for literary and cultural studies, and I have no interest in undermining or defaming it. However, I argue that despite Hall's critique of the growing textualist orientation of literary studies in the wake of theory, the project of cultural studies sustains critical theory's inflection of race studies in simply moving its deconstruction of language to the deconstruction of racial categories. What gets lost is a view of the literary marketplace as a whole and the racial inequality that drives it. I argue that it can be harder to see these things when "inequality" does not represent a major analytical keyword.

To this end, our MDW results point to a curious paradox: several distinctive terms that appear in the "After 1994" cohort are a set of years from the 1990s. This is curious because these results indicate that scholarship on race and literature from after 1994 is increasingly aware of its own contemporaneity, an implicit claim that *something was new and worth talking about* with contemporary literature.[46] Like Gates's mistaken belief that the postwar American literary field was rapidly changing along axes of race and gender, particularly an increase in black women writers, the scholarly discourse of race and literature through the optics of "cultural studies" also appears to assert that *something has changed in the contemporary and living moment*. And this becomes in part, again, an alibi for the emergence of new scholarly rhetorics to talk about race and writing in the postwar period. But yet again, this alibi comes at the expense of a critique of the red lines that continue to constitute the postwar American literary field, a reality that towers over what is in the end the ephemera of a few more black writers getting published at major presses, getting reviewed in magazines, winning book awards, and selling copies.

"RACIAL INEQUALITY" IN THE AGE OF *BELOVED*

To reiterate a point made in this book's introduction: I do not argue that literary scholars of race do not care about racial inequality or that the figure of inequality does not conceptually appear in their writings. It obviously does:

through the critique of racial oppression, through the critique of whiteness and hegemony, and through the critique of racial categories. Again, I marshal a series of statistics that show the gross sparsity of the term "racial inequality" in the scholarship not to manufacture a deficiency in the discipline but simply to point out that the term encodes an interpretative disposition and that this disposition encodes an aversion to quantitative reasoning and evidence. There are reasons to defend this aversion. However, in my previous two sections, I have shown that there are also significant unintended consequences to this aversion. In the case of postwar U.S. literary history, it has meant the neglect of a major, determining feature of the field—racial inequality through the field's phases of production, reception, and distinction as well as a set of consequent semantic and narratological patterns relevant for understanding modern American literature at scale and at the level of individual works, canonical and otherwise.

In this book, I have called for a stronger quantitative disposition for the study of American literature to supplement the discipline's already established and effective modes of criticism, theory, and historicism. Such an approach would perhaps begin with a greater awareness of the history of publication and reception, melding such statistical analysis with literary pattern recognition, to get at the question of how such structural inequalities enact aspects of literary form and content. And perhaps ironically, the use of these new computational methods might also rely significantly on a new orientation to reading itself: the way that we look at words on the page and how those words aggregate into broader text-level patterns of style and form and narrative and affect. In the final section of this chapter, I attempt to model a form of close reading that facilitates this reorientation, one that complements the modes of literary pattern recognition I have developed in the previous chapters of this book. The benefit of this approach is that it will allow us to see forms of "inequality," both at the scale of a single text and at that of a large corpus of texts, that we otherwise have overlooked or neglected through more traditional modes of analysis.

Where would we start? What authors? What texts? What period? Thus far, I have argued that the paradox of the canon wars was that its successes—the expansion of the canon to include a greater number of women and racial minorities—occurred during a time of severe and unchanging racial inequality within the literary field. In particular, as I have shown, the canon wars facilitated the development of "race" as a central topic for literary studies, what would take on synergy with other important new trends within the discipline, such as critical theory and cultural studies. But the paradox of this success is strong.

As I also have shown, our "race" topic begins to peak in the early 1990s—the same years that Random House begins to *decrease* its number of black novelists, after noticeably peaking in the mid-1980s (likely a direct effect of Morrison).

This paradox gains force when we look at a sample of the top six most discussed works of American fiction and prose writing published between 1800 and 2000, based on our JSTOR corpus (fig. 4.4).[47] The data tells us that literary scholars, Americanists in particular, were interested in rereading canonical works of literature, such as *Moby-Dick*, as well as reading new works of minority fiction, such as *Beloved*, in an effort to include a broader range of authors in the canon. In fact, the data says that scholars were more interested in the latter: of this sample, only two texts are increasing over time, and they were published, respectively, just as the canon wars were starting (*Sula* in 1973) and about to claim victory (*Beloved* in 1987).[48] The other texts are declining or unmoving—and in some cases plummeting, like *The Turn of the Screw*. Overall, literary scholars during this period were quite interested in contemporary literature; they just weren't very interested, as I've argued, in the contemporary U.S. literary marketplace.

In any case, if we want to identify the perhaps single most important novel that redefined how literary scholars, Americanists in particular, thought about race and writing in this period in order to create a new way of thinking about this topic—a greater attention to the affordances of quantification and "inequality" as keyword—*Beloved* would be the right text. Based on this data, this novel experiences the steepest growth of scholarly interest in this period,

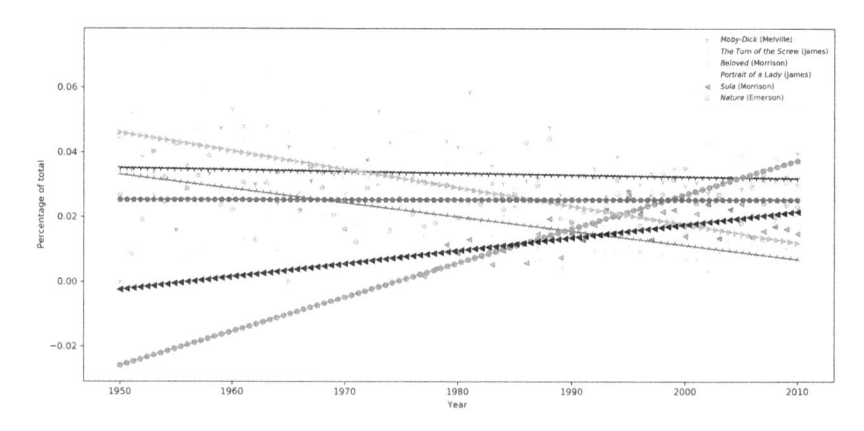

FIGURE 4.4 A scatterplot documenting a sample of six of the most discussed works of American prose or fiction by year in terms of how often they are mentioned in each document in the corpus as a percentage of all documents. Lines of best fit are added to visualize temporal trends.

surpassing such major canonical novels as *Moby-Dick* and *The Turn of the Screw*. Despite being published relatively recently in 1987, the novel quickly came to dominate scholarly discourse.

Literary criticism on *Beloved* often takes as its starting point the novel's epigraph: "Sixty Million and more."[49] The epigraph announces that its major "theme" will be the history of the Euro-American slave trade—specifically, the trans-Atlantic Middle Passage through which millions of Africans were shackled and transported. *Beloved* is a novel *about* slavery and its aftermath. But the text also already encodes an interpretative opportunity that scholars have been quick to leverage: *and more*. The second part of the epigraph articulates a form of knowing that stands in excess to what the first part—a quantitative description of life and death—can represent. This second part subverts or troubles the claims of the first. "Sixty million" signals the official account of the number of black people who died in the slave trade, the claims of the state, historians, and statisticians. The phrase "and more" instantly brackets that claim as limited or in some way faulty, by turning what is otherwise a firm value (*sixty million, no more no less*) into something unsure, unstable. Yes, we are fairly sure that at least sixty million people died in the Middle Passage. Yet there is a value, a quantity that moves beyond or outside that first value. It haunts that first value because that value cannot fully contain or represent the second value.

This scholarship largely derives from a version of postmodernism that critiques the limits of traditional historiography, particularly one rooted in empirical evidence or social scientific claims to knowable objectivity. For such literary scholars, the "and more" offers the real action of "history," whereas the epigraph's first declarative part simply attempts to provide false closure to that history. Kimberly Davis describes this problem, writing:

> Although the Middle Passage was a horrific historical reality, the estimated number is not a verifiable fact because the deaths of slaves were often deemed unworthy of recording. All the lives lost can never be accounted for, because our access to history is always limited by words and by those who have control of textual production. Thus, in beginning her novel with these epigraphs, Morrison seems both to ground her fictional work in historical reality and also to question the possibility of ever finding the historical referent outside of or preceding representation.[50]

Here we find a particularly effective merging of the rhetoric of critical theory with the rhetoric of cultural studies. Theory's interest in the unstable play of textual signs allows Davis to pivot to a more general claim about the instability of factual representation, all in service to problematize the novel's normative historical context. Other scholars, such as Linda Krumholz, in her reading of *Beloved*, have extended this insight: "[Morrison] counters a fact-based objective system with a ritual method, based on initiatory and healing rituals, in which the acquisition of knowledge is a subjective and spiritual experience. . . . Morrison denies the reader analytical explanations of slavery."[51] The novel does not merely challenge the quantitative foundations for understanding life and death in the slave trade. It challenges the fundamental epistemological grounds by which the very idea of "slavery" and its effects can be understood, not just counted. The novel is thus not only about slavery; it is also about the objective and subjective mechanisms we use to recall and narrate slavery, particularly how the first mechanism inscribes the second.

Much of this should be obvious both to literary scholars and to careful readers of *Beloved*; in several interviews, Morrison herself strongly invites this reading. But I want to sharpen this account of the research as specifically a skepticism toward data and quantification. Morrison often invokes the specter of data: "I want my fiction to urge the reader into active participation in the non-narrative, non-literary experience of the text, which makes it difficult for the reader to confine himself to a cool and distance acceptance of data."[52] In her reading of *Beloved*, Caroline Rody formalizes this resistance to "data" as the concept of "the numberless." Rody argues that a particularly destructive outcome of slavery was its total evisceration of black communities, and thus the subject of slavery is a subject who cannot be accounted for—who is quite literally "numberless."[53] Literary critics take up Morrison's invitation to grasp the body of the slave as "irreducibly particular"[54] and thus frame the scholar's task as reversing the process by which the black slave is aggregated into a number by instead asserting her lack of number.

As many scholars have noted, Morrison writes this critique into the content of the novel via the character of "Schoolteacher." Schoolteacher, we recall, is the slave owner who takes an especially degrading view of black persons as property by fixating on their measurable and quantitative worth as virtual livestock. Krumholz contends that Schoolteacher serves as a proxy for the "scientific method" as a device to dehumanize subjects deemed outside of standards of humanity within traditional Western thought. In a way, Schoolteacher's terror is more terrifying than brute physical violence because it imagines itself as the logical outcome of logical thought—"discourses, definitions, and historical methods"—that think of themselves as "objective."[55] In one rather horrific scene, the measuring rope that Schoolteacher uses to measure Paul D's limbs becomes the same rope used to lynch runaway slaves. Avery Gordon therefore asks the question: "How are we accountable for those who do the counting?"[56] Morrison's novel localizes the problem of "Sixty Million and more" as a problem of "scientific method."

Two types of understanding or reading are posited by the novel: first, the passive and uncritical acceptance of information ("data" and "facts") transmitted by institutions or figures of authority, like Schoolteacher, and second, a more active and critical engagement with the sites of knowledge that one lives within and experiences. The perils of the first are vividly rendered within the diegetic space of the novel. The second is implicitly written into the novel through its formal design. One distinct feature of the novel that has been widely celebrated by literary scholars is its discursive ambiguity and interpretative openness; as most critics and readers acknowledge, the novel often deliberately evades fixed meaning. Things are said or things happen in the novel, but it is never entirely clear what those things mean. Action, words, and their outcomes are usually indeterminate. For example, the text dilates time, past and present, to render cause and effect in the story's narrative opaque. This is, as scholars have noted, to illustrate the enduring effects of slavery in the lives of slaves, former slaves, and the children of slaves, both during and after its formal enactment. Slavery ended, but it never really ended. Valerie Smith writes: "the reader must be active, not passive; indeed, [Morrison] suggests that the reader must be actively engaged with the author in a dynamic process out of which textual meaning derives."[57]

The participation of the reader in the text's production of meaning facilitates the production of a larger regime of knowledge production, what scholars have described as "democratic." Judylyn Ryan argues: "Morrison's fashioning of language and narrative . . . supports a proactive commitment to constructing and advancing what I have called a democracy of narrative participation—a project that combines both narratological and ideological aspects."[58] The novel pits its own "democratic" version of knowledge making against the one posed by Schoolteacher in its diegesis. The problem of, as Gordon says, how to hold accountable those who count and define is in part resolved by the text's form. Readers undo what Schoolteacher has done.

This, too, I think will be obvious to many expert and lay readers of *Beloved*. But I am most interested in—to return to the focus of this chapter—how a scholarly discourse of "democracy" has come to overshadow a discourse of "inequality." Few scholars would disagree that the central theme of the novel is slavery and its postbellum manifestations, such as the chain gang and penal state, and few, I think, would disagree that slavery and the penal state, particularly in the second half of the twentieth century, represents a main driver of racial inequality in the United States. A number of historians and sociologists have argued that the modern prison system has simply reenacted the core principles of dehumanization and deprivation of resources implemented first by slavery.[59] This argument has begun to increasingly inflect *Beloved* scholarship. And so it is striking that the word "inequality" has largely yet to appear in this scholarship, even when scholars cite actual statistics from the Department of Justice about racial inequality and prisons.[60]

The task for literary scholars, I believe, is to create a critical discourse that threads the needle between empiricism as a way to register power imbalance and subjectivism as a way to render every black body visible. It is to recognize categories of person and quantities of things without using those categories and quantities as an excuse to control and dehumanize—as Schoolteacher does. It is to pay equal attention to both sides of the "Sixty million and more" formulation. Rather than exclusively use the latter as a basis to problematize the former, we can think both together. In the rest of this chapter, I sketch out what a version of this reading might look like. But before I begin, I need to make clear: this reading does not mean to erase or diminish existing readings of *Beloved* that foreground indeterminacy and reader participation—the text as a site of radical democracy making. As both scholars and Morrison herself make clear, the act of drawing attention to the singularity of the black body in and after slavery—indeed, the "and more" of the novel's epigraph—is crucial to challenging empirical, top-down histories of slavery and making possible new histories. The work of this democracy making is not only to defeat the diegetic force of Schoolteacher but also to defeat the ongoing legacy of his epistemology. Nonetheless, I argue that this approach should not elide "inequality" as keyword.

Let's begin. Consider this sequence from the novel in which the text's narrator reports the thoughts of Stamp Paid, after having a conversation with Baby Suggs. Even after slavery, Stamp argues, he can't get away from white supremacy. It's violent and terrifying and everywhere. He is sympathetic to Sethe because like him, "whitefolks had tired her out."[61] "Eighteen seventy-four and whitefolks were still on the loose. Whole towns wiped clean of Negroes; eighty-seven lynchings in one year alone in Kentucky; four colored schools burned to the ground; grown men whipped like children; children whipped like adults; black women raped by the crew; property taken, necks broken. [Stamp Paid] smelled skin, skin and hot blood."[62] Passages like this are rarely commented on in the scholarship. They are thought of as merely descriptive or fact bearing, as gateways to more essential narrative features, like an account of Stamp's conflicted interiority. But it bears a signification that goes beyond the merely descriptive, or it turns description itself into figuration: the figure of "whitefolks." Only three individual white characters appear in the novel: Amy Denver, Schoolteacher, and Edward Bodwin. Otherwise, white people appear as a mass entity or a descriptive aggregate: "whitefolks." This gesture, of course, is designed to refocus the story of slavery on those who endured it, rather than on those who inflicted it. Black people become the story's foreground; whiteness is its mere context. But this passage captures in detail the importance of measuring that whiteness as an overwhelming quantitative sum, something so large it cannot be counted. Anything that appears in relation to that massive sum—say, the "eighty-seven" black persons who were lynched—is dwarfed by that inequality. The eighty-seven is tiny compared to the infinite white.

As the passage develops, it becomes clear that the various numbers introduced are less important than what it provokes in Stamp. What disturbs him most is not the counts and figures and sums but instead the "smell" of human flesh he imagines—the smell of black bodies burnt by white people. But this passage would not be the same without its specific mention of "eighty-seven" black persons lynched in 1874. It is a mere "fact" or "detail," but it is an important one. It is valuable to measure one vastness—the profound vastness of American whiteness in 1874—against the vulnerable smallness of the other. The figure of "whitefolks" is less a pure abstraction than it is an index of some massive and unimaginable size. Whiteness is rendered uncountable not to obscure its quantity but to underscore its ubiquitous largeness. Inequality thus becomes implicit here: Stamp's world is a world in which there is and always will be so much more of one thing than the other, and that inequality of presence is the thing that perhaps most terrorizes him. Here, the passage attempts to mediate qualitative and quantitative forms of cognition. It matters that in Cincinnati in 1876 that *specifically* eighty-seven black people were murdered, and it matters that whiteness appears so vast and omnipresent as to appear uncountable. This is, again, a simple description of racial inequality. But it makes the rest of the passage possible.

Heather Love argues for a similar type of "surface reading" of the novel. In their influential essay "Surface Reading: An Introduction," Stephen Best and Sharon Marcus define surface reading as a form of literary interpretation that focuses on what is "evident, perceptible, and apprehensible in texts."[63] They position this approach against the discipline's more common method of "symptomatic reading," which seeks to unearth what a text allegedly represses or conceals. Best and Marcus argue that this approach is useful because often a text's most important meaning can be its literal meaning, which needs to be described, rather than extracted via close reading. For Love, this means "see[ing] Morrison's project as registering the losses of history rather than repairing them." She argues that "Morrison conveys the horrors of slavery not by voicing an explicit protest against it but by describing its effects."[64] Therefore, while passages like the one just quoted merely deliver "facts" about slavery, they also *describe* slavery's effects as actual effects and not just things to be imaginatively resisted. I would argue that the text's "eighty-seven" is a similar type of accounting. But I would also add that the text's attempt to account for and describe racial inequality is constituted by both description and figuration. "Whitefolks" points to a massive quantity as well as the thing that precisely cannot be counted because it is so vast. The passage holds taut this tension, encouraging both symptomatic and surface reading. It is the same tension that animates the novel's haunting epigraph, "Sixty million *and more*."

The novel sharpens this effect in its critical "chain gang" scene. In this passage, Paul D—after fleeing Sweet Home—is captured by the state authorities and placed on a chain gang with forty-six other black men. The scene describes in vivid detail the severe and dehumanizing process by which the men are forced to labor. In a persuasive reading, Dennis Childs argues that this passage aims to establish a homology between slavery and postslavery modes of black incarceration, particularly the modern prison, in delimiting black mobility and freedom after the nominal end of slavery.[65] This passage asserts that slavery ended but never ended.

Yet what also stands out is the passage's dilation of subjectivity. The text insists on thinking of the black men in the chain gang in the aggregate, as a category: "All forty-six men woke to rifle shot. All forty-six." Their quantitative sum is foregrounded. And as the passage unfolds, that sense of aggregate identity increases: "And one by one the blackmen emerged—promptly and without the poke of a rifle butt if they had been there more than a day."[66] Now, the forty-six have become "blackmen," a category. The text drifts into somewhat unfamiliar, if not perilous, territory. It reverses its usual intention of revealing the "irreducibility of black bodies" by combining black bodies into a kind of categorical type—forty-six blackmen who work along a chain gang. In most of the novel, we find the opposite. Black subjectivity emerges against the background of a homogenizing, general whiteness—"whitefolk." In this scene, blackness risks fading into generality—the faceless and nameless crowd of forty-six black prison workers.

One might argue that the novel deliberately creates this effect in order to represent the white perspective on the black laborers; that is, this is simply what the three white police officers see, a mere mass of faceless and nameless black men. But I contend that this effect also moves in a different direction. U.S. prisons stand as one of the major if not most important sites and drivers of racial inequality today. Despite representing only 12 percent of the U.S. population, blacks constitute 34 percent of its prisons.[67] In 1986, the year that *Beloved* was completed, that difference was even greater.[68] It's hard to think or write about African Americans and prisons without using the word "inequality." Yet in the scholarship, such as Childs's essay, which otherwise cites statistics on blacks and prisons from the U.S. Department of Justice, the word does not appear. The numbers are stark. The distance between 34 percent and 12 percent is a large and yawning abyss.

I argue that *Beloved* occasionally suspends its documentation of contingent and singular black subjectivity precisely to induce this quantitative cognition, however brief or passing in the text. Childs and other scholars have focused on the horrific conditions of the chain gang. They foreground its physical degradation. But the quantitative aspects of this subjection must be named to render this condition not just a degradation but also a systematic exploitation at the scale of the black population. The characters in this scene, including Paul D, must—however briefly—be absorbed into the wider category of "the blackmen" in order for the scene's broader sociological significance, "racial inequality," to emerge as cognizable and visible to the reader. There is a risk, of course. The text risks reproducing the cognition of the white policeman. But without that risk, we fail to see the empirical basis of a historical trajectory. We fail to see how 12 percent became 34 percent. While we can see the local effects of this degradation, we are not fully able to register how a group of persons, as a category, became numerically stretched out as a population—"blackmen" on a chain gang in the nineteenth century, 34 percent of prisoners today.

Again, literary scholars have tended to elide such passages, perceiving them, as Heather Love argues, as just "facts." For scholars, critical attention tends to drift to the other facets of narration, the parts that induce a participatory "democracy" between readers and text. My reading, however, has suggested a reversal of this notion of foreground and background. I argue that in foregrounding what otherwise has been viewed as mere context, the thing driving the real action of *Beloved*'s narrative, we can decipher new patterns of attention, namely, "inequality," the condition of one thing being much larger than another thing. Here, this means the quantitative terror of tens of thousands of violent white men hunting black men or the demographic stretching of black persons to fill prisons. There is value in just citing a statistic, as Childs does. But we also need to articulate that value in a framework of racial inequality—measuring the bigness of one thing compared to another. It reminds us that *Beloved* is indeed about the most significant and enduring animator of racial inequality in U.S. history. And that this inequality needs in part to be named as an accounting. Scholars like Madhu Dubey read *Beloved* as emphasizing the power of literacy as a way for the slave to resist the master's defining of the slave as a commodity.[69] Denver says, recalling a lesson from her father: "If you can't read, they can beat you." But we often forget the first part of his lesson: "If you can't count, they can cheat you."[70]

CONCLUSION: READING AND COUNTING

The question I want to close this chapter with is this: can novels like *Beloved* train or at least encourage readers (as well as literary scholars) to discern patterns of quantitative inequality as the basis to understand and recognize racial and social inequality? The simple answer is yes. The question is more: can literary scholars reorient their critical gaze to prioritize—to elevate to the position of central and essential—such patterns within the text? In my reading of the novel, I argue that this critical reorientation rests on shifting our usual notions as to what counts as background and foreground in contemporary novels like *Beloved*. If we can suspend, just for a moment, our usual reading protocols of underscoring contingency and particularity, our reconstruction of black life and death as irreducible to numbers, we can track other important historical effects that chart the equally destructive trajectories of black subjects as categories. The danger, as I have stressed, is in overprivileging those categories, as they are, ultimately, categories that belong to figures like Schoolteacher. But to neglect or fail to account for those numbers and figures is, as Denver reminds us, equally to empower Schoolteacher. We fail to see how 12 percent became 34 percent. Other transformations in the narrative—more contingent and local alterations of subjectivity—are critical, but this kind of transformation is also important, if not equally important.

The stakes of this reading go beyond a rereading of Morrison's *Beloved*. In each chapter of this book, I have insisted that what most defines the history of the postwar U.S. novel is racial inequality, the redlining of black and other minority authors from the coveted resources of mainstream book publishing, reception, sales, and prizes. I have insisted on the significance of a set of numbers—97 percent, 90 percent, 98 percent, and 91 percent—and the sheer durability of those numbers. The red line that separates white authors from the rest is unchanging—*things are not getting better; increasing diversity is an illusion.*

And most importantly, I have argued that these "facts," which might otherwise appear as merely sociological to scholars who prefer to closely read books rather than count them, have had profound effects on the development of postwar U.S. fictional discourse, form, and narrative. For example: postwar Random House fiction is defined by a literary whiteness in which white authors respond to an increasingly diverse society by narcissistically writing more about themselves, white authors; book reviewers determine that only a single form of minority writing is worth recognizing, thus marginalizing the majority of other types of nonwhite creativity; and, what most defines the postwar U.S. world of literary distinction is less the difference between high and low culture and more how they both exclude literary blackness.

Through each of these chapters, Toni Morrison has appeared as a complex figure at the heart of this inequality as the postwar literary period unfolds. I have stressed, over and over, that it would be absurd to "blame" Morrison for the dynamics of racial inequality she happens to find herself at the center of. American literature is obviously far better because Morrison worked as an editor at the most powerful publishing house in America for fifteen years, and the immense success achieved by novels like *Beloved* has had unequivocally positive benefits for the U.S. literary field as a whole, particularly minority authors. But this final chapter has argued that *somehow* the forms of critical and public attention we pay to Morrison has obfuscated wider patterns of an unrelenting and systematic racial inequality. In my analysis of *Beloved* scholarship, I argue that "inequality" does not enter its vernacular. By the year 2000, *Beloved* has become the defining American literary text for scholars, yet somehow, this surging interest does not map onto a growing interest in "inequality" as a keyword. It does not map onto a growing awareness of the unchanging racial inequality of the postwar American literary field, despite the importance of that field to *Beloved*'s success. We have two lines that look very different. One line—racial inequality in the literary field—is flat, while the other—scholarly interest in Morrison's novels—is rising.

My reading of *Beloved* has sought to model a form of critical analysis that allows us to better parse the gap between those two lines. The challenge, as it was with *Beloved*, is to reorient our sense of what counts as foreground and background. Like our readings of the characters of *Beloved*, like Sethe, we tend to focus on "Toni Morrison," the author of a group of profoundly brilliant and influential works of contemporary literature, as similarly a kind of singularity to be best understood on contingent and local terms. There have been some attempts to understand Morrison's rise in sociological terms, but few if any would move to reduce Morrison to the coarse and vague category of "black author."[71] Such a move would be flatly patronizing and offensive; it would reduce the singular brilliance of her work to a mere type, something that can be measured. It would be to play the role of Schoolteacher, with all of its attendant violences and dehumanizations. But I insist that refusing attention to this "background"—for example, the number of *other* black authors who get elevated to the status of the literary 1 percent in the postwar era—has consequences. Ninety-seven percent is also a kind of violence and dehumanization. Oppression in *Beloved* is not just Schoolteacher. It is also the vastness of "whitefolk" against the vulnerable smallness of "blackmen." That awful vastness is also a kind of terror, and it is a pattern of force that, in part, makes the novel's more particular and local instances of subjection possible.

In broad strokes, my argument for a new approach to the study of literature and race is straightforward. I argue that literary historians and critics need to start paying greater attention to patterns and quantity, or, rather, quantity against quantity, greater and lesser. To return to an earlier point, Morrison's *Beloved* itself indicates the importance of this approach. *If you can't count, they can cheat you. If you can't read, they can beat you.* Literary scholars have focused on the value of *reading* to unmasking the forms of racial violence and subjection that constitutes racial relations in America. We have tended to deprioritize the value of *counting* in performing this work, and this preference is reflected in how we have chosen to read *Beloved*—the novel that has effectively defined the scholarly discourse on race and American literature in the past three decades. In the dozens of articles and books I have read on *Beloved*, I have seen many references to this passage, but I have not found an instance where the scholar focuses on its second part: "if you can't count, they can cheat you." This elision analogizes what I have described in this book as the erasure or obfuscation of the various red lines that determine the postwar American literary field. Just as literary scholars have often ignored the first part of this passage, which marks the importance of the quantitative imagination to racial resistance, so too have we generally neglected a huge part of what constitutes and articulates the meaning of "race" within that field. We need to do both. We need to heed Denver's advice. We need to read, and we need to count.

CONCLUSION

In February 2020, the American bookseller Barnes & Noble undertook a rather curious marketing plan for Black History Month. They decided to use "artificial intelligence" (or more precisely, natural language processing) to analyze the contents of one hundred canonical Western novels to identify which texts omitted nonwhite protagonists. It found twelve specific novels that, based on their computational algorithm, did not feature any main racialized characters, and based on that, produced new book covers that imagined their white protagonists, such as Ahab from Melville's *Moby-Dick*, as a person of color. In their own words:

> We used artificial intelligence to analyze the text from 100 of the most famous titles searching the text to see if it omitted ethnicity of primary characters.... Our NLP algorithms accounted for the fact that when authors describe a character, they rarely outright state their race, but often use more poetic and descriptive language. Among the classics that didn't specify race or ethnicity, here are twelve that we have reimagined for Diverse Editions: *Alice's Adventures in Wonderland, The Count of Monte Cristo, Emma, Frankenstein, Dr. Jekyll & Mr. Hyde, Moby Dick, Peter Pan.*[1]

The new marketing campaign was immediately mocked and criticized on social media; Barnes & Noble quickly suspended it. The campaign had a laudable impulse—to reimagine "the classics" to acknowledge and celebrate racial diversity for an increasingly multicultural age. But as numerous commentators noted, the way they went about it was entirely misguided. The first problem is that the algorithm was not sophisticated enough to detect subtle forms of racial identification and racialized description. For example, *The Secret Garden*, one of the texts selected by Barnes & Noble for its campaign, is explicitly about British colonialism in India, and one of its main characters, Mary Lennox, expresses clear antipathy toward Indians.[2] Further, it's unclear why staff at Barnes & Noble didn't just read the novels—there were only one hundred of them—which would have represented a far more accurate way of identifying the presence or absence of racially marked characters. Finally, as L. L. McKinney argues on Twitter, if Barnes & Noble truly wanted to celebrate racial diversity in literature, they could have simply promoted examples of actual "classic" novels written by black and other racial minority authors rather than attempt to reimagine, via cover design, a group of texts written by white novelists.[3]

The outrage and frustration surrounding Barnes & Noble's campaign reflects a broader critique of the whiteness and racial inequality of contemporary book publishing (as seen in movements like #publishingsowhite) and American cultural production in general (as seen in movements like #oscarsowhite, which targets Hollywood). These protests remind us how little things have changed from the postwar period I've studied in this book (1950 to 2000). In my introduction, I mention that I in part wrote this book to correct a misperception, common among scholars, that postwar multiculturalism decisively transformed and diversified U.S. literary culture. I argue that this claim conflates the world of scholars and universities with the literary marketplace and that this misperception impedes efforts to positively change literary culture in not discerning the full scale of a problem that was unchanging in the 1980s and 1990s and apparently, based on recent studies, remains unchanged in the present.[4] It's become clear that academic researchers have lagged behind editors, writers, and even ordinary readers—those closest to contemporary literature—in understanding and recognizing the persistence and ubiquity of racial inequality in American culture. This book has tried to better align these two perspectives.

In particular, the Barnes & Noble marketing debacle shows us how little things have changed despite print culture's great technological changes in the past twenty years. The historical focus of this book is 1950 to 2000 because, as I explain in my introduction, this period represents a relatively coherent phase of American print culture and the literary marketplace; the post-2000 period is defined by new modes of writing and reading, production and consumption, facilitated by new internet services, such as Amazon, and online platforms, such as AO3. My belief is that this new digital environment has meaningfully altered the patterns of cultural redlining we see in the era before, and I leave it to future researchers to take up this question.

Yet despite its novelty of technological innovation (using "AI" to improve book marketing), this recent debacle reveals the persistence of some basic patterns of racial discrimination and inequality from our earlier multicultural moment. What it shows is that book publishers and more broadly the mainstream publishing world will always look for quick and easy solutions to difficult and complex structural problems. They will acquiesce to public pressure to promote greater racial diversity in the books and authors they publish and promote. But they will rarely provide solutions or countermeasures that are enduring and structurally transformative. For example, the Barnes & Noble AI campaign reminds me of the decision by Random House to hire its first black editor, Toni Morrison, in the late 1960s. Both have laudable goals: to increase racial diversity and promote a greater number of minority writers. But both lack a mechanism to create permanent and lasting change. Rather than just try to "reimagine" classic novels by white authors as works that emphasize nonwhite characters, Barnes & Noble should have thought about how to promote books by actual nonwhite writers. Similarly, as Morrison herself suggested, rather than just hire one single black editor over a fifteen-year period, Random House should have thought about creating an entire imprint or line to promote a range of nonwhite authors.[5]

Our Random House case study shows how hard it is to produce permanent and lasting change at a mainstream cultural institution. It's not just that the number of black authors nearly instantly regresses to its pre-1970s mean as soon as Morrison leaves in 1983; it's that the way that white and black characters get portrayed in fiction never really changes, despite an uptick in the number of black novelists published during Morrison's tenure. It's very difficult to change patterns of cultural representation—the *way* that writers write—especially when it comes to race. As we see with the Barnes & Noble example, it's much easier to produce the appearance of change—literally, redesigning book covers. It never occurred to the decision makers at Barnes & Noble that the things that really need changing are the words, characters, themes, and narratives that happen between the covers. All that we see with this example is the use of a fancier technology to produce a quick and easy take on racial inclusion, one that, again, doesn't do much to produce a lasting and durable structural transformation in publishing, reception, and sales.

This is not to end this book on a pessimistic note. I am encouraged by recent activism and efforts to engender greater racial diversity in the world of letters and literature in the past ten years, and I do believe things are changing, particularly as a result of the internet. I do not have any real data to this effect, but I intuit positive trends, including a greater number of racial minorities winning major literary prizes, such as Colson Whitehead's *The Underground Railroad*, which won the Pulitzer in 2017. But what this book's history teaches us is that we've been here before. From chapter 3, we will similarly recall an uptick in the number of minority authors winning prizes in the late 1980s, an increase that proves relatively ephemeral and nonlasting. We'll recall that this uptick didn't do much to effect broader patterns of language and narrative in the kinds of books that tend to win prizes—the literary whiteness of the American prizewinner remains essentially unchanged in the 1980s and 1990s. History teaches us to be cautiously skeptical of whatever seeming changes we see in literary culture in the present. Again, it's not entirely difficult to give a few more awards to nonwhite authors. It's far harder to change the broader *idea* of what the literary establishment defines as "prizeworthy" based on what's on the page.

This book has argued that in order to do this, we'll need some new tools and approaches, quantitative and computational methods in particular. Of course, the Barnes & Noble affair shows the dark side of this approach, and rightfully, writers and readers condemned their use of computers to understand literature. I am sympathetic to this critique, but it's unfortunate that in some instances, this critique has blended into a more general dismissal of "AI." In chapter after chapter, I have attempted to show the affordances of computation and data science to understand fiction at scale, often precisely in order to expose and critique racial inequality and whiteness. The problem with the Barnes & Noble marketing experiment was not that it used data to try to parse patterns of language and meaning in a corpus of texts. The problem is that the people who made the algorithm clearly had not read any of the novels they sought to parse and in general appeared to lack a basic critical understanding of the relationship between race and writing.

Despite the recent embarrassment, cultural institutions like Barnes & Noble will continue to use data to analyze, market, and sell novels. The question is how we writers, critics, academics, and ordinary readers will position ourselves in relation to this labor. We can continue to imagine ourselves as watchdogs, as the people who know the arts, and prevent these institutions from misusing technology to capitalize on it. There's great value in this position, and we should keep doing it. But we can also imagine another position or role: we can be the individuals who know culture and computation, data and the arts, equally well, and we can do more than just critique what institutions like Barnes & Noble try to do with technology; we can become the people who collaborate with them in order to build smarter algorithms that do the work we want them to do. In my view, this is also an empowered position. It says we are not just victims of capitalism and technology. We can play an active role in reconstructing algorithms to suit our needs better.

Methodologically, this book has offered a modest attempt to model this new type of reader, critic, and scholar. It responds to Tara McPherson's important critique of race and technology, which generously ends with a call for a new kind of researcher: "We need new hybrid practitioners: artist-theorists, programming humanists, activist scholars; theoretical archivists, critical race coders. We need new forms of graduate and undergraduate education that hone both critical and digital literacies."[6] One main thesis of this book is that racial inequality in literature is hard to change in part because it's been hard to see. And it's been hard to see because it partly exists at a scale that eludes traditional modes of readerly understanding and detection—what one can read on the page, in an archive. At a higher scale, the racial inequality of U.S. fiction in the 2010s and 2020s looks surprisingly similar to the racial inequality of the 1960s and 1970s, despite the multiculturalist interventions of the 1980s and 1990s. In the years to come, we have a chance to break this pattern. However, it will require a rapprochement with computers and data. It will require a lowering of the firewall that historically has separated the arts from technology, the humanities from the sciences. Readers, writers, critics, and scholars will have to start thinking about literature in new ways, in ways that might at first feel alien or awkward. But if we want to defeat cultural redlining, it'll be worth it.

NOTES

INTRODUCTION

1. Quoted in Danille K. Taylor-Guthrie, *Conversations with Toni Morrison* (Oxford: University Press of Mississippi, 1994), 133.
2. A helpful and accessible introduction to redlining and its aftereffects, especially as it played out in New York City, can be found at https://www.brickunderground.com/blog/2015/10/history_of_redlining. This piece cites Ta-Nehisi Coates's important journalistic history of redlining: "The Case for Reparations," *Atlantic*, June 2014.
3. This data represents a summary of the overall data presented in the rest of this book. For a more detailed explanation of the data and how these figures were computed, see the section in each of the book's chapters that are devoted to describing the data. For example, see the section "Random House by the Numbers" in chapter 1.
4. https://en.wikipedia.org/wiki/Historical_racial_and_ethnic_demographics_of_the_United_States.
5. Darryl Dickson-Carr, introduction to *The Columbia Guide to Contemporary African American Fiction* (New York: Columbia University Press, 2005), 1.
6. Michael Schudson, "General Introduction: The Enduring Book in a Multimedia Age," in David Paul Nord et al., *A History of the Book in America*, vol. 5: *The Enduring Book* (Chapel Hill: University of North Carolina Press, 2014), 16.
7. I am indebted to Caroline Levine for this formulation, which she presented at a lecture at McGill University in 2019.
8. For an excellent history of black publishers in America in the postwar period, see Donald Franklin Joyce, *Gatekeepers of Black Culture: Black-Owned Book Publishing in the United States, 1817-1981* (New York: Praeger, 1983). A good history of Broadside Press is Melba Joyce Boyd, *Wrestling with the Muse: Dudley Randall and the Broadside Press* (New York: Columbia University Press, 2003). For a history of Quinto Sol, see Jon Alba Cutler, "Quinto Sol, Chicano/a

Literature, and the Long March Through Institutions," *American Literary History* 26, no. 2 (Summer 2014).

9. I review this scholarship in greater detail in the first section of chapter 1; Dan Sinykin, however, has in particular identified the postwar U.S. literary-historical period as "the conglomerate era" in an important recent essay: "The Conglomerate Era: Publishing, Authorship, and Literary Form, 1965–2007," *Contemporary Literature* 58, no. 4 (Winter 2017).
10. Quoted in Evan Brier, *A Novel Marketplace: Mass Culture, the Book Trade, and Postwar American Fiction* (Philadelphia: University of Pennsylvania Press, 2009), 77.
11. Cited in Nick Levey, "Post-Press Literature: Self-Published Authors in the Literary Field," *Post-45: Peer Reviewed*, February 2, 2016.
12. See Sinykin, "The Conglomerate Era," 468–70, for a fuller account. I also cover this material in greater detail in the first section of chapter 1.
13. See Nord et al., *A History of the Book in America*, 5:211, for a longer description.
14. See Sinykin, "The Conglomerate Era," 470–71.
15. This included repeated attempts at communication with representatives at Random House, to no avail, and exhaustive web-based searches for this information, again to no avail. In the end, I used records of library holdings to get this data, which I describe at length in the "Random House by the Numbers" section in chapter 1.
16. Information about this archive is documented in detail in chapter 1.
17. Henry Louis Gates Jr., *Loose Canons: Notes on the Culture Wars* (Oxford: Oxford University Press, 1992), 91. Also see Gates, "To Be Raped, Bred, or Abused," *New York Times*, November 22, 1987, 12.
18. For example, see Stephen Marche, "Literature Is Not Data: Against Digital Humanities," *Los Angeles Review of Books*, October 28, 2012.
19. I simply identified how many articles in this corpus had the word "inequality" and divided that number by the total number of essays in the corpus. See the "Distant Reading the Canon Wars" section in chapter 4 for a more detailed account of how I assembled this data and the data's parameters.
20. See chapter 4 for more details on how these values were computed and on the underlying data.
21. See chapter 4 for more details on this analysis.
22. Article counts are drawn from the Web of Science and are based on searching for "inequality" in the "topic" field between 1995 and 2017. For "social sciences," the search was limited to the three fields of "sociology," "economics," and "political science." This resulted in 28,130 articles. For "humanities" I used all fields in the Arts and Humanities Citation Index. This yielded 3,013 articles. Over one-third of these belonged to the single field of history. Further, there does not appear to any increase in article counts over time, based on the data.
23. For example, here I think of Gayatri Spivak's important essays in *Outside in the Teaching Machine* (New York: Routledge, 1993), such as "More on Power/Knowledge," and classic essays by Hall, such as "The West and the Rest: Discourse and Power," in *Race and Racialization: Essential Readings*, ed. Tania Das Gupta et al. (Toronto: Canadian Scholars' Press, 2007).
24. Stuart Hall, ed., *Representation: Cultural Representations and Signifying Practices* (London: Sage, 1997), 41–51.
25. Hall, *Representation*, 44, 49.

26. See, for example, Stuart Hall, "New Ethnicities," in *Stuart Hall: Critical Dialogues in Cultural Studies*, ed. David Morley and Kuan-Hsing Chen (New York: Routledge, 1996), 441–49.
27. This is a method that instantly spoke to scholars of black culture and continues to resonate; see, for example, Hazel Carby's now canonical *Reconstructing Womanhood: The Emergence of the Afro-American Woman Novelist* (Oxford: Oxford University Press, 1987); and Alexander Weheliye, *Habeas Viscus: Racializing Assemblages, Biopolitics, and Black Feminist Theories of the Human* (Durham, NC: Duke University Press, 2014).
28. See, for example, Hall, "New Ethnicities," 445; and Stuart Hall et al., *Policing the Crisis: Mugging, the State, and Law and Order* (London: MacMillan, 1978).
29. David Grusky, "The Stories About Inequality We Love to Tell," in *The Inequality Reader: Contemporary and Foundational Readings in Race, Class, and Gender*, ed. David B. Grusky and Szonja Szelényi (New York: Routledge, 2018), 7.
30. Grusky, *The Inequality Reader*, would be a good place to start: Grusky's own essay is a fine critique, as well as Claude Fischer et al., *Inequality by Design: Cracking the Bell Curve Myth* (Princeton, NJ: Princeton University Press, 1996), of which the *Reader* provides an excerpt.
31. Here I am thinking of course of canonical work in whiteness studies, like Eric Lott, *Love and Theft: Blackface Minstrelsy and the American Working Class* (Oxford: Oxford University Press, 1993); and Toni Morrison, *Playing in the Dark: Whiteness and the Literary Imagination* (Cambridge, MA: Harvard University Press, 1992).
32. Mark McGurl, *The Program Era: Postwar Fiction and the Rise of Creative Writing* (Cambridge, MA: Harvard University Press, 2009); this claim suffuses McGurl's entire argument, particularly the introduction and page 74 in particular.
33. Here I more explicitly outline my position in relation to Walter Benn Michaels's important and influential writings on "inequality" in the context of contemporary U.S. cultural criticism—see, for example, his recent "The Political Economy of Antiracism," *Nonsite* 23 (February 11, 2018). My book also argues that the concept of inequality has an affordance for literary studies, but my point is less polemical and more methodological. I do not endorse Benn Michaels's position that literary scholars should pay less attention to racial diversity. However, I do agree that "inequality" in general can be a useful keyword for literary analysis, particularly in how it can reveal empirical forms of discrimination and oppression toward certain groups of writers. And I agree that data and statistics can provide a powerful form of evidence that supplements close reading. In sum, my interest in "inequality" as a critical keyword is not restricted to drawing attention to economic inequality (*pace* Benn Michaels). I believe that it has a greater utility and that it can help us trace patterns of power and oppression in general, which, as my book demonstrates, can indeed include racialized forms of inequality within literature and culture. Regarding Kenneth Warren's important contribution to this debate, I engage with his scholarship, particularly *What Was African American Literature?* in chapter 4.
34. Regarding this argument and claim, an anonymous reader of this manuscript assigned by Columbia University Press provided a number of incredibly lucid and eloquent formulations that I draw from and adapt in this paragraph. I am very grateful to this reader's highly engaged and intelligent comments and feedback.
35. Just to semiarbitrarily choose two prominent and relatively recent examples of postwar American literary history: Amy Hungerford, *Postmodern Belief: American Literature and Religion Since 1960* (Princeton, NJ: Princeton University Press, 2010); and Mark Greif, *The Age of*

the Crisis of Man: Thought and Fiction in America, 1933-1973 (Princeton, NJ: Princeton University Press, 2015).
36. I make this point in slightly greater depth, with more citations, in Richard Jean So, Hoyt Long, and Yuancheng Zhu, "Race, Writing, and Computation: Racial Difference and the US Novel, 1880–2000," *Journal of Cultural Analytics*, January 11, 2019.
37. For a general overview, see Stephen Jay Gould, *The Mismeasure of Man* (New York: Norton, 1980).
38. For a critique of PCA, see Gould, *The Mismeasure of Man*, esp. 264–350. For a recent example of the use of PCA to study literature, see Paul Vierthaler, "Fiction and History: Polarity and Stylistic Gradience in Late Imperial Chinese Literature," *Journal of Cultural Analytics*, May 23, 2016.
39. Cathy O'Neil, *Weapons of Math Destruction* (New York: Crown, 2016).
40. Safiya Noble, *Algorithms of Oppression: How Search Engines Reinforce Racism* (New York: NYU Press, 2018), 1.
41. An excellent example of recent scholarship that performs this type of work is Lauren Klein, "The Image of Absence: Archival Silence, Data Visualization, and James Hemings," *American Literature* 85, no. 4 (December 2013): 661–88, which represents a fantastic example of this emerging work.
42. Hazel V. Carby, "Becoming Modern Racialized Subjects: Detours Through Our Pasts to Produce Ourselves Anew," *Cultural Studies* 23 (2009): 628.
43. Tukufu Zuberi, *Thicker Than Blood: How Racial Statistics Lie* (Minneapolis: University of Minnesota Press, 2001), 110.
44. Beyond Zuberi, I have found the following two social scientific studies useful to this end: Angela James, "Making Sense of Race and Racial Classification," in *White Logic, White Methods: Racism and Methodology* (Lanham, MD: Rowman and Littlefield, 2008); and Quincy Thomas Stewart and Abigail Sewell, "Quantifying Race: On Methods for Analyzing Social Inequality," in *Rethinking Race and Ethnicity in Research Methods* (Walnut Creek, CA: Left Coast, 2011).
45. For more on the introduction of quantitative modeling into literary criticism, see Julia Flanders and Fotis Jannidis, "Data Modeling," in *A New Companion to Digital Humanities*, ed. Susan Schreibman, Ray Siemens, and John Unsworth (New York: Wiley, 2016), 229–38; Willard McCarty, "Modeling: A Study in Words and Meanings," in *A New Companion to Digital Humanities*, 254–72; Andrew Piper, "Think Small: On Literary Modeling," *PMLA* 132, no. 3 (2017): 651–58; and Richard Jean So, "All Models Are Wrong," *PMLA* 132, no. 3 (2017): 668–73.
46. See Andrew Piper, *Enumerations: Data and Literary Study* (Chicago: University of Chicago Press, 2018); Ted Underwood, *Distant Horizons: Digital Evidence and Literary Change* (Chicago: University of Chicago Press, 2019); and Katherine Bode, *A World of Fiction: Digital Collections and the Future of Literary History* (Ann Arbor: University of Michigan Press, 2018).
47. See again Hall, "New Ethnicities."
48. Weheliye, *Habeas Viscus*, 4.
49. Jessica Marie Johnson, "Markup Bodies: Black [Life] Studies and Slavery [Death] Studies at the Digital Crossroads," *Social Text* 36, no. 4 (2018): 57–79; Britt Rusert, *Fugitive Science: Empiricism and Freedom in Early African American Culture* (New York: New York University Press, 2017), 18.
50. Christina Sharpe, *In the Wake: On Blackness and Being* (Durham, NC: Duke University Press, 2016), 13.

51. Kim Gallon, "Making a Case for the Black Digital Humanities," in *Debates in the Digital Humanities*, ed. Matthew K. Gold (Minneapolis: University of Minnesota Press, 2016), online version, unpaginated.
52. See Nord et al., *A History of the Book in America*, vol. 5; Brier, *A Novel Marketplace*; and Schudson, "General Introduction"; as well as John Thompson's work, which I cite and discuss in greater detail in chapter 1. See also Sinykin, "The Conglomerate Era."
53. See, for example, Levey, "Post-Press Literature"; and Sinykin, "The Conglomerate Era." Also see Mark McGurl, "Everything and Less: Fiction in the Age of Amazon," *Modern Language Quarterly* 77, no. 3 (2016); and Aarthi Vadde, "Amateur Creativity: Contemporary Literature and the Digital Publishing Scene," *New Literary History* 48, no. 1 (2017).
54. See for example, Michael Hill, Lawrence Jackson, and Kenneth Warren's work, all of which I cite and discuss at length in chapter 4.
55. I explain in detail how I determined this fact in the final section of chapter 4.
56. A very brief sample of such writings might include: Robyn McGee, "The Overwhelming Whiteness of the Publishing Industry," *Bitch Media*, January 27, 2016; April Reign, "#OscarsSoWhite Is Still Relevant This Year," *Vanity Fair*, March 2018; and, most recently, Laura McGrath, "Comping White," *Los Angeles Review of Books*, January 21, 2019; and Michael Nava, "Big Lit Meets the Mexican Americans: A Study in White Supremacy," *Los Angeles Review of Books*, January 2, 2020.

1. PRODUCTION: ON WHITE PUBLISHING

1. Quoted in Evan Brier, *A Novel Marketplace: Mass Culture, the Book Trade, and Postwar American Fiction* (Philadelphia: University of Pennsylvania Press, 2009), 77.
2. See, for example, John Tebbel, *Between Covers: The Rise and Transformation of Book Publishing in America* (Oxford: Oxford University Press, 1987).
3. Loren Glass, *Counterculture Colophon: Grove Press, the* Evergreen Review, *and the Incorporation of the Avant-Garde* (Palo Alto, CA: Stanford University Press, 2013), 15.
4. See, for example, Charles Kadushin, Lewis A. Coser, and Walter W. Powell, *The Culture and Commerce of Publishing* (Chicago: University of Chicago Press, 1985), 19.
5. Bennett Cerf, *At Random: The Reminiscences of Bennett Cerf* (New York: Random House, 2012), 65.
6. For an excellent comprehensive history, see David Paul Nord et al., *A History of the Book in America*, vol. 5: *The Enduring Book* (Chapel Hill: University of North Carolina Press, 2014), 35–51.
7. Quoted in Kadushin, Coser, and Powell, *The Culture and Commerce of Publishing*, 19.
8. See Brier, *A Novel Marketplace*, 130–31.
9. See Nord et al., *A History of the Book in America*, 5:211.
10. Lewis Coser, "Publishers as Gatekeepers," *Annals of the American Academy of Political and Social Science*, 421, no. 1 (1975): 16.
11. Cited in Nick Levey, "Post-Press Literature: Self-Published Authors in the Literary Field," *Post-45: Peer Reviewed*, February 2 (2016), unpaginated.
12. I describe in the introduction the underlying data for this graph and how this graph was produced.

192　1. PRODUCTION

13. The question of sales is important here, but I have found it impossible to gather reliable sales data from the publisher, and such figures have proven extremely difficult to estimate. However, I implicitly take on the question of sales in my third chapter in its analysis of "the bestseller."
14. See, for example, Michael Schudson, "General Introduction: The Enduring Book in a Multimedia Age," in Nord et al., *A History of the Book in America*, vol. 5.
15. For example, consider this popular essay that covers Toni Morrison's tenure at Random House: Rachel Kaadzi Ghansah, "The Radical Vision of Toni Morrison," *New York Times*, April 8, 2015. Ghansah interviews several prominent editors from Random House from the 1980s onward, and they claim that the press was more open minded to black editors and thus black literature than their peers.
16. Quoted in Henry Louis Gates, "The Black Person in Art: How Should S/he Be Portrayed?," *Black American Literature Forum* 21, no. 2 (1987): 3, 4.
17. Zora Neale Hurston, "What White Publishers Won't Print," *Negro Digest*, April 1950, 5.
18. See Jason Epstein, *Book Business: Publishing Past Present and Future* (New York: Norton, 2011).
19. See John Thompson, *Merchants of Culture: The Publishing Business in the Twenty-First Century* (London: Polity, 2010).
20. For example, see Kadushin, Coser, and Powell, *The Culture and Commerce of Publishing*.
21. See Kadushin, Coser, and Powell, *The Culture and Commerce of Publishing*, 112.
22. Cited in Ghansah, "The Radical Vision of Toni Morrison."
23. Kadushin, Coser, and Powell, *The Culture and Commerce of Publishing*, 166.
24. Cited in Robyn McGee, "The Overwhelming Whiteness of the Publishing Industry," *Bitch Media*, January 2016.
25. Albert Greco, *The Book Publishing Industry* (New York: Routledge, 2004), 281.
26. Quoted in Glass, *Counterculture Colophon*, 147.
27. See Glass, *Counterculture Colophon*, 151.
28. Quoted in Danille K. Taylor-Guthrie, *Conversations with Toni Morrison* (Oxford: University Press of Mississippi, 1994), 133. Also see Lawrence Jackson, *The Indignant Generation: A Narrative History of African American Writers and Critics, 1934-1960* (Princeton, NJ: Princeton University Press, 2010), who argues that by 1954 all of the major U.S. publishing houses had picked up a black author—like Harper touting Richard Wright—but that such a gesture was always token and never sweeping. Each publisher typically had one black writer but rarely more than one.
29. André Schiffrin, *The Business of Books: How the International Conglomerates Took Over the Publishing Industry and Changed the Way We Read* (New York: Verso, 2001), 57.
30. Dudley Randall, "Black Emotion and Experience: The Literature for Understanding," *American Libraries* 4, no. 2 (1973): 87.
31. Donald Joyce, *Gatekeepers of Black Culture: Black-Owned Book Publishing in the United States, 1817-1981* (New York: Praeger, 1981), 101.
32. Nancy Larrick, "The All-White World of Children's Books," *Journal of African Children's and Youth Literature* 3 (1991/1992): 2.
33. Larrick, "The All-White World of Children's Books," 2-3.
34. Quoted in Larrick, "The All-White World of Children's Books," 3.
35. Larrick, "The All-White World of Children's Books," 10.

36. Alice Mayhew, "Confidential Report on Candidate for Fellowship," January 5, 1970; "Lucille Clifton—Good News—Manuscripts" Folder, MS 1048, Box 1516, Random House Records, Columbia University Archives, Columbia University, New York, New York.
37. Nan Talese, "Memo to Nancy Caulkins," 5/22/72, "Lucille Clifton—Good News—Manuscripts" Folder, MS 1048, Box 1516.
38. Quoted in Boris Kachka, "Who Is the Author Toni Morrison," *New York*, April 29, 2012.
39. See, for example, the exchange with Epstein over Lucille Clifton's poetry. Morrison to Epstein, April 22, 1977, "Lucille Clifton—An Ordinary Woman—Production" Folder, Box 1515, MS 1048.
40. See, for example, Epstein to Morrison, March 7, 1979, "Gayl Jones—Your Book—Palmares" Folder, Box 1521, MS 1048.
41. Morrison, "Reader Report for the Black Critique," May 14, 1975, "Morrison Correspondence 1975 M–Z" Folder, Box 1527, MS 1048.
42. Morrison, "Memo to Design and Copyediting," July 30, 1979, "Toni Bambara Salt Eaters Production" Folder, Box 1511, MS 1048.
43. See Taylor-Guthrie, *Conversations with Toni Morrison*.
44. Hoyt Fuller to Morrison, October 23, 1974, "Dumas Henry 1974–1976 Author-Editor Correspondence" Folder, Box 1518, MS 1048.
45. Carole Parks to Morrison, October 31, 1974, "Dumas Henry 1974–1976 Author-Editor Correspondence" Folder, Box 1518.
46. Parks to Morrison, October 31, 1974.
47. Morrison to Parks, November 7, 1974, "Dumas Henry 1974–1976 Author-Editor Correspondence" Folder, Box 1518.
48. Cheryl Wall, "Toni Morrison, Editor and Teacher," in *The Cambridge Companion to Toni Morrison*, ed. J. Tally (Cambridge: Cambridge University Press, 2007), 139.
49. Morrison to Parks, November 7, 1974.
50. See, for example, Brier, *A Novel Marketplace*, 3.
51. At least during Morrison's tenure there; see Wall, "Toni Morrison," 139.
52. I created my list of English-language novels published at Random House between 1950 and 2000 in the following way. First, I scoured the records of WorldCat to identify every book published by Random House in this period that was also marked as a novel. This returned 3,525 texts. Now, this is an imperfect process. A book will only appear in WorldCat if it is currently held in a library somewhere in the world. Surely there are novels published by Random House that were never acquired by a library. However, I will argue that the vast majority of books it published will have made it into at least one library and that those that didn't represent a very small population. What is held at libraries represents a nontrivial sample of what Random House has published and is adequate to capture the major trends in its literature. Further, there is the question of what has been marked as a "novel." Here, we are dependent on subjective judgment. Yet, I will argue that what is defined as a novel is always subjective, and the judgments of librarians who create the WorldCat standard represent a coherent baseline (if one admittedly bound to the institution of "libraries"). Finally, I focus on the period between 1950 and 2000 because that is the overall focus of the book—a period that has become generally understand as in part defined by the rise and victory of multiculturalism and in scholarship has gone by the name of the "postwar period" and "post-45."

53. The following process was used to perform this task: two researchers had to independently find a scholarly source, or an instance of author self-identification, that marked that author as a specific gender and/or racial category, and the researchers had to agree in their findings. If this standard could not be reached, the author was left unmarked. To create a finite number of racial categories, we used three that are commonly employed in the scholarship: "white," "black," and nonblack racial minority or person of color (or POC).
54. The average year is 1983, and the standard deviation is 14 years. This means that the corpus leans toward the present and that some years, such as years in the 1990s, tend to have more novels than earlier years, such as the 1950s. That difference hovers around 14 texts a year. As with our identity metadata, this additional metadata was collected by hand.
55. The percentage of men and the percentage of women in this data is decreasing and increasing, respectively, at a statistically significant rate ($p < 0.01$), based on fitting the data to a linear regression model. Lines of best fit have been added to the graph to visually depict trends over time.
56. The percentage of white men and white women is decreasing and increasing, respectively, at a statistically significant rate ($p < 0.01$), based on fitting the data to a linear regression model.
57. HathiTrust was able to provide 1,371 digital texts of the overall corpus. To determine if there are any meaningful skews in this sample, I completed some basic statistical analyses to compare the two corpora. There is no meaningful racial skew. The Hathi corpus is slightly less white, at 96.6 percent. There is no real chronological skew: its mean year for publication is 1980, with a standard deviation of 14, basically comparable to the original corpus's mean of 1983 and standard deviation of 14. And there is no national skew. Hathi is 75.5 percent American, nearly identical with the original corpus. However, I found a nontrivial skew with gender. The Hathi corpus is 68 percent male versus 59 percent male in the original corpus. Yet because gender is not a key variable I explore in this analysis and the skew is not so massive (above 10 percent) that it might alter the core composition of the corpus, I have decided that this slant is acceptable. The genre distribution for the Hathitrust corpus though has a larger skew. Fifty-two percent of the fiction in the corpus belongs to the "literary" category, while the young adult (YA) category is significantly underrepresented compared to its representation in the full corpus (3.5 percent versus 28.6 percent). However, I will not be primarily focusing on literary genre, and the limited genre analysis I do perform is through the lens of "literary" versus "genre" fiction.
58. Ruth Frankenberg, *The Social Construction of Whiteness* (New York: Routledge, 1992), 1. Some other works that are influential, as well: Catherine Jurca, *White Diaspora: The Suburb and the Twentieth-Century American Novel* (Princeton, NJ: Princeton University Press, 2001); Birgit Rasmussen et al., *The Making and Unmaking of Whiteness* (Durham, NC: Duke University Press, 2001); Eric Lott, *Love and Theft: Blackface Minstrelsy and the American Working Class* (Oxford: Oxford University Press, 2013); Richard Dyer, *White: Essays on Race and Culture* (London: Routledge, 1997).
59. Toni Morrison, *Playing in the Dark* (Cambridge, MA: Harvard University Press, 1992), 59.
60. Frankenberg, *The Social Construction of Whiteness*, 2. See also Eduardo Bonilla-Silva, *Racism Without Racists: Color-Blind Racism and the Persistence of Racial Inequality in America* (New York: Rowman and Littlefield, 2017).

61. Sara Ahmed, "Declarations of Whiteness: The Non-Performativity of Anti-Racism," *Borderlands* 3, no. 2 (2004). See also Robyn Wiegman, "Whiteness Studies and the Paradox of Particularity," *boundary 2* 26, no. 3 (1999).
62. David Roediger, *The Wages of Whiteness: Race and the Making of the American Working Class* (London: Verso, 2007), 100.
63. John Firth, "A Synopsis of Linguistic Theory 1930–1955," in *Selected Papers of J. R. Firth*, ed. F. R. Palmer (London: Longmans, 1968), 168–205.
64. For this first analysis, I used an automated process to extract "white" and "black" characters from our novels. Specifically, I wrote a script to identify every time a category of person such as "man" or "woman" or "person" (including cognates like "child" as well as independent markers of racial identity such as "Caucasian" and "Negro") appears with the racialized marker "white" or "black." It will find every instance of "white man," "black woman," etc. The limit of this approach is that it will only discover *explicit* mentions of racialized characters. It will *miss* unmarked examples of racialized characters. Later in this section, I describe how I implement a word embeddings model to start addressing this limitation.
65. And of course, normalizing the results, so what appear on the y-axis of the graph are percentages, not raw counts.
66. Again, the results have been normalized. I also performed this same analysis on characters marked as "white" and found similar results; as a space-saving measure, I do not include this graph, however. Interested readers can implement my code (contact author) to produce this graph.
67. I use the flexibility of word embeddings to create a more robust idea of "white characters" and "black characters." I created a vector where I took the term "white" and used vector arithmetic to add an array of terms that describe humans, such as "man" and "woman" as well as "boy" and "person," to identify "white characters." Simply creating the vector with "white man" and so forth as a single term would constrain our ability to identify the characterness of whiteness and contradict my theoretical assumptions described earlier. I am looking for a flexible, capacious notion of white characterness, albeit one rooted in concrete terms. I then also used vector arithmetic to "subtract out" character blackness (terms such as "black" and "Negro") to make sure that what the model finds is not just racialized characterness in general. I also subtracted out common words for color such as "blue," so the model did not fixate on nonracialized color terms. I did the same but in reverse to identify "black characters."
68. I used the Python-based Gensim implementation version of word embeddings with the following specifications. First I used a fairly simple, bespoke "fast" tokenizer (code can be provided on request) at the word level and then tokenized by sentence because the Gensim implementation requires sentences as input. I used the skip-gram training algorithm, a window of 5 for the maximum distance between current and predicted word, 100 as the dimensionality of the word vector, a minimum word count of 5, an alpha of 0.025, 100,000 as my target size of batches of examples, and an iteration value of 5. Finally, after running the model, I computed the 30 most similar terms (using Gensim's built-in "most similar" function (which computes the most similar terms by measuring cosine similarity) to my originally created "white character" and "black character" vectors.
69. In note 67, I describe the parameters I use, in particular vector subtraction, to create this model.

70. See Frankenberg, *The Social Construction of Whiteness*; Morrison, *Playing in the Dark*.
71. Cosine similarity was employed to compute the distance between word vectors, and then I used a multidimensional scaling algorithm (the "MDS" package in Python's Scikit Learn) to visualize the relations between words in two dimensions (selecting two ["2"] components).
72. An important caveat is the version of word embeddings I implement via Gensim (word2vec) is a form of predictive modeling, which means that each time I run the model, the results will potentially differ. Thus, if one runs my code on the data, one will possibly arrive at different results (i.e., a slightly different list of "most similar" terms). Computer scientists are currently developing methods to stabilize the results of models like word2vec, but an implementation was beyond what was possible during the research of this chapter. However, I ran the model (for both white and black characters) an additional ten times for each and found that 95 percent or more of the terms documented in each graph appeared with each run of the model. This made me confident that the model was producing essentially stable results.
73. John Updike, *Rabbit Is Rich* (New York: Random House, 1996), 94.
74. In technical terms, I ran a permutation test on the data to determine whether we can reject the null hypothesis that the racialized representations of characters by white authors are *no different* from the racialized representation of characters by white and black authors *combined*. If we cannot reject this hypothesis, it indicates that black authors do not directly change the racialized representation of characters in the corpus; i.e., they have no measurable effect. I ran the following test. (1) I created two subcorpora—a corpus of white-only writers and then a corpus of white+black authors. I then computed a racialized character vector for each of the subcorpora that combines both "white" and "black" figurations of characterness from the previous model. Next, I wanted to see how different these two corpora are. I computed the fifty most similar terms for each vector and used the Levenshtein distance algorithm to compute how semantically different they are. This produced a score. (2) However, I needed a test to see if this score is significant or not. This is where I used a permutation test. I took my two subcorpora but now randomly shuffled the labels of the racial identity of each text; i.e., each text now has a "fake" identification for the racial identity of its author. Then, I performed step (1) on these fake subcorpora, but I did this one hundred times to create a null distribution of scores. (3) Last I wanted to see where our "real" difference score fell in this distribution; if it falls outside the bounds of the 2.5 percent and 97.5 percent intervals, thus rejecting the null hypothesis at the 0.05 level, we can be confident that the difference is statistically significant at that level. However, I found the opposite. The true score falls squarely in the middle of the distribution. We cannot reject the null hypothesis. There is no statistically significant difference between the racialized representation of characters in our white-only corpus and our white+black writers corpus based on our word embeddings model output.
75. Here I implement the model developed in W. Hamilton, J. Leskovec, and D. Jurafsky, "Diachronic Word Embeddings Reveal Statistical Laws of Semantic Change," *Association for Computer Linguistics* 1 (2016). I did so with the help of Ryan Heuser's Python implementation, which takes as its input Gensim word embeddings model output and essentially aligns the output of multiple Gensim models. In my case, of course, the output is divided by decades.

76. Again I have already noted an important caveat regarding the potential instability of results with word2vec; this is a particular concern for this analysis by decade, where the number of texts per decade is smaller, of course, than for the entire period. To ensure the robustness of these results, I ran the model ten additional times for each decade-pair and found that 95 percent or more of the terms appear with each run; further, each of the eight terms I highlight in my chart appeared in every run of the model. Finally, the cosine similarity score that indicates the amount of semantic shift for each decade-pair changed with each run, but I found that the direction of the difference remained stable with each (i.e., the scores for white characters was always greater than for black characters), and the magnitude of that difference was always greater than a factor of 2.
77. See Jason Stevens, *God-Fearing and Free: A Spiritual History of America's Cold War* (Cambridge, MA: Harvard University Press, 2010).
78. See Matthew Frye Jacobson, *Whiteness of a Different Color: European Immigrants and the Alchemy of Race* (Cambridge, MA: Harvard University Press, 1999), 13–90.
79. Ann Beattie, *Another You* (New York: Vintage, 2011), 176.
80. A useful aspect of Heuser's Python implementation of Hamilton et al.'s model is that it computes a value to measure the "relative semantic shift for this word [vector] between these two models." This value is simply computed by calculating the cosine distance between our two word vectors (in my case, the 1950s vector for "white characters" versus the 1960s vector for "black characters," and so forth). In my chart, I simply report these scores for each decade pair, i.e., 1950–1960 and so forth. A caveat, though, naturally: it's difficult to interpret the meaning of this value of its "effect size"—what I am thus interested in is their relative difference. What the charts indicate is that for black characters there is virtually no change in any of the decades whereas for white characters there is a great deal of change in each decade pair.
81. Nell Irvin Painter, *The History of White People* (New York: Norton, 2010), 387.
82. See Wiegman, "Whiteness Studies and the Paradox of Particularity." This also is echoed in a different context by Ahmed, "Declarations of Whiteness."
83. See Mark McGurl, "Introduction: Hall of Mirrors," in *The Program Era: Postwar Fiction and the Rise of Creative Writing* (Cambridge, MA: Harvard University Press, 2011).
84. This is what I did. For the entire corpus, I identified every instance in which a racially marked person appears in the text (white or black). I then identified all of the terms that appear within 4 words (before and after) of that entity (stop-words removed). I then created a probabilistic distribution of terms that indicate what I argue is the "racial imagination" of the entire corpus: what words it tends to use when describing white and/or black characters. I describe this as my corpus's "racialized character vector." Next, I created this vector, using the same procedure as described earlier, for each novel in the corpus. I then computed the semantic distance between each text to the overall corpus vector using cosine similarity as my measurement. This then produced a score for each novel. Last, I ranked each novel based on that score. This is admittedly a coarse approach, but I believe it helps identify a basic signal regarding the intensity of racial representation for each single text in relation to the corpus as a whole. It is meant simply to draw our attention to a list of novels that would be appropriate to investigate more closely via close reading. It is not meant as a definitive ranking of novels in terms of how they enact "racial identity."
85. James Michener, *The Drifters* (New York: Dial, 1971), 594.

86. For a very fine account of Dumas and his work for a popular audience, see Scott Saul, "The Devil and Henry Dumas," *Boston Review*, October 4, 2004.
87. See, for example, Eleanor Traylor, "Henry Dumas and the Discourse of Memory," *Black American Literature Forum* 22, no. 2 (Summer 1988).
88. Nathan Ragain, "A 'Reconcepted Am': Language, Nature, and Collectivity in Sun Ra and Henry Dumas," *Criticism* 55, no. 4 (Fall 2012); Amiri Baraka, "Afro-Surreal Expressionist," *Black American Literature Forum* 22, no. 2 (Summer 1988): 164; Eugene Redmond, "Introduction: The Ancient and Recent Voices Within Henry Dumas," *Black American Literature Forum* 22, no. 2 (Summer 1988): 150.
89. Scholarship on Dumas is indeed thin. Other than the *Black American Literature Forum*'s special issue on Dumas's work (already cited), I have found no more than a handful of essays on his writings—the Saul and Ragain essays being recent, notable exceptions.
90. Henry Dumas, *Jonoah and the Green Stone* (New York: Random House, 1976), 47.
91. Dumas, *Jonoah and the Green Stone*, 28.
92. Dumas, *Jonoah and the Green Stone*, 36.
93. Dumas, *Jonoah and the Green Stone*, 15–16.
94. Here I am mainly drawing from the work of Phillip Brian Harper, *Abstractionist Aesthetics: Artistic Form and Social Critique in African American Culture* (New York: New York University Press, 2015).
95. William Faulkner, "Dry December" (1931), http://engl273g-finnell.wikispaces.umb.edu/file/view/william-faulkner-dry-september.pdf.
96. Dumas, *Jonoah and the Green Stone*, 109.
97. These statistics can be found in Joyce, *Gatekeepers of Black Culture*, 101. See Joyce also for more on this book history.

2. RECEPTION: MULTICULTURALISM OF THE 1 PERCENT

1. Cheryl A. Wilson, "Placing the Margins: Literary Reviews, Pedagogical Practices, and the Canon of Victorian Women's Writing," *Tulsa Studies in Women's Literature* 28, no. 1 (Spring 2009): 58. See also Jon Klancher, *The Making of English Reading Audiences, 1790-1832* (Madison: University of Wisconsin Press, 1987); and Frank Donoghue, *The Fame Machine: Book Reviewing and Eighteenth-Century Careers* (Palo Alto, CA: Stanford University Press, 1996).
2. Quoted in Wilson, "Placing the Margins," 58.
3. Robert Avrett, "Waning Art of Book Reviewing," *South Atlantic Bulletin* 14, no. 4 (March 1949): 1.
4. Elizabeth Hardwick, "The Decline of Book Reviewing," *Harper's*, October 1959, 138.
5. See Charles Kadushin, Lewis A. Coser, and Walter W. Powell, *The Culture and Commerce of Publishing* (Chicago: University of Chicago Press, 1985), 323–24.
6. Quoted in Kadushin, Coser, and Powell, *The Culture and Commerce of Publishing*, 318.
7. See Susanne Janssen, "Reviewing as Social Practice: Institutional Constraints on Critics' Attention for Contemporary Fiction," *Poetics* 24, no. 5 (1997).
8. See Wendy Griswold, "The Fabrication of Meaning: Literature Interpretation in the United States, Great Britain, and the West Indies," *American Journal of Sociology* 92, no. 5 (March 1987).

9. C. J. van Rees, "How Reviewers Reach Consensus on the Value of Literary Works," *Poetics* 16, no. 3–4 (August 1987): 290. Also see C. J. van Rees, "How a Literary Work Becomes a Masterpiece: On the Threefold Selection Practiced by Literary Criticism," *Poetics* 12, no. 4–5 (November 1983).
10. Quoted in Carolyn Denard, ed., *Toni Morrison: Conversations* (Oxford: University of Mississippi Press, 2008), 243.
11. I used the same process to tag authors by race and gender as described in my first chapter; see that chapter's section "Random House by the Numbers" for a full elaboration.
12. I fit a linear regression model to the data. White authors are decreasing at a statistically significant rate ($p < 0.01$), but the coefficient of decrease is trivial at a value of −0.0024. Or, in lay terms, the percentage of white authors per year being reviewed in this corpus is decreasing at a rate of less than 1 percent per year. In my view, this effect size is trivial and essentially indistinguishable from zero. Similarly, POC authors are increasing over time at a significant rate ($p < 0.01$), but again, the coefficient is trivial at a value of 0.0019, or less than 1 percent per year.
13. Coser, Kadushin, and Powell, *The Culture and Commerce of Publishing*, 311.
14. One concern is that this resource has some latent ideological bias and excludes certain types of journals from its collection. I could find no underlying bias. Its list of periodicals is exhaustive. It contains a vast range of mainstream and niche journals. Extremely specialized periodicals with tiny print runs, from science-fiction magazines to academic journals focused on highly specific topics, are included. In total, there are 310 unique titles. I could not think of any journals or magazines that had been excluded, and while necessarily the *Book Review Index* will miss some more obscure journals, the index's exclusive aim, it appears, is to be as comprehensive and inclusive as possible.
15. Also, while the *Index*, again, originally publishes its information in the form of physical issues, they also produce larger compilations that aggregate such issues. For example, there exists a single volume that compiles all of the *Book Review Index* issues for 1965 to 1982. I used these volumes.
16. I estimate that the volumes record metadata for nine million unique books. My goal was to reduce this mass of data to a more manageable size to facilitate research. I assembled a team of research assistants, and we undertook the following steps. First, we combed through the entire list of book reviews and identified the top 1 percent most-reviewed titles. That is, we determined an order for books based on their number of reviews and took the top 1 percent of that list. We performed this filtering on the entire period at once, rather than year by year. One worry is that this would underrepresent titles from the earlier years. Indeed, the number of titles in the 1 percent corpus increases as we move to the year 2000. However, this skew is not so significant as to make problematic statistical analysis, and, further, it likely reflects the underlying reality of the number of novels being published per year and thus being reviewed each year in periodicals. We lack a definitive account of the number of novels published in North America and the United Kingdom between 1965 and 2000 by year, but based on estimates by R. R. Bowker and other scholars, I find that the increase in titles by year in our 1 percent book-review corpus to mirror what has been estimated to be the increase in the number of books published in this period. I argue that the skew in our data has its basis in reality. In our dataset, there is a clear increase in the late 1980s and another increase in the 1990s in the number of book reviews by year. This increase,

however, mirrors an estimate of the number of new fiction titles published in the United States from 1940 to 2010 by Matthew Wilkens, "Contemporary Fiction by the Numbers," *Post-45: Peer Reviewed*, March 11, 2011. Wilkens similarly finds a steady increase in titles in the 1990s, which accelerates by 1999 and 2000 and explodes by the early 2000s. The broader trend is a steady increase in titles from 1990 to 2010, which is reflected in our data.

We now had a more manageable dataset of approximately 9,000 titles. The next task, already alluded to, was to reduce this corpus further to include only *novels written by American or U.S.-based authors*. This filtering would keep authors, of course, who are American citizens and identify as such but also naturalized American citizens as well as non-American authors who have had extended residences in the United States and strongly identify with the U.S. literary community, such as Salman Rushdie. After this next bit of filtering, there now remained 1,776 unique titles in the corpus, representing 1,003 unique authors. Finally, we wanted to know more about the identity of each author. My team of research assistants researched each author and inputted their race and gender. The standard for inputting such metadata was high—we would only input data if we could find a credible source for such information or the author self-described him- or herself in such identity-based terms. If this standard of evidence could not be reached, we left that information blank. We also researched and recorded the publisher information for each title. This work represented a more straightforward task; we gathered this data via WorldCat searches. The only complication was dealing with book reprints. For this metadata, we inputted the *original* publisher of the novel, ignoring reprint information.

17. I fit a linear regression model to the data; decreases or increases for the percentages of men and women novelists were both statistically significant ($p < 0.01$).
18. Two very accessible and authoritative introductions to network analysis that would interest literary scholars are Albert-László Barabasi, *Linked: The New Science of Networks* (New York: Perseus, 2002); and Duncan J. Watts, *Small Worlds: The Dynamics of Networks Between Order and Randomness* (Princeton, NJ: Princeton University Press, 2003).
19. Three relatively recent examples of network science applied to literary history are Richard Jean So and Hoyt Long, "Network Analysis and the Sociology of Modernism," *boundary 2* 40, no. 2 (2013); Anne Dewitt, "Advances in the Visualization of Data: The Network of Genre in the Victorian Periodical Press," *Victorian Periodicals Review* 48, no. 2 (Summer 2015); and Ruth Ahnert and Sebastian Ahnert, "Protestant Letter Networks in the Reign of Mary I: A Quantitative Approach," *ELH* 81, no. 1 (Spring 2015).
20. Ahnert and Ahnert, "Protestant Letter Networks in the Reign of Mary I," 32.
21. I used the "Center" function from Python's NetworkX to compute the nodes that represent its "center" (the nodes in which eccentricity equals radius), and given the structure of this network, more than 50 percent of the nodes passed this test. And they were a random distribution of white and nonwhite authors, so one cannot say that there exists a discrete "center" to this graph or that it is constituted by one racial group or another.
22. I created two bipartite network projections of my graphs, one in which authors represent nodes and then one in which individual texts represent nodes (using the weighted_projected_graph function in NetworkX). I computed EC scores based on NetworkX's Eigenvector_centrality function for both of these graphs and then simply ranked the titles or authors by this score. There are, of course, many other ways to determine the "influence" of a node—other measurements include between-ness, centrality, and page rank—but I found EC

tends to produce the most distinct results, and it is the method most commonly used by computational literary scholars. For example, it is a key measurement used by Ahnert and Ahnert, "Protestant Letter Networks in the Reign of Mary I."

23. The mathematical definition of the Gini coefficient can be found at https://en.wikipedia.org/wiki/Gini_coefficient. I first used a scaling algorithm (Scikit Learn's MinMax Scaler function) to transform the eigen scores for white and black authors to fall on a range between 0 and 1 in order to make them comparable; I then used Python to implement the Gini coefficient formula to compute Gini scores for white and black writers, respectively.
24. Quoted in David Streitfeld, "Author Toni Morrison Wins Nobel Prize," *Washington Post*, October 8, 1993.
25. Michael Hill, "Toni Morrison and the Post–Civil Rights Novel," in *The Cambridge History of the American Novel*, ed. Leonard Cassuto (Cambridge: Cambridge University Press, 2011), 1076, 1072.
26. Valerie Smith, *Toni Morrison: Writing the Moral Imagination* (New York: Wiley, 2012), 41.
27. Douglas Graham, review of *Song of Solomon*, *Manchester Guardian Weekly*, October 15, 1989.
28. Reynolds Price, "The Adventures of Macon Dead," *New York Times*, September 11, 1977.
29. Quoted in Gay Wilentz, "Civilizations Underneath: African Heritage as Cultural Discourse in Toni Morrison's Song of Solomon," *African American Review* 26, no. 1 (Spring 1992): 137.
30. Wilentz, "Civilizations Underneath," 138.
31. Judylyn Ryan, "Language and Narrative Technique in Toni Morrison's Novels," in *The Cambridge Companion to Toni Morrison*, ed. Justine Tally, online ed. (Cambridge: Cambridge University Press, 2007).
32. Toni Morrison, *Song of Solomon* (New York: Doubleday, 2007), 337.
33. Brent Wade, *Company Man* (Chapel Hill, NC: Algonquin, 1992), 1.
34. Wade, *Company Man*, 47.
35. Michael Harris, "When Black Is Dutiful: *Company Man*," *Los Angeles Times*, March 29, 1992.
36. Morrison, *Song of Solomon*, 178.
37. Review of *Song of Solomon*, *Kirkus*, September 1, 1977.
38. Earl Frederick, "The Song of Milkman Dead," *The Nation*, November 19, 1977.
39. Susan Willis, "Eruptions of Funk: Historicizing Toni Morrison," *Black American Literature Forum* 16, no. 1 (Spring 1982): 38, 35.
40. Jeffrey B. Leak, "An Interview with Brent Wade," *African American Review* 32, no. 3 (1998): 430.
41. Review of *Company Man*, *Publisher's Weekly*, February 1992.
42. When I computed eigenvector centrality scores for black authors based on a network of elite journal reviews for all authors, these three authors rank 43, 44, and 55, respectively, out of a total of 60 black authors in this dataset. Morrison, of course, ranks first.
43. We do not have enough data on black and POC authors or titles to conduct a reliable linear regression analysis to determine if either or both of those groups are statistically increasing or decreasing over time with regard to their EC scores. This part of the analysis was conducted with the help of Jessica Young (statistics, University of Notre Dame), who confirmed that fitting a linear regression model to this specific data would be inappropriate.
44. Given the scale of the data (550,869 rows based on 550,869 unique edges based on the data) and the complexity of the regression model (more than a dozen predictor variables), I again required the assistance of Jessica Young. We have produced a full write-up of the model

and output, which is available on request. Here I provide a brief summary. The model was specified as: connections_books ~ BothBlack + BothWhite + BothMale + BothFemale + ACAD_Match + BLACK_Match + GENRE_Match + LIT_Match + MISC_Match + TRADE_Match + P_0_Match + P_1_Match + P_2_Match + P_3_Match + P_4_Match + P_5_Match + P_6_Match + P_7_Match + P_8_Match + P_10_Match. A Poisson regression model was used. The first set of variables indicate racial and gender variables and whether they matched; the next set represents the type of journals (e.g., ACAD for academic) being connected and whether they match, and the final variables indicate whether the publisher type (e.g., P_1 for mainstream publishers) for the novels matched. Thus, we control for gender, race, journal type, and publisher type. The model predicts, for each author, how many more or less connections, times the average, that author will have (connections_books). Significant coefficients are reported for the race variable in the visualization. We find no particularly meaningful patterns with the journal or publisher variables, but we do find an interesting pattern regarding gender: values for male authors are decreasing, while values for female authors are increasing over time, essentially switching places by the 1991 to 1995 time interval. These results are outside the bounds of this chapter but warrant further analysis. Further documentation can be produced on request.

45. More technical readers may wish to have more information about the model, such as the baseline number of connections per year, to evaluate its robustness. This documentation can be provided upon request.

46. The Networkx package in Python implements the popular Louvain algorithm for community detection. The full documentation is here: https://media.readthedocs.org/pdf/python-louvain/latest/python-louvain.pdf.

    The technical description of the Louvain algorithm on Wikipedia is generally accurate, and I quote it here: "The inspiration for this method of community detection is the optimization of Modularity as the algorithm progresses. Modularity is a scale value between –1 and 1 that measures the density of edges inside communities to edges outside communities. Optimizing this value theoretically results in the best possible grouping of the nodes of a given network, however going through all possible iterations of the nodes into groups is impractical so heuristic algorithms are used. In the Louvain Method of community detection, first small communities are found by optimizing modularity locally on all nodes, then each small community is grouped into one node and the first step is repeated." A formal paper that validates the method is Vincent D. Blondel, Jean-Loup Guillaume, Renaud Lambiotte, and Etienne Lefebvre, "Fast Unfolding of Communities in Large Networks," *Journal of Statistical Mechanics: Theory and Experiment*, October 2008.

47. I fit a multinomial logistic regression model to the data in which the predictor variables were RACE and GENDER as categorical variables (RACE as white, black, and POC; GENDER as male and female), and the response variable was the community identified (0, 1, or 2). The model indicates that authors identified as POC have a greater odds of appearing in community 2 (odds ratio 3.2, 95 percent confidence intervals 1.5, 6.8), holding community 1 as the baseline, when compared to authors identified as white, at a statistically significant level ($p < 0.01$). This test was done under the supervision of Dr. Jose Correa, lecturer in statistics at McGill University. Code and data can be provided upon request.

48. Interested readers can review the relevant output as provided by the author as part of the project's release. In the end, the recognition of some authors as "elite" or more "elite" than

others is highly subjective. Here, I simply appeal to a perceived consensus held by current literary critics and scholars; for example, that Morrison represents perhaps the most celebrated and "elite" of black authors and, similarly, that authors like Philip Roth, John Updike, and Joyce Carol Oates represent their white counterparts.

49. Quoted in Melanie McAlister, "(Mis)reading the *Joy Luck Club*," *Asian American: Journal of Culture and the Arts* 1 (1992): 2. This essay also has an excellent account of the overall media reception of Tan's novel.
50. Sau-ling Wong, "'Sugar Sisterhood': Situating the Amy Tan Phenomenon," in *Amy Tan's The Joy Luck Club*, ed. Harold Bloom (Philadelphia: Chelsea House, 2002), 86.
51. McAlister, "(Mis)reading the *Joy Luck Club*," 6.
52. Wong, "'Sugar Sisterhood,'" 93.
53. McAlister, "(Mis)reading the *Joy Luck Club*," 14.
54. A good, relatively recent example is Tara Fickle, "American Rules and Chinese Faces: The Games of Amy Tan's *The Joy Luck Club*," *MELUS* 39, no. 3 (Fall 2014).
55. See, for example, Patricia Chu, *Assimilating Asians: Gendered Strategies of Authorship in Asian America* (Durham, NC: Duke University Press, 2000), 158.
56. See, for example, McAlister, "(Mis)reading the *Joy Luck Club*."
57. Quoted in Lisa Dunick, "The Silencing Effect of Canonicity: Authorship and the Written Word in Amy Tan's Novels," *Melus* 31, no. 2 (Summer 2006): 17.
58. McAlister, "(Mis)reading the *Joy Luck Club*," 7, 9.
59. Amy Tan, *The Joy Luck Club* (New York: Random House, 1989), 312.
60. Merve Emre, *Paraliterary: The Making of Bad Readers in Postwar America* (Chicago: University of Chicago Press, 2018).
61. Orville Schell, review of *The Joy Luck Club*, *New York Times*, March 19, 1989.
62. Looking at all individual titles and computing eigencentrality vector scores for each of them, *Necessary Roughness* ranks 67 out of 75 total novels by POC authors.

3. RECOGNITION: LITERARY DISTINCTION AND BLACKNESS

1. See Andreas Huyssen, *After the Great Divide: Modernism, Mass Culture, Postmodernism* (Bloomington: Indiana University Press, 1986); and Paul DiMaggio, "Classification in Art," *American Sociological Review* 51, no. 4 (August 1987): 440–55.
2. I've already cited several scholars who have asserted these positions in my introduction.
3. For more on this scandal, see James English, *The Economy of Prestige: Prizes, Awards, and the Circulation of Cultural Value* (Cambridge, MA: Harvard University Press, 2005), 152.
4. Darryl Dickson-Carr, introduction to *The Columbia Guide to Contemporary African American Fiction* (New York: Columbia University Press, 2005), 1.
5. Here I am thinking both of foundational studies in the field like Houston Baker Jr., *Blues, Ideology, and Afro-American Literature: A Vernacular Theory* (Chicago: University of Chicago Press, 1987); and more recent outstanding works in the field, like Salamishah Tillet, *Sites of Slavery: Citizenship and Racial Democracy in the Post-Civil Rights Imagination* (Durham, NC: Duke University Press, 2012).
6. See, for example, Graham Huggan, "Prizing 'Otherness': A Short History of the Booker," *Studies in the Novel* 29, no. 3 (Fall 1997): 412–33.

7. In *The Economy of Prestige*, James English argues for the "rising prestige of African American literature" (245).
8. For example, this is the approach taken by John Unsworth in constructing a definitive "Bestseller Database" for American fiction. See his curated website for more information: https://bestsellers.lib.virginia.edu/.
9. Two scholars researched each novelist and only identified the gender and/or race of that author if definitive evidence of an identification was found either in the scholarship or through self-declaration. If evidence could not be found or the two researchers could not agree, the author remained untagged by race or gender.
10. I drew a random sample of 224 texts from the original list (more than 33 percent) written by 118 unique individual authors, based upon which texts I was able to acquire digital copies of. This subcorpus of bestselling American novels constitutes the corpus to be text-mined in the next steps of this chapter. The demographic distribution of this sample is commensurable with the master corpus. In terms of gender: 71 percent male, 29 percent female; and race: 97 percent white, 1 percent black, and 2 percent POC. The distribution of texts over time is also commensurable.
11. A full list of the prizes used for this study can be provided on request.
12. I created a random sample of 225 texts written (I chose this sample value to be roughly equivalent with the size of our bestseller corpus) by 164 unique individual authors from this original list of prizewinning American novels (more than 40 percent of that total), which I was able to get digital copies of. The demographic distribution of this corpus is commensurable with the original corpus. By gender: 71 percent male, 29 percent female; by race: 91 percent white, 6 percent black, and 3 percent POC. And the distribution of texts over time is also basically the same.
13. Specifically, I identified the 100 most commonly held novels by black authors published between 1950 and 2000 in libraries based on WorldCat records, of which 67 I was able to acquire digital copies of. I added these 67 texts to our 162 texts to create a final corpus of 229 texts written by 165 unique individual authors (nearly the same exact size as our American bestseller and prizewinning corpora), constituting our "novels by black authors" corpus. The distribution of novels over time is commensurable with that of bestseller and prizewinning corpora. The gender distribution of this corpus is less skewed toward men than in our other two corpora (60 percent male, 40 percent female), yet it still presents a proportion that is directionally comparable. Overall, this corpus of novels includes a mixture of canonical and noncanonical literary texts, such as *Beloved*, by Toni Morrison; *Black Betty*, by Walter Mosley; and *True American*, by Melvin Van Peebles.
14. See Pierre Bourdieu, *The Rules of Art* (Palo Alto, CA: Stanford University Press, 1996), 248, 158.
15. Here we can think of Janice Radway's canonical *Reading the Romance: Women, Patriarchy, and Popular Literature* (Chapel Hill: University of North Carolina Press, 1991) or, more recently, in the context of quantitative literary criticism, Andrew Piper and Eva Portelance, "How Cultural Capital Works: Prizewinning Novels, Bestsellers, and the Time of Reading," *Post45: Peer Reviewed*, May 10, 2016.
16. See, for example, Ted Underwood, *Distant Horizons* (Chicago: University of Chicago Press, 2019). Also see Katherine Bode, *A World of Fiction: Digital Collections and the Future of Literary History* (Ann Arbor: University of Michigan Press, 2018).

17. Underwood, *Distant Horizons*, 65.
18. This is an argument I develop further in two coauthored methodological pieces: Richard Jean So, Hoyt Long, and Yuancheng Zhu, "Race, Writing, and Computation: Racial Difference and the U.S. Novel, 1880–2000," *Journal of Cultural Analytics* (January 11, 2019); and Richard Jean So and Edwin Roland, "Race and Distant Reading," *PMLA* 135, no. 1 (January 2020).
19. For this feature, I specifically track part-of-speech *bigrams* rather than *unigrams*. That means that rather than simply identify and record each single word's syntactical identity (such as: "dog" will be identified as NOUN), I identify and record pairs of words and their syntactical identity (such as: "dog ran" will be NOUN-VERB). I did this because after a great deal of data exploration and testing, I found that syntactical bigrams rather than single unigrams encode a greater deal of information related to the syntactical ambitions of a text. Unigrams were too coarse.
20. Here follows a more technical discussion of feature selection: these novels were transformed into three types of feature sets: *term frequency*, *Part-of-Speech bigram frequency*, *style*, and our so-called *narrative-feature frequency*. These features were produced thanks to the BookNLP pipeline, developed and distributed by David Bamman. Term frequencies were tabulated from lower-cased entries in the pipeline's "originalWord" output. Although stopwords are often removed at this stage, I included them in the model, since they are understood to mark genre and authorial style. Part-of-Speech tags were tabulated from the pipeline's "pos" output, which reports tags in the Penn Treebank format and relies on the Stanford POS tagger. These were then counted as bigrams of consecutive tags within sentence boundaries. Narrative features included tabulated frequencies of NER and Super Sense tags, from the "ner" and "sst" output columns. This pipeline uses the Stanford NER tagger and Wordnet Super Sense Tagger (SST). For example, these tag references to any PERSON or LOCATION and OBJECT or ACTION in the novel. In addition to these, I also counted the share of the text that consists of dialogue (from the "inQuotation" output), the share of the text that consists of character mentions (i.e., total character space; from the "characterId" output), and the number of unique characters normalized by text length (also from the "characterId" output). Finally, for the "style" features, I computed the following measurements for each text: type token ratio, conditional entropy, average sentence length, Yule's K, and Guiraud's Constant. Each of these values help measure the amount of lexical complexity in a text.
21. Here I provide some more technical details about the implementation of classification: my statistical model relies on logistic regression for its binary classification. Specifically, I used the implementation made available in the *scikit-learn* package for Python. To ensure the model's generalizability, I employed L1-regularization, which selects a small number of features to use for its predictions. Cross-validation with ten folds (k = 10) was used to assess and validate the predictive performance of the model. The accuracy scores I report in the body of the text represent the average of the ten scores. In the next section, I refer to "significant features"—the significant features to which we refer have nonzero weights in the model and pass a z-test, indicating that they have different mean values among the types of novels being compared. In this case and all others where significance is tested, I employ a 95 percent confidence threshold. However, in all cases, that threshold is adjusted by the conservative Bonferroni correction. In effect, we require $p = 0.05$ / [*# of observations*]. All

features were normalized and turned into standard units to ensure comparability across features across all texts and across all categories of texts.

22. Here and elsewhere in this chapter, I report simple accuracy scores (number of correctly classified divided by the total number of classified texts) rather than AUC, F-1, or other common types of accuracy scores reported by data scientists and social scientists in order to maximize the legibility of the results to my primary intended audience—literary scholars—who often do not have existing literacy in these types of metrics. I did not want to get bogged down in explaining these metrics in the flow of my argument.

23. The probability that a text belongs to a given category is a native feature of logistic regression, which previous computational literary scholarship has embraced and which I emphasize here. Each text was assigned its probability through leave-one-out cross validation, where each text is set aside during training and afterward receives predictions. Thus, each text has a probability value for belonging to class 0 and class 1 (e.g., prizewinner versus novels by black authors, etc.). I then simply plotted these values over time where the y-axis is the probability score and the x-axis time by year.

24. It is worth acknowledging that feature selection is based entirely on the researcher's subjective belief in what features are worth including and are significant; I have done this selection, however, with regard to the scholarship, what literary scholars have identified as important to understanding what makes different genres of writing distinct from one another, particularly novels by black authors.

25. Charles Kadushin, Lewis A. Coser, and Walter W. Powell, *The Culture and Commerce of Publishing* (Chicago: University of Chicago Press, 1985), 30.

26. Thomas Whiteside, *The Blockbuster Complex: Conglomerates, Book Publishing, and Show Business* (Middletown, CT: Wesleyan University Press, 1981).

27. John Sutherland, *Bestsellers: Fiction of the 1970s* (London: Routledge, 1981), 34.

28. Elizabeth Long, *The American Dream and the Popular Novel* (London: Routledge, 1985), 45.

29. Gordon Hutner, *What America Read: Taste, Class, and the Novel, 1920–1960* (Chapel Hill: University of North Carolina Press, 2009), 4.

30. For example, see Hutner, *What America Read*, 271.

31. Henry Louis Gates Jr., *The Signifying Monkey: A Theory of African-American Literary Criticism* (Oxford: Oxford University Press, 1988); and Houston Baker Jr., *Blues, Ideology, and Afro-American Literature: A Vernacular Theory* (Chicago: University of Chicago Press, 1984).

32. Mae Henderson, "Speaking in Tongues: Dialogics and Dialectics and the Black Woman Writer's Literary Tradition," in *Changing Our Own Words*, ed. Cheryl Wall (New Brunswick, NJ: Rutgers University Press, 1989), 5.

33. Quoted in Bernard Bell, *The Contemporary African American Novel* (Amherst: University of Massachusetts Press, 2004), 198.

34. Quoted in Danille K. Taylor-Guthrie, *Conversations with Toni Morrison* (Oxford: University Press of Mississippi, 1994), 166.

35. This information was reported in Michael Pakenham, "Judith Krantz, a Phenomenon, with Everything Hanging Out," *Baltimore Sun*, May 28, 2000.

36. Judith Krantz, *Scruples* (New York: Random House, 1978), 328.

37. The National Book Award was first created in 1936, and it gave a series of awards to works of fiction under various prize names until 1941 but was only reconstituted in its modern form in 1950.

38. See English, *The Economy of Prestige*, 152, for a good account of this scandal.
39. English, *The Economy of Prestige*, 245.
40. The data was highly skewed toward values of 1 or near 1, so I had to use a one-inflated beta regression to fit a model to the data. The model indicates that there is no effect; there is no significant association between our year variable and our predicted probability value (p-value = 0.9).
41. These two terms appear on the longer list of most distinctive features.
42. I should note that this result was noisier than compared to the prominence of adverbs as a distinctive feature for bestsellers versus novels by black authors. The adverb bigram feature is ranked less highly than as it appears for bestsellers. Further, other types of syntactical bigrams, such as verbs, appear as distinctive for prizewinners versus novels by black authors. However, looking at the bag-of-words diction features makes me confident that adverbs represent a distinctive feature for prizewinners versus novels by black authors, even if the machine does not explicitly identify adverb-based bigrams as distinctive in terms of the POS-tag features inputted into the model. The most highly ranked diction features tend to be adverbs, such as "enormous" and "delicately."
43. In other words, these are examples of texts that the model predicts to belong to the category of prizewinner with 99.9 percent certainty.
44. See, for example, Catherine Jurca, *White Diaspora: The Suburb and the Twentieth-Century Novel* (Princeton, NJ: Princeton University Press, 2001). Also consider this, from Percival Everett: "But certainly John Updike's work is influenced by his being white in America, but we never really discuss that. I think readers black and white are sophisticated enough to be engaged by a range of black experience, informed by economic situation . . . just as one accepts a range of so-called white experience." Quoted in Bell, *The Contemporary African American Novel*, 327.
45. John Updike, *Rabbit Is Rich* (New York: Random House, 1981), 186.
46. See Jurca, introduction, in particular.
47. For example, see Piper and Portelance, "How Cultural Capital Works."
48. More precisely, a text was identified as "misclassified" if the machine predicted its class to be different than what the text was originally labeled as: thus, for example, we labeled *Parable of the Sower* as a "novel by a black author" based on the existing scholarship, but the machine predicted it to belong to either the prizewinner and/or bestseller class (i.e., assigned a probability score greater than 0.5), and, thus, the text has been "misclassified" by the machine.
49. Specifically, our model misclassifies *Clay's Ark* as a prizewinning novel when prizewinners are classified against novels by black authors; it correctly classifies *Parable of the Sower* but shows a degree of uncertainty; it makes its correct prediction with only a 70 percent predicted probability, thus indicating that the novel creates a certain degree of confusion for the machine. Our model misclassifies *Parable of the Sower* when bestsellers are classified against novels by black authors, with a near 99 percent predicted probability. Finally, when we classify novels by black authors against a combined bestseller/prizewinner corpus, the machine misclassifies both *Clay's Ark* and *Parable of the Sower*. All of the other novels by Butler in our corpus (including *Patternmaster*, *Kindred*, *Imago*, and several others), however, are correctly classified with each pairwise classificatory scheme.
50. Quoted in Phoenix Alexander, "Octavia E. Butler and Black Women's Archives at the End of the World," *Science Fiction Studies* 46 (2019): 342.

51. Quoted in Lincoln Michel, "Read Octavia E. Butler's Inspiring Message to Herself," *Electronic Literature*, February 2, 2016.
52. Mark Dery, "Black to the Future: Interviews with Samuel R. Delany, Greg Tate, and Tricia Rose," in *Flame Wars: The Discourse of Cyberculture*, ed. Mark Dery (Durham, NC: Duke University Press, 1994).
53. Kodwo Eshun, "Further Considerations on Afro-Futurism," *CR: The New Centennial Review* 3, no. 2 (Summer 2003): 293.
54. To reiterate, to turn this classification problem into a binary case, I classified novels by black authors against a combined corpus of bestsellers and prizewinners where I simply merged those two corpora into a single corpus. All features were normalized and turned into standard units to ensure comparability across features across all texts and across all categories of texts. I then look specifically at the most distinctive features for *Parable of the Sower*, removing any features that do not pass a test of significance, as described in note 21, and ranked by their feature weight as reported by the model.
55. Octavia Butler, *Parable of the Sower* (New York: Seven Stories, 2017), 241 (my emphasis).
56. Eshun, "Further Considerations on Afro-Futurism," 299.
57. Phillip Brian Harper, *Abstractionist Aesthetics: Artistic Form and Social Critique in African American Culture* (New York: New York University Press, 2015), 159.
58. Butler, *Parable of the Sower*, 328 (my emphasis).
59. See, for example, Mark A. Tabone, "Rethinking *Paradise*: Toni Morrison and Utopia at the Millennium," *African American Review* 49, no. 2 (Summer 2016).
60. Tabone makes the point that both writers, especially *Paradise* and Butler's *Parable* books, are interested in this shared theme of "utopia."
61. I use the same method as described in footnote 54 but applied now to *Paradise*. Syntactical features for adverbs and modal verbs are positive, as with *Parable of the Sower*.
62. Based on my earlier classifications and feature reports, the word "neighborhood" is the highest-ranked feature in terms of feature importance for *Parable of the Sower* and the fiftieth most important for *Paradise*.
63. Alexander, "Octavia E. Butler and Black Women's Archives at the End of the World."

4. CONSECRATION: THE CANON AND RACIAL INEQUALITY

1. See, for example, Elaine Showalter, *A Literature of Their Own: British Women Novelists from Brontë to Lessing* (Princeton, NJ: Princeton University Press, 1977); Adrienne Munich, "Notorious Signs, Feminist Criticism, and Literary Tradition," in *Making a Difference: Feminist Literary Criticism*, ed. Gayle Greene and Coppélia Kahn (London: Methuen, 1985); and Henry Louis Gates Jr. and Kwame Anthony Appiah, eds., *"Race," Writing, and Difference* (Chicago: University of Chicago Press, 1986), which includes essays by Gates and Baker.
2. See Leslie Fiedler and Houston Baker Jr., eds., *English Literature: Opening Up the Canon* (Baltimore, MD: Johns Hopkins University Press, 1981); and David Palumbo-Liu, introduction to *The Ethnic Canon*, ed. Palumbo-Liu (Minneapolis: University of Minnesota Press, 1995), 1.
3. Henry Louis Gates Jr., *Loose Canons: Notes on the Culture Wars* (Oxford: Oxford University Press, 1992), 33. This is Gates's language.

4. Michael Bérubé, "*Canons and Context* in Context," *American Literary History* 20, no. 3 (Fall 2008): 459.
5. See John Guillory, *Cultural Capital: The Problem of Literary Canon Formation* (Chicago: University of Chicago Press, 1993).
6. Cornel West, "Minority Discourse and the Pitfalls of Canon Formation," *Yale Journal of Criticism* 1, no. 1 (1987): 198.
7. Guillory, *Cultural Capital*, 339.
8. In terms of raw counts, we counted 37 identified white prose/fiction writers, 13 black or African American prose/fiction writers, and 11 "person of color" prose/fiction writers. *The Norton Anthology of American Literature*, ed. Robert Levine, 9th ed., vol. 2 (New York: Norton, 2016). These numbers were arrived at by simple counting (and then division). Authors were identified by race and gender based on the scholarship, using the same methods of research and validation described in my previous chapters.
9. *The Norton Anthology of American Literature*, ed. Gottesman et al. (New York: Norton, 1979).
10. We counted 39 identified white prose/fiction writers, 9 black prose/fiction writers, and 0 POC prose/fiction writers.
11. This data was procured through a request made to the JSTOR Data for Research service in 2017, under the aegis of the McGill Text Lab's legal agreement with JSTOR (managed by the lab's director, Andrew Piper). We requested all articles published by journals assigned to their "literary studies" category between 1950 and 2016. They delivered metadata and n-gram (up to 3-gram) text files for 83,255 articles, spanning this period. For the purpose of this chapter, I decided to only focus on journal articles published from 1950 to 2010. After this temporal filtering and removing empty files from the JSTOR dataset, I was left with 63,397 essays total. This will be the corpus I use for all statistical and text-mining analysis, moving forward.
12. See Amy Earhart, *Traces of the Old, Uses of the New: The Emergence of Digital Literary Studies* (Ann Arbor: University of Michigan Press, 2015).
13. A few examples include Andrew Goldstone and Ted Underwood, "The Quiet Transformations of Literary Studies: What Thirteen Thousand Scholars Could Tell Us," *New Literary History* 45, no. 3 (Summer 2014); Lisa M. Rhody, "Topic Modeling and Figurative Language," *Journal of Digital Humanities* 2, no. 1 (Winter 2012); Matthew L. Jockers and David Mimno, "Significant Themes in 19th-Century Literature," *Poetics* 41, no. 6 (2013); and Timothy Tangherlini and Peter Leonard, "Trawling in the Sea of the Great Unread: Sub-Corpus Topic Modeling and Humanities Research," *Poetics* 41, no. 6 (2013).
14. See Goldstone and Underwood, "The Quiet Transformations of Literary Studies," 378.
15. Benjamin Schmidt, "Words Alone: Dismantling Topic Models in the Humanities," *Journal of Digital Humanities* 2, no. 1 (Winter 2012).
16. Andrew Piper, *Enumerations: Data and Literary Study* (Chicago: University of Chicago Press, 2018), 70.
17. Jonathan Culler, *Framing the Sign: Criticism and Its Institutions*. (Norman: University of Oklahoma Press, 1988), 32–33.
18. Houston A. Baker Jr., "Generational Shifts and the Recent Criticism of Afro-American Literature," *Black American Literature Forum* 15, no. 1 (Spring 1981): 16.
19. See Henry Louis Gates Jr., "Editor's Introduction: Writing 'Race' and the Difference It Makes," *Critical Inquiry* 12, no. 1 (Autumn 1985).

20. See Barbara Christian, "The Race for Theory," *Feminist Studies* 14, no. 1 (Spring 1988).
21. Joyce A. Joyce, "'Who the Cap Fit': Unconsciousness and Unconscionableness in the Criticism of Houston A. Baker, Jr., and Henry Louis Gates, Jr.," *New Literary History* 18, no. 2 (Winter 1987): 378.
22. Henry Louis Gates Jr., "'What's Love Got to Do with It?': Critical Theory, Integrity, and the Black Idiom," *New Literary History* 18, no. 2 (Winter 1987): 352.
23. Elizabeth Abel, "Black Writing, White Reading: Race and the Politics of Feminist Interpretation," *Critical Inquiry* 19, no. 3 (Spring 1993): 476.
24. I used Scikit Learn's implementation of the Latent Dirichlet Allocation topic modeling algorithm via Python. This version implements the popular online variational Bayes algorithm as its learning method. The number of topics was chosen semiarbitrarily; the results from selecting 50 topics proved most coherent and convincing to the eye, based on scholarly expertise. Other important parameters selected were 50 for the maximum number of iterations (again chosen semiarbitrarily, but well above the often-used threshold of 10 to increase accuracy) and 50 for learning offset. Last, simple counts were employed via Scikit Learn's CountVectorizer function. See the full Scikit Learn documentation for more information: https://scikit-learn.org/stable/modules/generated/sklearn.decomposition.LatentDirichletAllocation.htm. I also need to describe the preprocessing of the data: in order to maximize the coherence of the topics and avoid the overdetermination of topics by stopwords, proper names, and so forth, I reduced each text to words that belong to a curated list of 3,000 words. This list was developed by Andrew Piper and I, after a significant amount of trial and error, to identify a finite list of words that best represented the substantive terms in the corpus and that thus, again, would produce the most coherent and distinctive topics.
25. The number of words (25) chosen to represent "topics" was selected semiarbitrarily. Fewer than 25 failed to produce a comprehensive and substantial version of the topics, while more produced a too diffused and incoherent version, based on domain expertise. Also, it must be noted here that because the modeling algorithm is probabilistic, the results are slightly different with each run; that is, the "top 25 constitutive words" may be different each time the model is run. The model does not provide stable results. However, at the scale of more than 60,000 documents, I have found that the results are relatively stable, although I have not been able to quantify this finding yet.
26. First, I identified all articles in the corpus, by year, that express the "race" topic at or above a threshold of 0.10 (10%) based on the model's output, which reports topic distributions per document. Then I simply computed the percentage of articles that express that topic at that threshold by year and plotted those values from 1950 to 2010.
27. I computed the Pearson correlation coefficient value for "Theory" and "Race" topics and found they were positively correlated (r = 0.963).
28. Gates, *Loose Canons*, 91. Also see Gates, "To Be Raped, Bred, or Abused," *New York Times*, November 22, 1987.
29. See chapter 3, "The Data of Distinction" section.
30. See the arguments and data presented in chapters 1 and 3.
31. Here I am thinking of Gayatri Spivak, "Three Women's Texts and a Critique of Imperialism," *Critical Inquiry* 12, no. 1 (Autumn 1985); and Gates's editorial work on the Harriet Jacobs text.

32. Kenneth Warren, *What Was African American Literature?* (Cambridge, MA: Harvard University Press, 2011), 65.
33. I simply sorted all of the articles in the corpus based on their "race" and "theory" topic shares.
34. Naomi Pabst, "Blackness/Mixedness: Contestations Over Crossing Signs," *Cultural Critique* 54 (Spring 2003): 179.
35. Based upon computing Pearson correlation coefficient scores for "Race" and "Cultural Studies" topics and comparing them to the scores for "Theory," "Gender," and "Colonialism" topics.
36. See, for example, Stuart Hall, *Cultural Studies 1983: A Theoretical History* (Durham, NC: Duke University Press, 2016), for a good overview of the field from the viewpoint of the 1980s. See Graeme Turner, *British Cultural Studies* (London: Routledge, 2002) for a more recent history of the field, particularly its British origins and instantiation. See John Hartley and Roberta E. Pearson, eds., with Eva Vieth, *American Cultural Studies: A Reader* (Oxford: Oxford University Press, 2000) for an account of the field's movement into the U.S. academy.
37. Carby earned her PhD at Birmingham; Denning earned his MA at Birmingham before completing his PhD at Yale University.
38. Quoted in Hazel V. Carby, "Becoming Modern Racialized Subjects: Detours Through Our Pasts to Produce Ourselves Anew," *Cultural Studies* 23 (2009): 626.
39. Stuart Hall, "Cultural Studies and Its Theoretical Legacies," in *Cultural Studies*, ed. Lawrence Grossberg, Cary Nelson, and Paula Treichler (New York: Routledge, 1992), 285.
40. I simply identified all of the articles in the corpus that express the race topic above the 0.10 threshold and computed the rate by which the word "inequality" appears in the articles by year as a function of all of the words that appear in the articles. The 0.10 threshold was chosen semiarbitrarily; I determined that this rate represented a nontrivial occurrence of a topic in a document after inspecting a number of documents that had a rate below or above this rate. For this analysis, I used the original 1-gram corpus of texts provided by JSTOR rather than my curated corpus that only includes words that belong to a list of 3,000 words.
41. I fit a negative binomial regression model to the data using the original count data, with the total number of words as an offset. The model indicates no effect; there is no association between year and the number of times that the word "inequality" appears in the corpus (p-value = 0.32).
42. First, I kept only the articles in the corpus that express the race topic above the 0.10 threshold. Then, I split that corpus into two sub-corpora—those published before and after 1994, the year of interest. Then I implemented a standard Mann-Whitney U test in Python (implementing the mannwhitneyu function) to identify which terms are most distinctive of each class (pre and post 1994) based on their computed "rho values." Ted Underwood has provided a good rationale for using Mann-Whitney for Most Distinctive Words tests for literary texts, rather than Dunning's Log-Likelihood or any other popular test. See https://tedunderwood.com/2011/11/09/identifying-the-terms-that-characterize-an-author-or-genre-why-dunnings-may-not-be-the-best-method/. See also Adam Kilgarriff, "Comparing Corpora," *International Journal of Corpus Linguistics* 6, no. 1 (2001): 97–133, which Underwood draws from.
43. Of course, one can point to Hall's own cultural studies textbook, *Representation: Cultural Representations and Signifying Practices* (London, Sage: 1997), which helped to articulate the

analysis of the "circuit of culture" as a main feature of cultural studies, and the wealth of scholarship that would then take up his approach.

44. I make an important distinction here. My point is limited to the uptake of cultural studies within literary studies and the analysis of race; I necessarily bracket out the uptake in fields like sociology or the emerging autonomous discipline of "cultural studies" itself (particularly as it developed in the United Kingdom), where the interest in the demographics of cultural production obviously was taken on more explicitly and directly.

45. Stuart Hall, "New Ethnicities," in *Black Film, British Cinema*, ed. K. Mercer (London: Institute of Contemporary Arts, 1988), 28.

46. One might worry that this result is simply an artifact of the data; however, I can confirm that the publication year (as well as footnotes that might also contain publication dates) of each essay is removed from the text that has been text mined, so what we are not seeing is merely an artifact of the metadata or footnotes encoded in the text data. When terms like "1993" and "1971" appear in texts, it is because the author or authors refer to a specific temporality and date in their essay, and as I argue here, talking about the decade or specific year in which one is writing is more distinctive in the post-1994 period than it is for the pre-1994 period. However, further analysis has not revealed any further strong patterns. For example, identifying the most common terms that tend to co-occur with "1993" and "1994" reveals no apparent signal.

47. I extracted this information in the following way. First, I restricted my focus to American prose because the research of this book is focused on U.S. fiction and I want my analysis of the canon to be commensurable with this book's previous analysis; also, much of the canon debates focused on U.S. literature and the novel in particular, and this focus allows a relatively coherent frame of analysis. Next, I compiled a list of all works of U.S. prose mentioned in *The Norton Anthology of American Literature* and *The Heath Anthology of American Literature*. For this, I used the most recent versions of these two texts: the 8th edition (New York: Norton, 2011) of the *Norton* and the 2013 version of the *Heath* (Boston: Wadsworth, 2013). This would cover the most-discussed works of U.S. fiction in the scholarship. Last, I counted the number times each work appeared in our JSTOR corpus, tallied the most-mentioned works of U.S. fiction, chose a sample of five of the top twenty, and plotted their values over time. As a final point: pattern matching for articles that discuss the titles in our *Norton* and *Heath* lists was rigorous. An article had to contain *both* the author's full name and the full title of the text; only then was a "match" reported. For example, an article had to contain both "Herman Melville" and "Moby-Dick" for that text to count as a match. The JSTOR data provides trigram versions of the texts, and matching was done with those files. For titles with greater than trigram-length titles, such as "The Turn of the Screw," the most distinctive parts of the title (in this case, "Turn of the") was searched for as the text's "title." Still, errors will exist. For example, it is possible that an essay will discuss an author such as "Toni Morrison" and refer to a topic or object such as "beloved" without discussing the text itself. Such errors are likely very rare, though.

48. I fit linear regression models to all six texts and found that *Sula* and *Beloved* are the only ones of this sample of most-cited works statistically increasing ($p < 0.01$).

49. Toni Morrison, *Beloved: A Novel* (New York: Vintage, 2004), n.p.

50. Kimberly Chabot Davis, "'Postmodern Blackness': Toni Morrison's Beloved and the End of History," *Twentieth Century Literature* 44, no. 2 (Summer 1998): 248.

51. Linda Krumholz, "The Ghosts of Slavery: Historical Recovery in Toni Morrison's *Beloved*," *African American Review* 26, no. 3 (Autumn 1992): 406.
52. Quoted in Valerie Smith, *Toni Morrison: Writing the Moral Imagination* (New York: Wiley-Blackwell, 2012), 5.
53. Caroline Rody, "Toni Morrison's *Beloved*: History, 'Rememory,' and a 'Clamor for a Kiss,'?" *American Literary History* 7, no. 1 (Spring 1995): 98.
54. Cynthia Dobbs, "Toni Morrison's *Beloved*: Bodies Returned, Modernism Revisited," *African American Review* 32, no. 4 (Winter 1998): 565.
55. Krumholz, "The Ghosts of Slavery," 399.
56. Avery Gordon, *Ghostly Matters: Haunting and the Sociological Imagination* (Minneapolis: University of Minnesota Press, 2008), 189.
57. Smith, *Toni Morrison*, 3.
58. Judlyn Ryan, "Language and Narrative Technique in Toni Morrison's Novels," in *The Cambridge Companion to Toni Morrison*, ed. Justine Tally (Cambridge: University of Cambridge Press, 2007), 152.
59. For example, see Loïc Wacquant, "The New 'Peculiar Institution': On the Prison as Surrogate Ghetto," *Theoretical Criminology* 4, no. 3 (2000): 377–89.
60. See, for example, Dennis Childs, "You Ain't Seen Nothin' Yet: *Beloved*, the American Chain Gang, and the Middle Passage Remix," *American Quarterly* 61, no. 2 (2009): 271–97.
61. Morrison, *Beloved*, 212.
62. Morrison, *Beloved*, 212.
63. Stephen Best and Sharon Marcus, "Surface Reading: An Introduction," *Representations* 108, no. 1 (Fall 2009): 9.
64. Heather Love, "Close but Not Deep: Literary Ethics and the Descriptive Turn," *New Literary History* 41, no. 2 (Spring 2010): 386.
65. See Childs, "You Ain't Seen Nothin' Yet," 280.
66. Morrison, *Beloved*, 126.
67. A summary of recent research that reports these statistics can be found on Wikipedia at https://en.wikipedia.org/wiki/Incarceration_in_the_United_States.
68. For historical data, see Patrick A. Langan, "Race of Prisoners Admitted to State and Federal Institutions, 1926–1986," U.S. Department of Justice, May 1991. The percentage of blacks incarcerated in 1986 was 44 percent.
69. See Madhu Dubey, "The Politics of Genre in *Beloved*," *Novel: A Forum on Fiction* 32, no. 2 (Spring 1999): 187–206.
70. Morrison, *Beloved*, 245.
71. See, for example, Malin LaVon Walther's review essay of Toni Morrison scholarship: "And All of the Interests Are Vested: Canon-Building in Recent Morrison Criticism," *Modern Fiction Studies* 39, no. 3/4, (Fall/Winter 1993): 781–94.

CONCLUSION

1. Quoted in Jenny McGrath, "Barnes & Noble Used A.I. to Make Classic Books More Diverse. It Didn't Go Well," *Digital Trends*, February 6, 2020.
2. A point made on Twitter by Hanna Alkaf, quoted in McGrath, "Barnes & Noble Used A.I."

3. Quoted in McGrath, "Barnes & Noble Used A.I."
4. See, for example, Robyn McGee, "The Overwhelming Whiteness of the Publishing Industry," *Bitch Media*, January 27, 2016; and Laura McGrath, "Comping White," *Los Angeles Review of Books*, January 21, 2019.
5. See this book's introduction.
6. Tara McPherson, "Why Are the Digital Humanities So White?," in *Debates in the Digital Humanities* (Minneapolis: University of Minnesota Press, 2016).

INDEX

Adventures of Augie March, The (Bellow), 129
African Americans, 2, 159; authors, book sales, 4, 11, 109, 157; racism and, 91; stereotypes, 30–31, 48. *See also* slavery
Afrofuturism, 134, 139
Ahmed, Sara, 42, 43
Aiiieeeee!, 106
algorithms: "black character" vector with multidimensional scaling, *49*; classification, 113, 206n22; community detection, 96, *97*, 202n46; computational, 16, 181–82; Louvain, 202n46; multidimensional scaling, *48*, *49*, 196n71; of oppression, 16; skip-gram training, 195n68; topic modeling, 26, 149–51, *155*, 210n24; whiteness and, 63
Alkaf, Hanna, 214n2
All the Pretty Horses (McCarthy), 70
"All-White World of Children's Publishing, The" (Larrick), 33–34
American Academy of Arts and Letters, 86
American Journal of Education, 72
Another You (Beattie), 54
antiblack racism, 91
AO3, 24, 182
Appiah, Kwame Anthony, 153

artificial intelligence, 113, 181
Asian Americans, 4, 70, 73, 93, 145; fiction, 5, 102; as model minorities, 99
Atlantic, The, 73
authors, *81*, *97*; POC, 79, 92, 95–98, 145, 199n12; publication with reviews of two same-race, 93, *94*; race and most influential, 25. *See also* black authors; nonwhite authors; novelists; white authors
Avrett, Robert, 68
awards. *See* book prizes; prizewinners
Awkward, Michael, 154

bag of gold, 90–91
Baker, Houston, 152–53, 154, 159, 163
Baldwin, James, 5, 35, 97, 98, 99, 104
Bambara, Toni Cade, 1, 9, 10, 11, 29, 35, 37, 92, 157
Bamman, David, 207n21
Barabási, Albert-László, 76
Baraka, Amiri, 61
Barnes & Noble, 181–83
Beattie, Ann, 54
Beet Queen, The (Erdrich), 92
behavioral data, 76
Bellow, Saul, 70, 79–80, 119, 129

Beloved (Morrison), 76, 85, 109, 128, 134, 179; epigraph, 171–76; racial inequality and, 168–78, *170*
benign narrative, of inequality, 14
Bernstein, Bob, 35
Bertelsmann AG, 28
Best, Stephen, 175–76
bestsellers: book reviews and, 68; Bourdieu on, 112–13; distinctive features of, *121*; list, *New York Times*, 106, 110; list, *Publisher's Weekly*, *107*, 110, 139; with machine color line, reading, 122–31; promotion of, 8; Random House with racial identity of novelists and, 3, *4*; rationalization and, 10; rise of, 27, 28. *See also* literary distinction, blackness and
bias, in literary journals, 199n14
bigrams, 205nn20–21, 207n43
Black Arts Movement, 4, 5, 60, 61, 65, 105, 152
black authors, *84*, *119*, *120*, 192n28; African Americans and book sales, 4, 11, 109, 157; book reviews and, 69–70; as marketable, 32; novels by, 50; valorization of, 11, 82–83, 91–92; white and, 196n74
"black character" vector: by decade, *54*; eight novels semantically similar to, 58–59, *59*; Gensim word2vec embeddings model and similar terms to, *49*, *54*; racial inequality and, 56–57; semantic variance with white and, *56*
black fiction, 61, 91–92, 134
Black History Month, Barnes & Noble and, 181–82
#blacklivesmatter, 12
blackness, 13, 110. *See also* literary distinction, blackness and
"Blackness/Mixedness" (Pabst), 160–61, 163
Black Power, 140
black press, 83
black publishers, 33
black studies: critical theory and, 151–59, *155*, 157; humanism and, 20
Black Woman, The (Bambara), 157
Black World (literary magazine), 37–39
Blockbuster Complex, The (Whiteside), 28, 122

Bluest Eye, The (Morrison), 86, 157
Bode, Katherine, 19, 114
book discipline, 148
BookNLP pipeline, 207n21
book prizes, 86, 99; distinctive features of American novels winning, *121*; economics of, 109; prizewinners, 3, *4*, 86, 105, 108, 127; racial inequality and, 3. *See also* literary distinction
Book Review Index, 72, 74–75, *80*, *81*, *84*, 199nn14–15
book reviews: black authors and, 69–70; book sales and bestsellers, 68; *Company Man* and *Song of Solomon*, 84–92; *The Joy Luck Club*, 100–101; with networks of literary attention, 75–79; nonwhite authors and, 11; power of, 25, 78; race and, 67–72; racial inequality and, 2, 3, 11, 69–70; Random House with racial identity of novelists and, 3, *4*; *Song of Solomon*, 89; as system of influence, 25. *See also* multiculturalism, of 1 percent
book sales, 5, 113, 144, 146, 159, 178, 183; for authors, African American, 4, 11, 109, 157; book reviews and, 68; data, 192n13; racial inequality and, 3, 110; with white supremacy in children's literature, 34. *See also* bestsellers
Bourdieu, Pierre, 68, 107, 112–13
Bowker, R. R., 199n16
Boyd, Melba Joyce, 187n8
Bradley, David, 85
Broadside Press (Detroit), 7, 33, 66, 187n8
Butler, Octavia, 83, 92, 141, 207n50, 208n55; *Parable of the Sower* by, 116, 131–39, *135*; as prizewinner, 132–33

canon, 146; wars, 143, 147–51. *See also* racial inequality, canon and
Carby, Hazel, 17, 162–63, 167, 211n37
Carmichael, Stokely, 29
CARP (Combined Asian Resources Project), 4, 105
Carroll, Hamilton, 42
"Case for Reparations, The" (Coates), 187n2

Cerf, Bennett, 8, 27–28
Cheever, John, 129
Children's Book News, 72
children's literature, 8, 33–34, 103
Childs, Dennis, 176, 177
Chin, Frank, 97
Choi, Susan, 96, 97
Christian, Barbara, 30–31, 153, 154
Christian identity, 51–52
civil rights, 30, 33, 34, 56, 62, 86, 89
classification algorithm, 113, 206n22
Clay's Ark (Butler), 132, 133, 207n50
Clifton, Lucille, 34
Coates, Ta-Nehisi, 187n2
collocations approach, 43–45
Color Purple, The (Walker), 85
Columbia Guide to Contemporary African-American Fiction, The (Dickson-Carr), 4
Columbia University, 10
Columbia University Press, 189n34
Combined Asian Resources Project. *See* CARP
community detection, 96, 97, 202n46
Company Man (Wade): black women in, 89; book reviews and, 85, 91; narratological complexity and style of, 87–88, 89; social alienation and, 90; *Song of Solomon* versus, 84–92; starling in, 88, 89
computational algorithms, 16, 181–82
computational criticism, 20, 21
Confessions of Nat Turner, The (Styron), 70
conglomeration: corporatization and, 27, 28; engine of racial inequality, 7–11; print culture and rise of, 24
"coon," 43–45
corporatization, 8–9, 27–28, 68, 122
Coser, Lewis, 28–29, 31–32, 72, 85, 103
crime, race and, 13
Critical Inquiry (Gates), 153, 157
critical race studies, 17, 20, 48, 145–46, 152
critical theory, 148; black studies and, 151–59, *155*, 157; race and, 160
criticism: computational, 20, 21; quantitative, 18, 19
critique: cultural, 20, 160; power of, 13; racial, 16, 17

Culler, Jonathan, 152
cultural analytics, 17, 21, 114
cultural critique, 20, 160
Cultural Critique, 160
cultural identity, whiteness as, 42
cultural redlining, 2, 5–7, 23, 183, 185
cultural studies: 1983 and after, 159–68; race and theory topics as percentage of all topics, *162*; scholarly articles on race and, *160*
culture, 187n8; economics and, 161; inequality and, 189n33; postwar print, 9. *See also* print culture

data: behavioral, 76; book reviews as, 72–75, *74*, *75*; book sales, 192n13; of distinction, 110–12; metadata, most-reviewed novels, 70, 199n16; prizewinners, 107, *107*, *108*, 111; Random House, numbers and, 40–42, *41*, 194nn53–57; resistance to, 172; science, 17, 18, 20, 23, 184; Web of Science, 12, 188n22
Davis, Angela, 92, 161
Davis, Kimberly, 171–72
Davis, Ossie, 81
Dean's December, The (Bellow), 70
Delany, Samuel, 92, 112
DeLillo, Don, 98, 104
Denning, Michael, 162, 163, 211n37
Derrida, Jacques, 151, 156, 161
Dery, Mark, 134
"Diachronic Word Embeddings Reveal Statistical Laws of Semantic Change" (Hamilton, Leskovec, and Jurafsky), 196n75
Dickens, Charles, 18
Dickson-Carr, Darryl, 4, 106, 109
Didion, Joan, 98
discourse, 13
disease, racial identity and, 17–18
Donoghue, Frank, 67
Dreaming in Cuban (García), 92
Drifters, The (Michener), 59–60
Drue Heinz Literature Prize, 111
"Dry December" (Faulkner), 64
Dubey, Madhu, 178
Du Bois, W. E. B., 30, 31

218 INDEX

Dumas, Henry, 1, 22; Black Arts Movement and, 61, 65; legacy of, 65; patterns, breaking of, 24, 30, 60–65; scholarship on, 198n89; support for, 37–38; work and life of, 60
Dyer, Geoff, 42

Earhart, Amy, 148
economics, 18, 32, 59, 113, 154, 207n45; of American literature, 5; bag of gold and, 90–91; culture and, 161; Gini coefficient and, 82, 83, 201n23; inequality, 82; literary-prize, 109; mobility, upward, 123; opportunities and racial inequality, 14; race and, 138; redlining, 2, 6; social sciences and, 12, 14, 188n22; socioeconomic alienation, 90–91; valorization of, 90, 123
EC scores. *See* eigenvector centrality scores
eigenvector centrality (EC) scores, 79, *80–81*, 84, 86, 92, 102, 200n22, 201n42
Ellison, Ralph, 15, 29, 34, 60, 81, 127
Emre, Merve, 100
English, James, 127–28
Epstein, Jason, 7–8, 27, 31, 35–37
Erdrich, Louise, 92, 95, 102
Eshun, Kodwo, 134, 137
Essence, 72
eugenics, 16, 115
Everett, Percival, 207n45

Farrell, James T., 28
"Fate of Writing in America, The" (Farrell), 28
Faulkner, William, 8, 64, 111
Federal Housing Administration, 2
fiction, 4; Asian American, 5, 102; black, 61, 91–92, 134; science, 111, 115, 132–34, 137, 199n14; YA, 103; by year and most discussed works, *170*
Firth, John, 44
Fixer, The (Malamud), 122
Fools Die (Puzo), 122
Foucault, Michel, 13, 151, 156, 162

Four Walls Eight Windows, 133
Frankenberg, Ruth, 42–43, 45
fugitive science, 2020, 16–20
Fuller, Hoyt, 37–38

Gaines, Ernest, 85
Gallon, Kim, 21
Gatekeepers of Black Culture (D. F. Joyce), 187n8
Gates, Henry Louis, Jr., 11, 143, 152–54, 157–59, 161, 163, 168
gender: inequality, 41; of novelists with top 1 percent most reviewed titles, *74*; race and, *74*, *107*, 111, 200n16, 202n47, 204n9; Random House novels written by male versus female writers, 1950 to 2000, 41, *41*, 194nn55–56; white female authors, 41; white male authors, 2, 41, 107, 143
"Generational Shifts and the Recent Criticism of Afro-American Literature" (Baker), 152–53
genres: analysis, 54; role of, 52; "white character" vector by, *53*
Gensim word embeddings, *48*, *49*, *51*, *54*, 195n68, 196n72, 196n75
geometry, of whiteness, 42–45
Ghansah, Rachel Kaadzi, 192n15
Gini coefficient, 82, 83, 201n23
Glamour, 99
Golden Age of publishing, 27
Goldstone, Andrew, 150
Gordon, Mary, 79
Grafton, Sue, 69
Granovetter, Mark, 76
Graves, Robert, 28
Gravity's Rainbow (Pynchon), 70
Graywolf Press, 40, 66
"Great Change," in publishing, 27–30, 31
"Great Divide," 105, 106
Griswold, Wendy, 68–69
Grove Press, 40, 66
Grusky, David, 14
Guggenheim fellowship, 34
Guillory, John, 144, 145

INDEX 219

Haley, Alex, 32
Hall, Stuart, 17; cultural critique and, 20; cultural studies and, 161, 163–64, 167–68; with inequality, 13–14; quantification and, 19
Hamilton, W., 196n75
Hardwick, Elizabeth, 68, 69
Harper, Phillip Brian, 137–38
HarperCollins, 40, 102
Harper's Magazine, 68, 73
HarperTeen, 103
Hartman, Saidiya, 21
HathiTrust library, 42, 194n57
Heinemann, Larry, 127
Hemingway, Ernest, 127
Henderson, Mae, 124
Heuser, Ryan, 196n75, 197n80
Hill, Michael, 85
Hoggart, Richard, 161
HOLC. *See* Home Owners' Loan Corporation
Hollander, John, 68
Home Owners' Loan Corporation (HOLC), 2
homosexuality, 89–90, 112
Hugo Award, 111
humanism, 20, 55–56
Hurston, Zora Neale, 31
Hutner, Gordon, 123–24

identity: social, 41, 101, 112; valorization of Christian, 51–52; whiteness as cultural, 42. *See also* racial identity
I'll Take Manhattan (Krantz), 122
immigrants, 2, 5
Incidents in the Life of a Slave Girl (Jacobs), 158
Indignant Generation, The (Jackson), 192n28
inequality, 41, 82; as keyword, 11–16; literary analysis and, 189n33; literary marketplace as map of, 2; power and, 14–15, 40; race and, *165*; social sciences and, 14. *See also* racial inequality
Invisible Man (Ellison), 29, 34, 127

Jackson, Lawrence, 192n28
Jacobs, Harriet, 158
James, Angela, 17, 18
James, Henry, 143, 170, 171, 212n47
Jen, Gish, 97
Jews, 5, 81
Jihad Productions (Newark), 33
Johnson, Barbara, 153
Johnson, Charles, 83
Jones, Gayl, 1, 9, 10, 35, 39, 85, 92, 93
Jonoah and the Green Stone (Dumas): leverage and, 22, 65; Morrison and, 60, 61, 64; pattern-recognition analysis and, 2; racial abstraction and, 64; racial language in, 62–65; whiteness and, 63
journals, categories of, 148
Joyce, Donald Franklin, 32, 187n8
Joyce, James, 8, 28
Joyce, Joyce A., 153–54
Joy Luck Club, The (Tan): book reviews of, 100–101; revolution, 92–103; success of, 99
JSTOR scholar services, 26, 148–49, 151, 170, 209n11, 211n40, 212n47
Jurafsky, D., 196n75
Jurca, Catherine, 130

Kadushin, Charles, 32, 72, 85, 103
Kincaid, Jamaica, 83, 98
Kindred (Butler), 132
Kingston, Maxine Hong, 92, 95, 96, 97–98, 99, 102, 104, 105, 127
Kirkus Reviews, 73, 95
Klancher, Jon, 67
Klopfer, Donald, 8, 27–28
Knopf, 28, 140
Krantz, Judith, 122, 126–27, 130–31
Krumholz, Linda, 172

Lahiri, Jhumpa, 98
language: bigrams, 205nn20–21, 207n43; collocations approach and, 43–45; "coon" as racial slur, 43–45; model, 116–22, *132*; NLP, 6, 18, 118; racial, 62–65; racist, 43–45; topic modeling and, 27, 149–51, *155*, 210n24; white, 45. *See also* word embeddings
Larrick, Nancy, 33–34
Larsen, Nella, 112
Latin Americans, 5

Latinx, 70, 73, 93, 145
Lee, Harper, 116
Lee, Marie Myung-Ok, 102–3
Leskovec, J., 196n75
leverage: getting, 20–23; history of, 22, 23; *Jonoah and the Green Stone* and, 22, 65; Tan and, 99
Lewis, Sinclair, 28
linear regression, 16, 74, 194nn55–56, 199n12, 200n17, 201n43, 212n48
Linton, Eliza Lynn, 67
literacy rates, 7, 32
literary analysis, inequality and, 189n33
literary attention, 47, 70–71, 75–79, 82, 91, 92
literary distinction, blackness and: American winners by race, between 1950 and 2000, *108*; American winners by race and gender, between 1950 and 2000, *107*; data of, 110–12; distinctive features of American prizewinning novels, *121*; distinctive features of bestsellers, *121*; machine, reading color line, 122–31; machine classification and, 112–16, *118*, *119*; 98 and 91 percent, 105–10; novels misclassified by language model, 131–39, *132*, 207n49; *Paradise* and, 139–41; probability of bestseller novels by black authors, 1950 to 2000, *119*; probability of prizewinning novels by black authors, 1950 to 2000, *120*; race and, 116–22; textual features, types of, *117*
literary gatekeepers, 25, 80–83
literary journals, bias in, 199n14
literary marketplace, inequality and, 2
literary modeling, 19
literary studies essays, 12, 147
literary studies journals, 12, 26
literary whiteness, 5, 7, 20; inequality and, 14; patterns of, 45–57; prizewinners and, 184; Random House and, 45–57, *46–49*, *51*, *53–54*, *56*, 179; redlining and, 22
Lolita (Nabokov), 122
Long, Elizabeth, 123
Lott, Eric, 14, 42

Louvain algorithm, 202n46
Love, Heather, 175–76, 177

MacDonald, Dwight, 106
machine: classification, 112–16, *118*, *119*; color line, reading, 122–31
Mailer, Norman, 81
Malamud, Bernard, 122
Malice (Steel), 122
Marcus, Sharon, 175–76
Marxism, 161
Master of Fine Arts (MFA) degree, 57
Mayhew, Alice, 34
McAlister, Melanie, 99, 100–102
McCarthy, Cormac, 70, 98
McGurl, Mark, 15, 57, 189n32
McKinney, L. L., 182
McMillan, Terry, 106
McPherson, Tara, 16–17, 185
Melville, Herman, 170, 171, 181
metadata, most-reviewed novels, method for, 70, 199n16
MFA degree. *See* Master of Fine Arts degree
Michaels, Walter Benn, 15, 189n33
Michener, James, 58, 59–60
Milgram, Stanley, 76
misclassification of novels, language model and, 131–39, *132*, 207n49
mobility, upward economic, 123
Moby-Dick (Melville), 170, 171, 181
Momaday, N. Scott, 127
Moore, Lorrie, 79, 80
Morrison, Toni, 14, 50, 98, 99, 104, 125, 134, 157; from archives of, 36–39; on book reviews and racial inequality, 69–70; criticism of, 38–39; influence of, 5, 85, 179; with *Jonoah and the Green Stone*, 60, 61, 64; with literary attention, networks of, 76; NBA and, 127–28; *Paradise* by, 139–41; as prizewinner, 86, 105, 106, 109; "The Radical Vision of Toni Morrison," 192n15; at Random House, 1–2, 8–9, 10, 24, 29–30, 32, 34–40, 61, 66, 92, 133, 158, 183; "Toni Morrison effect," 78–84; Updike and, 93; valorization of, 11; on whiteness, 42

multiculturalism: acceptance, myth of, 4, 30; conglomeration and, 7–8; evolution of, 26; influence of, 24–25; prizewinners and, 108, 127; racial inequality and, 4, 30; rise of, 4–5

multiculturalism, of 1 percent: black authors in top ten with most reviewed titles, *84*; book reviews as data, 72–75, *74*, *75*; *Company Man* versus *Song of Solomon*, 84–92; *The Joy Luck Club* revolution, 92–103; male versus female novelists with most reviewed titles, *74–75*; mirages, 103–4; most reviewed titles and top ten authors, 1965 to 2000, *81*; networks of literary attention and, 70–71, 75–79, 82, 91, 92; race and gender of novelists with most reviewed titles, *74*; race and reviews, 67–72; race of novelists with most reviewed titles, *71*; racial inequality and, 24–25; "Toni Morrison effect" and, 78–84; top ten novels with most reviewed titles, 1965 to 2000, *80*

multidimensional scaling algorithm, *48*, *49*, 196n71

Munich, Adrienne, 143

Nabokov, Vladimir, 122
National Book Award (NBA), 99, 106, 111, 127–28, 133
National Book Critics Circle Award, 86, 99
Native Americans, 70, 73, 145
Native Son (Wright), 106
natural language processing (NLP), 6, 18, 181
NBA. *See* National Book Award
Nebula Award, 111, 133
Necessary Roughness (M. M. Lee), 102–3
neighborhood, 2, 140–41, 208n63
network analysis, 18, 25, 71, 76–77, 200n18
network science, 76, 77, 200n19
New Literary History (J. A. Joyce), 153–54
New Republic, 73
Newton, Huey, 35
New Yorker, 2, 3, 69, 72, 73; *The Blockbuster Complex* in, 28, 122; book reviews in, 77–78, 83
New York Times, 72, 85, 95, 99; bestseller list, 106, 110; whiteness and, 11

New York Times Book Review, 68, 69, 72
Ng, Fae Myenne, 96, 102
NLP. *See* natural language processing
Nobel Prize in Literature, 105, 106, 140
Noble, Safiya Umoja, 16, 21
No-No Boy (Okada), 22
nonwhite authors: book reviews and, 11; with novels, most-reviewed, 25; POC, 79, 92, 95–98, 145, 199n12
Norton Anthology of American Literature, The, 145, 146, 147
novelists: most reviewed titles, male versus female, *74–75*; with race and gender, top 1 percent most reviewed titles, *74*; with race and top 1 percent most reviewed titles, *71*; Random House, 1950 to 2000, racial identity of published, 2, 3, *3*, *4*, 29
novels: by black and white authors, 50; distinctive features of American prizewinning, *121*; language model and misclassified, 131–39, *132*, 207n49; multiculturalism of 1 percent, 1965 to 2000, reviews and top ten, *80*; from Random House, 193n52; Random House with "black" characters, 1950 to 2000, *47*; Random House with "white" versus "black" characters, 1950 to 2000, *46*; at Random House written by male versus female writers, 1950 to 2000, 41, *41*, 194nn55–56. *See also* metadata, most-reviewed novels

Oates, Joyce Carol, 80
Occupy Wall Street, 12
O'Connor, Flannery, 5, 15
O'Hara, John, 27
Okada, John, 6, 22
Old Man and the Sea, The (Hemingway), 127
1 percent. *See* multiculturalism, of 1 percent
O'Neil, Cathy, 16, 21
operationalization, 77
orchestration, with book reviews, 69
Orientalism, 99–102
Outside in the Teaching Machine (Spivak), 188n23

Pabst, Naomi, 160–61, 163, 164
Paco's Story (Heinemann), 127
Painter, Nell Irvin, 57
Palmares (Jones), 35
Palumbo-Liu, David, 144
Pantheon Books, 8, 28, 33
paperback rights, 99, 126
Parable of the Sower (Butler), 116, 207n50, 208n55; distinctive features of, *135*; literary distinction, blackness and, 131–39; plot, 133–34
Paradise (Morrison), 139–41
Parks, Carole, 38–39, 40
part-of-speech bigrams, 205nn20–21
Patternmaster (Butler), 132
peer-review journal, 12
PEN/Faulkner, 111
Penguin, 30
periodization, 24
Perkins, Maxwell, 27
permutation test, 196n74
person of color (POC), 2, 70, 73; authors, 79, 92, 95–98, 145, 199n12
Piketty, Thomas, 14
Piper, Andrew, 19
Play Ebony, Play Ivory (*Poetry for My People*) (Dumas), 37–38
POC. *See* person of color
Poetry for My People. *See Play Ebony, Play Ivory*
poststructuralism, 154, 167
postwar print culture, 9
poverty, 2, 7, 13, 44
Powell, Walter, 31–32, 72, 85, 103
power: Black Power, 140; of book reviews, 25, 78; critique of, 13; inequality and, 14–15, 40; of literary gatekeepers, 25, 80–83; of whiteness, 43–45; of white publishers, 125; white publishing and, 72; of word embeddings, 45
print culture, 11, 24
prison system, 174, 176–77
prize juries, whiteness and, 11
prizewinners: Bourdieu on, 112–13; Butler as, 132–33; data, 107, *107*, *108*, 111; literary whiteness and, 184; with machine color line, reading, 127–31; Morrison as, 86, 105, 106, 109; multiculturalism and, 108, 127; probability of prizewinning novels by black authors, 1950 to 2000, *120*; Random House with racial identity of novelists and, 3, *4*; Updike as, 119. *See also* book prizes; literary distinction, blackness and
Program Era, The (McGurl), 15
Project on the History of Black Writing, 112
prose, by year and most discussed works, *170*
publishers. *See* black publishers; white publishers
Publisher's Weekly, 69, 72, 73; bestseller list and, *107*, 110, 139; scholarly consensus on, 110
publishing: evolution of, 8–9; Golden Age of, 27; monopoly, 29; race and, 31. *See also* white publishing
Pulitzer Prize, 106, 109, 111, 127, 133, 184
Putnam, 99
Puzo, Mario, 98, 122
Pynchon, Thomas, 15, 70, 104

quantification, 6, 16–17, 19, 167, 170, 172
quantitative criticism, 18, 19

Rabbit Is Rich (Updike), 49–50, 129–30
Rabbit Redux (Updike), 119
Rabbit Run (Updike), 76
race, 24; with authors, most influential, 25; book reviews and, 67–72; canon and, 149; as categorical variable, 17; crime and, 13; critical race studies, 17, 20, 48, 145–46, 152; critical theory and, 160; distinctive words for documents expressing, *166*; economics and, 138; fluidity of, 112; gender and, 74, *107*, 111, 200n16, 202n47, 204n9; inequality and, *165*; language and, 62–65; literary distinction, blackness and, 116–22; of novelists with top 1 percent most reviewed titles, *71*, *74*; publishing and, 31; scholarly articles on cultural studies and, *160*; with theory topics as percentage of all topics, *156*; with theory topics computed by topic modeling, *155*
"Race, Writing, and Difference" (Appiah), 153

"Race for Theory, The" (Christian), 153
racial abstraction, 64
racial critique, 16, 17
racial identity: disease and, 17–18; multiculturalism and, 24; network analysis and, 25; of novelists published by Random House, 1950 to 2000, 2, 3, *3*, *4*, 29; stereotypes, 65
racial imagination, 197n84
racial incognizance, 43
racial inequality: book reviews and, 69–70; book sales and, 3, 110; conglomeration, engine of, 7–11; economic opportunities and, 14; literary whiteness and, 22; multiculturalism and, 4, 30; multiculturalism of 1 percent and, 24–25; Random House and, 66; redlining and, 15, 178; systemic, 2–4, 6, 8–10; with white and black characters, 56–57; white authors benefiting from, 3
racial inequality, canon and: *Beloved* and, 168–78, *170*; black studies and critical theory, 151–59, *155*; cultural studies, 1983, and after, 159–68; cultural studies, race and theory topics as percentage of all topics, *162*; distant reading of, 147–51; distinctive words for documents expressing race, *166*; "inequality" and "race" as terms, *165*; problem with 61 percent, 143–47; prose or fiction by year, most discussed works, *170*; race and theory topics as percentage of all topics, *156*; race and theory topics computed by topic modeling, *155*; reading and counting, 178–80; scholarly articles on cultural studies and race, *160*
racial realism, 134, 137, 138–39
racism, 43–45, 91, 154
"Radical Vision of Toni Morrison, The" (Ghanash), 192n15
Randall, Dudley, 33
Random House, 188n15; "black" characters in novels, 1950 to 2000, *47*; civil rights and, 30; cultural redlining and, 6; growth of, 8, 9, 27–30; literary whiteness and, 45–57, 179; Morrison at, 1–2, 8–9, 10, 24, 29–30, 32, 34–40, 61, 66, 92, 133, 158, 183; novelists published and racial identity, 1950 to 2000, 2, 3, *3*, *4*, 29; novels from, 193n52; novels written by male versus female writers, 1950 to 2000, 41, *41*, 194nn55–56; numbers and data, 40–42, *41*, 194nn53–57; Pantheon Books and, 8, 28; with power, 72; racial inequality and, 66; redlining and, 12; with valorization of black authors, 11; whiteness and, 11; "white" versus "black" characters in novels, 1950 to 2000, *46*. See also white publishing
rationalization, 9, 10
RCA, 8, 28
redlining, 20, 187n2; cultural, 2, 5–7, 23, 183, 185; economic, 2, 6; literary whiteness and, 22; racial inequality and, 15, 178; Random House and, 12; technological, 16. See also inequality
Redmond, Eugene, 61
Reed, Ishmael, 35
Representation (Hall), 13
Rody, Caroline, 172
Roediger, David, 43, 45
Roots (Haley), 32
Rose, Tricia, 134
Roth, Philip, 80, 98, 104
Rusert, Britt, 20
Rushdie, Salman, 200n16
Ryan, Judylyn, 87, 173

Salt Eaters, The (Bambara), 37
Schell, Orville, 100–102
Schmidt, Benjamin, 150–51
Schudson, Michael, 5, 8
science: data, 17, 18, 20, 23, 184; network, 76, 77, 200n19; 2020 and fugitive, 16–20
science fiction, 111, 115, 132–34, 137, 199n14
Sciffrin, André, 33
Scruples (Krantz), 126–27, 130–31
Seize the Day (Bellow), 119
Sharpe, Christina, 21
Showalter, Elaine, 143
skip-gram training algorithm, 195n68

slavery, 137–38, 154, 171–78
Smiley, Jane, 52
Smith, Valerie, 173
social alienation, 90
social identity, 41, 101, 112
social sciences, 12, 14, 18, 188n22
socioeconomic alienation, 90–91
Song of Solomon (Morrison), 5; bag of gold in, 90–91; book reviews, 89; *Company Man* versus, 84–92; conclusion, 87; narratological complexity and style of, 86–87, 89; peacock in, 88–89; social alienation and, 90; women in, 89
Southern Illinois University Press, 38
Spillers, Hortense, 154
Spivak, Gayatri, 13, 153, 188n23
standpoint, 42, 43
star system, 10
Steel, Danielle, 122
stereotypes: Asian Americans, 99; black, 30–31, 48; poverty, 7; racial identity, 65
St. Martin's, 133
Styron, William, 58, 70, 79
Sula (Morrison), 86
Sutherland, John, 123

Tabone, Mark A., 208n61
Talese, Nan, 34
Tan, Amy, 92, 96, 98; leverage and, 99; popularity of, 100, 102. See also *Joy Luck Club, The*
Tate, Greg, 134
technological belonging, 21
technological redlining, 16
Terkel, Studs, 8
textual classification, 25
textual features, types, *117*
Third World Press (Chicago), 33
Thompson, E. P., 161
Thompson, John, 31
Time, 73
To Kill a Mockingbird (H. Lee), 116
"Toni Morrison effect," multiculturalism of 1 percent and, 78–84
topic modeling, 26, 149–51, *155*, 210n24

Tripmaster Monkey (Kingston), 92
Troupe, Quincy, 61
True to the Game (Woods), 108
Turn of the Screw, The (H. James), 170, 171, 212n47
Twain, Mark, 143
Tyler, Anne, 79

Underground Railroad, The (Whitehead), 184
Underwood, Ted, 19, 114–15, 150, 211n42
University of Kansas, 25, 112
Updike, John, 2, 5, 49–50, 52, 69, 76, 78, 207n45; bestsellers and, 129–31; book reviews and, 79–80; influences on, 207n45; Morrison and, 93; as prizewinner, 119

valorization: of black authors, 11, 82–83, 91–92; of Christian identity, 51–52; by decision makers, 128, 144, 158–59; of economics, 90, 123
Van Rees, C. J., 68–69
Vidal, Gore, 81
Viking Press, 60, 72
Village Voice, 72
Vitale, Alberto, 8, 28
Vonnegut, Kurt, 8, 28

Wade, Brent, 83, 85
Walker, Alice, 81, 85, 124, 127, 157
Wall, Cheryl, 39
Wallace, David Foster, 98
Wapshot Chronicle, The (Cheever), 129
Warren, Kenneth, 15, 159, 189n33
Washington Post, 99
Watts, Duncan, 76
"weapons of math destruction," 16
Web of Science database, 12, 188n22
Weheliye, Alexander, 20
West, Cornel, 144, 145
What Was African American Literature (Warren), 159
"What White Publishers Won't Publish" (Hurston), 31
white: language, 45; "Why Are the Digital Humanities So White," 16–17

white authors: black and, 196n74; book reviews and, 69–70; decreasing in number, 199n12; females, 41; males, 2, 41, 107, 143; *New Yorker* with, 3; in *The Norton Anthology of American Literature*, 145; with novels, most-reviewed, 25; novels by, 50; racial inequality benefiting, 3. *See also* nonwhite authors

"white character" vector: by decade, *51*; eight novels semantically similar to, 58–59, *59*; by genre, *53*; Gensim word2vec embeddings model and similar terms to, *48*, *51*; humanism and, 55–56; racial inequality and, 56–57; semantic variance with black and, *56*

Whitehead, Colson, 184

"white man effect," 107

white narcissism, 60

whiteness: in children's literature, 33–34; as cultural identity, 42; geometry of, 42–45; *Jonoah and the Green Stone* and, 63; Morrison on, 42; with power and inequality, 14–15; power of, 43–45; print culture and inertia of, 11; standpoint with, 42, 43. *See also* literary whiteness

white publishers: black stereotypes and, 30–31; power of, 125; publishing and, 30–34

white publishing: archive, view from, 34–39; Dumas and breaking patterns, 24, 30, 60–65; with "Great Change" and nonchange, 27–30, 31; with nonwhite staff, 32; power and, 72; publishers and, 30–34; with still untold story, 65–66; with token black authors, 192n28; with whiteness, geometry of, 42–45

Whiteside, Thomas, 28, 122

white supremacy, in children's literature and book sales, 34

"Why Are the Digital Humanities So White" (McPherson), 16–17

Wideman, John Edgar, 85

Wilentz, Gay, 87

Wilkens, Matthew, 200n16

Williams, Raymond, 161

Willis, Susan, 90

Wilson, Cheryl, 67

Woman Warrior, The (Kingston), 105

women, 74, 89, 105, 157

Wong, Sau-ling, 99–100, 102

Woods, Teri, 108

word2vec, *48*, *49*, *51*, *54*, 196n72, 197n76

word embeddings: approach, 24, 44–45, 47–48, 50–54, 195n64, 195n67, 196n74; Gensim, *48*, *49*, *51*, *54*, 195n68, 196n72, 196n75; power of, 45; racial inequality and, 30

WorldCat, 193n52, 200n16, 204n13

Wrestling with the Muse (Boyd), 187n8

Wright, Richard, 106

YA fiction. *See* young-adult fiction

Yale Review, 72

Young, Jessica, 200nn43–44

young-adult (YA) fiction, 103

Zuberi, Tukufu, 17, 18